THE
ITALIAN
AMERICANS
Troubled Roots

THE
ITALIAN
AMERICANS
Troubled Roots

by Andrew Rolle

University of Oklahoma Press: Norman

Library of Congress Cataloging-in-Publication Data

Rolle, Andrew
  The Italian Americans.

   1. Italian Americans—History. I. Title.
E184.I8R63   973'.0451   84-40282
ISBN: 0–8061–1907–1 (paperback)

There she lies, the great
Melting-Pot— . . . Ah, what a
stirring and a seething! Celt
and Latin, Slav and Teuton,
Greek and Syrian—black and
yellow—Jew and Gentile . . . how
the great alchemist melts and
fuses them with his purging
flame! Here shall they all unite
to build the Republic of Man
and the Kingdom
of God. . . .

ISRAEL ZANGWILL, 1909

CONTENTS

Acknowledgments ix

Introduction xi

I.   A Vision of the New Land 1

II.   Dispersal 16

III.   Seeking Shelter 28

IV.   Birds of Passage 47

V.   The Roots of Discrimination 56

VI.   A Touch of the Gutter: La Mafia and Crime 78

VII.   La Famiglia: Defending the Old Ways 110

VIII.   La Famiglia: Reaching Out 127

IX.   Politics 140

X.   The Amenities 154

XI.   Making It Big and Small   169

XII.   A New Identity or Assimilation?   179

Notes   191

Essay on Sources   196

Index   208

ACKNOWLEDGMENTS

AT ONE TIME OR ANOTHER the following persons have aided in the writing of this volume: Angus Cameron, Ray Billington, Martin Ridge, John Lahr, Lois Douglass, Grace Allen, Marie Caldiero, and the members of Marie Briehl's Child Analysis Seminar at the Southern California Psychoanalytic Institute. I am grateful to that institute for my analytic training over a period of four years, as well as to the Psychiatric Division of the Cedars Sinai Medical Center in Los Angeles for several more years of attendance at seminars and case conferences. These experiences were invaluable in helping me to clarify the roles of immigrant children and parents. At Sinai, Saul Brown, M.D., Stuart Turkel, M.D., Allan Weiner, M.D., and Richard Kettler, M.D., were particularly kind. In a less formal way I am indebted to Warren Jones, M.D., and to those psychiatrists and psychoanalysts who have become personal friends. Thanks also go to Luigi Barzini, Jr. and to Colin Jones. Myra Moss, Ph.D., restructured the manuscript and suggested its title.

A. R.

INTRODUCTION

THIS VOLUME MOVES BEYOND the boundaries of immigration history. Its approach is related to psychiatry more than to sociology or social psychology. The book attempts to fuse psychoanalysis with history in order to understand the dynamics of specific individuals and groups. It makes no attempt to demean, but seeks insights and motivations. Sigmund Freud suggested that the development of a people can resemble the clinical histories of individuals. The group's repressed wishes bear a similarity to those experienced by the patient. Yet, the history of immigrants is not necessarily one of pathological disability.

Historians, however, need to focus much more attention upon the internal hurts that foreigners experienced. Indeed, one of the most misunderstood aspects of America's development concerns the immigration experience of its people. The story of our country's "ethnics" is related to that of all of us. Each person wants to feel that he comes from somewhere and shares his homeland's heritage. We cling to tradition in order to measure our worth as humans with a usable past.

In 1909 a minor English writer of Jewish extraction, Israel Zangwill, wrote a play entitled *The Melting Pot*. This work expressed the massive distortion against which my own book struggles today. For Zangwill's play achieved a cultural significance totally disproportionate to its literary pretensions. He created a symbolic mythology about what millions of our forebears encountered in coming to the New World. Immigrants, their children, and later interpreters seized upon the "melting pot" concept, which perpetuated confusing explanations of what had actually happened.

While crossing the Atlantic, millions of persons approached not only a melting pot or the Statue of Liberty. A psychological barrier of differentness also lay across the foamy sea. Ever since these newcomers streamed down the splintered gangplanks along the American waterfront, they and we have been perplexed by what they saw and sought.

Former peasants who suffered initial feelings of anomie scarcely realized that part of their unease lay in the primitive past from which they had emerged. Deprivations suffered in Italy's Mezzogiorno had masked insecurities not to be remedied by America's so-called melting pot.

The immigrants' progeny today have virtually discarded that term. Few choose to remember their forebears as bubbles in a melting pot. Those who felt the heat of the flames beneath the pot achieved an assimilation that reeked of the loss of selfhood. Today's third-generation ethnics tend to see their ancestors as torn away from origins that were somehow heroic though deprived.

The savage streets of America swallowed up these forebears. Among them were persons whose weaknesses were taken advantage of; not even all of these became "neurotics." The unlucky were sometimes hurt. Most struggled through, huddling together and yearning to break free, as the words at the base of the Statue of Liberty promised. We still admire and wonder, indeed, how they so quickly accomplished outward success. Emotional crosscurrents, made up of frailties, enmities, and gnawing doubts, clouded their vision. With linkages and bonds of their past distorted, the immigrants often sought escape from what Carl Jung called our collective unconscious. Total flight proved impossible. What the newcomers had been in the Old World remained, sometimes festering in the confusion of their repressed thoughts. A people's linguistic and cultural characteristics cannot be totally erased. The ties to family, clan, or region form a part of being civilized.

How do historians dig up the roots of a people's past? We know that humans conduct their relationships on the surface of life, but that beneath there flows an underground river of the unconscious mind. In healthy persons the roots of assurance, which we all crave, grow slowly to the surface. Because the reconstruction of these deeper impulses is so difficult, writers have preferred to deal with the immigrants' social milieus and material conditions.

Admittedly, poverty creates personal deficits. A sterile and narrow materialism has indeed consigned ethnics and non-ethnics who are poor or elderly to the bottom of America's socioeconomic heap. Yet the disadvantaged hunger for more than food; they yearn for a sense of identity. In our zeal to ferret out discrimination in the American past, historians have troweled over emotional disabilities. Immigration history is heavily clouded by a focus upon economic attainments.

The descendants of immigrants, too, rather than admit to a history of shame, believe a kind of historical lie. By stressing the deprivations that our forefathers encountered, we have denied the emotions that they actually experienced. Out of faded photographs they seem to stare at us disbelievingly.

To see more clearly the confusing panorama that immigrants faced after landing on Ellis Island requires interpretation in the light of modern psychiatric and psychoanalytic insights. In order to drop the veil of illusion about what they experienced, we need to live vicariously with these people. By focusing less on hard data (names, dates, and disputable facts) and more on soft (inchoate emotions and unconscious feelings), we can view them anew—inside out, as it were.

The "new psychohistory" (there is no "old" one) is concerned with uncovering buried impulses. As we explore these underlying emotions they seem countervailing, if not ambivalent and contradictory. Yet historians must learn how to interpret important accumulations of unconscious feelings (id, ego, and superego impulses). In the history of painting, the nineteenth-century impressionists moved boldly beyond illustration. Similarly, we need to know more about what motivated those troubled immigrants whose faces stare at us out of the pages of America's history.

Psychohistorians have in common with medical doctors the task of analyzing the covert problems of persons in pain, individuals who are perplexed by their anxieties. Our goal is not to overemphasize their pathologies but to understand complex behavior. There is no purpose in repudiating the role of the senses (intrapsychic) in history. We wish to unmask legendry. The ultimate reductionism is denial of the role of emotion in the lives of human beings.

I have written several books about one of the most misunderstood of America's minorities. The first of these (*The Immigrant Upraised*) was cast in a different vein from that of standard immigration histories. That volume looked at the social, political, and economic record of Italians who had deserted New York's Mulberry Street for the twenty-two states west of the Mississippi River. I did not deny that foreigners encountered prejudice and adversity but argued that their acculturative pattern varied markedly from section to section.

I do not quite see America's immigrants as uprooted, defenseless pawns adrift in a sea of confusion and despair. That gloomy and joyless approach obscures the challenges of "making it" in the New World. Out west the immigrant developed an independence not characteristic of his countrymen left behind in east coast ghettoes. The stereotype of the organ-grinding Italian with rings in his ears and a monkey on a leash fell down in the western setting. The brutalities of factory life were not fully duplicated there, despite injustices practiced against immigrant workers. My book also had application to reappraising the role of other national groups. It was called the first systematic account of one nationality in the states west of the Mississippi. Yet that book was limited by geography and by the examination of conscious-level factors, as was my later *The American Italians*.

We should seek to dissect misleading clichés that have encrusted what the immigrant experienced in the New World. At the mercy of strange forces, in an untried environment, he utilized a variety of emotional defenses to quiet his anxieties. Survival with self-respect required the maintenance of internal control (sometimes rationalized as material success).

To quiet their anxieties our forebears from abroad sought not to face the pain that they felt. Indeed, their intrapsychic maneuvers have led to continuing misinterpretations of the great peasant and urban movements out of Europe. The participants sometimes depicted themselves as the heroic figures of a New World epic. They promoted a Ulysses-like mythology that flavored their mixed accounts of facts and lies, of affirmation and negation, of defensive and boastful tales. Before immigrants ever left their home ports, a heroicized mythology had been built up in their minds. Upon arrival, they were encouraged to forget past allegiances. More immediate than indulging one's memories about Naples or Catania was the need to conform to the pressures of American life. So, confused newcomers vowed to succeed American style—at whatever cost. But their repressions proved damaging for some of them.

Psychoanalysts have devised a vocabulary to describe mechanisms that we use to protect our egos. For bewildered immigrants, emotions that they could not express openly were pushed back into the unconscious mind through "denial" (a kind of convenient forgetfulness), "isolation of affect" (emotions), and by "undoing" what seemed most painful in both past and present. Troubled immigrants also "acted out" their frustrations in dramatic attempts to ward off daily humiliations.

Embittered by indignities of all sorts, Italians, Poles, and Greeks nursed irrational guilts about abandoning parental and other powerful childhood ties. Some newcomers sought to cover over the shame of illiteracy and poverty by damning the feast that America temptingly offered.

Even those who seemed euphoric about what lay ahead buried feelings of anger and fear. Only at baptisms, weddings, or funerals was a blend of anxiety and nostalgia apt to well up tearfully. Between such events, a rigid pattern of concealment convincingly distorted the record.

Some immigrants became shredded personalities who sold their souls for the gold of America. Rejection of the last remnants of village feudalism reversed the family's traditional authority system and placed harsh strains upon both parents and children. When the latter grew to know more about the new land than did their elders, imitation of past family patterns was no longer prized. A restless tension between the generations seemed to alter Freud's classic Oedipal struggle in unprecedented ways. A son's envy became sidetracked. Victorious over their families by virtue of abandonment, rather than confrontation, children who had humiliated their fathers nevertheless carried guilt within them.

America's peasant strangers had themselves made the basic decision to discard their material and emotional baggage. When asked later in life why they had come to America, most said they were glad to leave the old country behind. Required to make emotional changes greater than those that peasants had experienced in preceding centuries, these transplanted villagers replaced not only their old pots and pans but also loyalties to the past.

"Americanization" forced upon them, self-preservation meant adopting different products, folkways, and laws. And acceptance of a harsh materialism, based upon a Protestant ethic unfamiliar to Italian *contadini*, created severe personal contradictions. While America encouraged the material accumulation of goods, its middle-class orthodoxy imposed outward conventionality as one price of upward mobility.

The enormous cities of America promised emancipation from the barren villages and decayed urban centers of the past. But this new land imposed demeaning adjustments—indeed the sacrifice of selfhood itself—to a crushing materialism. Racist biases, too, accompanied the concentration of wealth. If one did not conform, one almost certainly could not succeed.

Only in the 1960s did a virtual ethnic explosion occur. Called a race revolution by some, this outburst reflected the indignation of America's minorities over the inconsistencies that masked a promised American Dream. Born of disappointment with over-sold slogans, and reflective of the maldistribution of wealth (particularly among blacks, Chicanos, and Indians), a "new ethnicity" suddenly, if temporarily, became ideologized. It was as though this represented an angry eruption from the unconscious over the hurts of the past.

Without denying prejudice against which some minorities have finally rebelled, I continue to encounter in the records of European immigrants an unusual capacity to manipulate the surface environment. Faced with inferior status, the foreigner opted for expediency (ego controls) rather than run the risks of misplaced altruism (uncertainty). A Calabrian saying comes to mind: "He who depends on others will sing but won't eat." In the New World, peasant pragmatism remained intact. (Later, "practicality" helped to produce hard-hat ethnic clods, whose prejudices today resemble those of bigots in the dominant culture.)

One way by which immigrants could reconcile their intense tradition of family privatism with having to swallow a loss of identity was to deny "things psychological." Indeed, this denial has made it necessary to write not just another history of a minority. My book thus concerns the underlying moods, injuries, and motivations of a vast sea change.

There is no need to remake the immigrant experience into either an apologia or an attack. By looking at how they coped, we can see patterns that were both injurious and healthy. What seems truly significant was the impact of trying to mediate between two drastically different ways of life. So-called success, furthermore, involved subtle repudiations of a previous identity, whether Italian or Greek or Polish.

It is difficult to unravel myths in history, to look behind the highlights and the heroes who made good. Although America was a nation of immigrants, they were, paradoxically, viewed in a hostile manner. By reinterpreting our darker past we may come to see all of our people with greater compassion. One can take better measure of oneself by knowing where one came from. Unresolved turmoil among the members of any minority belongs to all of us.

In stressful situations, faulty internal images arise. As forms of self-hatred are projected outward onto others, the underlying motivations of national behavior become obscured. It is important that we reexamine the internal imagery that propels each of us in the twentieth century. The United States is not a small, homogeneous country like Sweden or Norway, but a giant, turbulent society in which ethnicity remains a misunderstood aspect of American life.

A. R.

A VISION
OF THE NEW LAND

PEOPLE WHO LEAVE THEIR HOMELANDS remind one of a child who takes his first faltering steps across a room. One sees in both curiosity and a wish for autonomy. There is also the prospect of loss. We all fear separating from our parents or from our homeland. Encountering the unfamiliar involves abandoning security. Why, then, does an individual break with his past? Psychiatry describes a process of attachment by the child to its mother that is anaclitic—a leaning, emotional closeness. When this parental *imago* is disturbed the results can be distortive. The immigrant's departure from his mother country evoked a sadness like that associated with separating from the mother. With his homeland no longer available for succor, the immigrant leaving for America—almost like a small child—took his first confusing, yet venturesome, steps off Ellis Island toward autonomy.

We have read enough about the externals of immigrant life—about inflated levels of achievement and barbaric working conditions. These are useful ideas but it is more important to unlock the hidden fears and aspirations stored in the unconscious mind of the supposedly stolid immigrant. Only rarely did casual expressions, feasts, mottoes, or folkways suggest a deeper anxiety. The stereotypes that clutter the "outer history" of ethnic groups generally have not dealt with such subsurface ambivalence.

If we look through a different window of time, only superficially does it seem paradoxical that millions of Italians abandoned their attractive peninsula. These immigrants left behind the blue Mediterranean, their olive trees, craggy hilltops, vines in the sun—in short, a beautiful terrain and a climate seldom excessively hot or cold—and brought with them a set of indelible memories. Despite all the pervasive sentimentality about Italy's romantic attractions, we may properly question whether "normality" has ever existed there. Southern Italy remains much as it was fifty years ago. A peasant society still struggles with poverty and oppression, as well as with insecurity. Denial of these disabilities has hardly helped to solve the problems of a narrow and rigid culture. From the late nineteenth century onward Sicily, Campania, and the Abruzzi region in particular experienced a disintegration of the traditional ligaments and cellular structure of their culture. Poverty-stricken peasants and urban dwellers alike grew up in an atmosphere of disorder and breakdown. A complex of depressing social, political, and economic conditions encouraged the flight of 8.5 million Italians prior to the first world war.

After the middle of the nineteenth century a significant rise in the European birthrate created a bulge of discontented persons below the age of thirty. Although they had achieved working status, *contadini* were enraged by an authoritative, inflexible social system administered by entrenched older persons. In their peasant villages the young felt blocked and defeated. And actually, however much the Italian immigrants later sought to sentimentalize the places they had left behind, there was a meanness and defeatism that weighed down upon many a village back in the old country. The children of remote mountain hamlets were quite capable of stoning a stranger to death. The saffron-colored houses of the nobility towered over the stone huts of commoners, in-

2

directly tithed in order to maintain their economic masters in the style to which the idle-rich were accustomed. For most peasants, life was not only unpromising, but bleakness itself.

The whole system of Italian life seemed to encourage ignorance and lack of opportunity. For example, some peasants near Palermo in Sicily firmly believed that crops cultivated with a hoe would produce a greater yield. Absentee landlords did little to modernize their estates, on which the *contadini* worked for long hours.

Angry at their inability to own land, south Italian peasants produced a folk song whose vengeful, anarchistic overtones were directed at rapacious landowners:

> *Today, landlord, you will plow your own field*
> *Because we are leaving for America.*

It was natural that resentment over social incompetence would produce endemic distrust of forces outside the shelter of the family. Rule by a succession of corrupt political regimes strengthened reliance upon the emotional shelter of the family.

Not only the peasants, but impoverished town dwellers also, remained at the mercy of economic cycles that threw them repeatedly out of work. After 1873 a sharp drop in the demand for Sicilian textiles created an immigration reservoir of unemployed weavers, spinners, and sheepherders. At a time when unemployment became rampant all over Europe, the foreign born were sorely needed in the United States. Between the Civil War and 1920 the quickening pace of mechanization fired America's most explosive period of growth.

Disease, hunger, epidemics, and political corruption had darkened the lives of too many young peasants. Their exploitation by absentee landlords and avaricious merchants produced a wage system that was scandalous, even by European standards. In 1902 Sicilian *braccianti*, common laborers, received the equivalent of $.25 for twelve hours of hard work. In the large cities of the United States a newcomer could usually count upon wages of $1.50 to $2.00 per day. Even an ignorant street hawker or peanut vendor (especially if he had an accordian with a monkey on a leash) might make $10.00 to $15.00 per week. It is true that wages in the American South, as we shall see, were considerably lower, but few Italians made their way southward; they tended to remain on the east coast or to move toward the Middle and Far West.

Achievement could best take place by expatriation, a process that demanded the transcending of one's kinship ties. Thus the voyage to America connoted rebellion. At least, those older folk who were left behind—parents, aunts, uncles, and grandparents—were apt to see the departure of the young as defection, even abandonment. As for those forced to turn away from their fathers and mothers, there was also rage, which had to be repressed. Although these young emigrants were to attempt to reestablish their family lives in America, many were saddened and even depressed by the necessity of leaving their homeland.

On the surface, however, the majority of these troubled immigrants saw America as a magnificent, hopeful alternative to despair. We must also remember that not a few of them were genuinely happy to leave, and it is these folk who have been most vocal about their successes. For all immigrants America presented a vast arena whose towns were bursting out into the countryside. The new land, furthermore, seemed to need each one of them, at least superficially. No wonder, then, that some of Italy's villages were virtually depopulated, or *spopolati*, in one of the great migrations of modern times.

The Italian novelist Carlo Levi has pointed out that, among the hundreds of myths cherished by Italy's peasants, one stood out over the rest, providing a perfect escape from unpleasant realities. This was "their version, magical and real at the same time, of an earthly paradise, lost and then found again: the myth of America." Trite though such a concept may seem today, we ought not to underrate its idealistic impetus, admittedly once overestimated.

At the deepest level, the voyage to America involved a fantasy of escape thrown up by the unconscious. Stories of such quests are ancient. The Roman writer Virgil's *Aeneid* describes how Aeneid and some friends left the burning city of Troy in order to found a new paradise in Italy. In the same way, the Israelites escaped from bondage in Egypt to set up a new home in the Promised Land. This theme of the quest for a new homeland is, thus, an age-old one in the literature of the world. Jason's fiercest tests of courage, however, occurred *after* the exodus from his old homeland—when he had arrived in the land of the Golden Fleece, Colchis.

The expansive clichés about America that once seemed so true are now time-worn by sentimental repetition. One was the conviction that any American, regardless of origin, could rise to the top. Another was the belief that America was a refuge for the maltreated. Her vaunted appeals of fair play and equal opportunity were prospects that unlocked the immigrant heart. One folk saying seemed especially to apply: *Vivere e lasciar' vivere* ("Live and let live").

Actually, young migrants, lugging along battered suitcases tied with ropes, turned their faces toward years of hard work and almost immediate misunderstanding. A north Italian woman named Olympia told me, when she was almost ninety, of her mixed feelings about arriving at Ellis Island after the turn of the century. She was a well-bred, carefully dressed city girl from Piedmont who wanted to make the best possible impression upon docking. Instead, she befuddled the immigration inspectors. Her hair was elaborately piled in proper Victorian tresses high atop her head, fastened with combs and pins. Her long embroidered skirt swept the floor. Beneath various petticoats were tiny shoes, not the clodhoppers of the fields that most peasants wore. All of these accoutrements, and her immaculately done nails, had caused her to be invited to the captain's table aboard ship. But in America she encountered immediate debarkation problems. She burst into tears when an insensitive inspector suggested that she might be a prostitute coming to New York to ply her trade. United States government immigration officers were used to seeing young peasant wives who suckled their children at the breast. It seemed inconceivable that a youthful Italian woman should step off a dirty

5

ship not clad in somber and tattered clothing. Clichés about the immigrants, thus, were abuilding even before they left Ellis Island.

In his novel *The Watch*, Levi described going to America as an act that demanded self-denial:

> This gesture, with all it stood for, was the American baptism. And that renunciation was required and always will be required from everyone, whether they were born in America or had arrived singing psalms on sailing ships, or had disembarked from third-class transatlantic liners with poor valises and swollen sacks across their shoulders. This individual renunciation is the American revolution, and it is repeated every day by thousands of new men. With this gesture they renounce the gods and also the possibility of creating or fabricating new ones.

Foreign laborers were to play a critical role in constructing the railroad tunnels and bridges, waterworks, and the farm system of a new continent. Everywhere in this prodigal land there was much to do. With factories to man, roads to build, houses to erect, and forests to clear, at first the foreigner seemed overwhelmed by the challenge.

In America the land was ready for man's exploitation. In Italy peasants had carved terraces out of rocky slopes in order to provide the barest strips of flat arable land. In contrast to the stone walls needed to hold together these manmade earthworks were the endless prairies of the American West. In the eastern United States, too, new virgin tracts of land were waiting to be cultivated. And all about him the immigrant saw woods ready to provide the lumber with which to build new cities.

Only about 20 percent of the American Italians went west. Those who became miners, loggers, or ranchers, furthermore, do not suit the ethnic stereotypes created by historians. And indeed most of the Italian immigrants seemed content to construct replicas of their home villages along the city blocks of new "Little Italys." Pasquale D'Angelo put it this way: "We fellow townsmen in this strange land clung desperately to one another. To be separated from our relatives and friends and to work alone was something that frightened us, old and young. So we were ready to undergo a good deal of hardship before we would even consider breaking up the gang." Also it was in the cities that most jobs were available. However much newcomers might admire the richness of America's countryside, propertyless latecomers had to rely upon whatever employment was offered. A Como silk worker might be put to shining shoes on the Bowery; a baker from Calabria began life in Pittsburgh cleaning out boilers; an organist from Turin had a first American job unloading bananas from boats anchored in Boston harbor.

As former peasants ventured awkwardly out into American life, an observer wrote: "As soon as they step outside of the Italian colony, they are almost as helpless as babies, owing to their lack of knowledge of the language, customs and laws of this country." Thus, immigrants chose the gray life of the slums rather than separation from their countrymen. "It is the instinct," he continued, "that makes all living creatures band together in time of storm." Stores where immigrants shopped were operated by Italians whose customers (*clientela*) spoke Italian. Americanization was impeded whenever there was easy access to foreign stores, newspapers, physicians, and churches.

We have the greatest amount of information about the immigrants who settled in large cities, and the data tend to be economic. An 1890 United States Bureau of Labor report indicated that a Calabrian helper in a Chicago bakery, as head of a family of four, worked forty-eight weeks. His average weekly wage was $7.00 and his hours of work per week, sixty. His earnings for the period were $336, and no other member of the family was a wage earner. (The four weeks lost from work were ascribed to bronchitis.) By 1910, a United States Immigration Commission report stated that the average Italian-born male in the United States earned only $396 per year. The national average salary at that time was $666. Blacks earned an average of $445 that year.

In 1907 one in every four immigrants to the United States came from Italy. About eighty men arrived for every twenty women. One tends to forget how many single males there were and that life expectancy in the United States around the turn of the century was only a little more than age forty. Bachelors, in their most productive years, sought to earn enough money with which to send for their families. They might wander from job to job once they paid the debts acquired in getting to America.

The separation of wives from husbands, sometimes for years, disrupted family life. Although the toll on some families proved disastrous, the majority of young breadwinners sent home remittances and did not abandon their wives. In 1908 more than half of the Italians who had migrated into the country that year returned, at least for a while, to their families in the homeland.[1]

After World War I whole families (like the Jews at an earlier date) increasingly migrated together. They came in large numbers from Calabria, Campania, and Sicily, southern Italy's Mezzogiorno. Many were from one particular town, Basilicata, in the Abruzzi.

Angelo Pellegrini has written a description of the landing on Ellis Island in 1913 of his family and of their eight-day train ride across the continent. The *abbondanza* of the new land was overwhelming. Only ten years old, Pellegrini was astounded by the great mounds of apples under the trees in the state of Washington. As the train neared the frontier lumber town of Macleary, he recalled:

> When I saw those apples and remembered that in Italy I once was nearly beaten to death by a peasant whose single apple tree I had raided and he chased me and flailed me for one lousy apple, I said to myself, 'Chiasimo, we have arrived.' [Pellegrini went on to praise the way in which one could acquire land easily out west.] I mean, for once, for once in our lives, we knew the extraordinary delight of turning sod, and every shovelful was a loaf for us.[2]

A variety of popular writers contributed to the theme of what America might offer its newcomers. D.H. Lawrence, for instance, saw the United States rejecting its European past much as a child seeks omnipotence and independence from its elders. He believed that the mass migration to the New World occurred not so much because of a search for freedom or economic opportunity but because most wanted to drift away from a sense of authority inherent in the paternalistic structure of Europe. Lawrence wrote about the immigrant "sloughing off the old skin." The Piedmontese author Cesare Pavese described non-immigrant Americans of the preindustrial era as men who had themselves reestablished contact with the land. Admiring the Jeffersonian concern for the soil and for the region, Pavese felt uprooted back in the cities of Italy, rather than in America. He saw in the writings of William Faulkner, Sherwood Anderson, and Louis Bromfield an allegiance to soil, rather than a revolt against village origins. Although Pavese never emigrated, his writings are pervaded by a search for a new start amid the spacious and the primitive.

The New World seemed to promise a chance to combine brawn with delicate artisanship. Sigmund Freud's *Civilization and Its Discontents* discusses this creative urge in terms that are almost Italian: "Beauty has no obvious use; nor is there any clear cultural necessity for it. Yet civilization could not do without it." The Italians provided a humanizing ingredient in a harsh industrial society. Today one can still see the fading mosaics they carefully fashioned in the New York subways and the terrazzo and statuary work they executed on the country estates of the Rockefellers and the Huntingtons.

Whether they were mosaic workers who decorated the New York subways or, in the case of the eccentric Simon Rodia, built high towers at Watts, immigrants sought a way to reconcile themselves with the new America. Their work was an offering, a feast, a celebration that today seems both touching and tragic. Wanting the new land to know something of the old, they poured out their fantasies and aspirations. Illiterate hod carriers and cement mixers alike brought beauty into their daily menial work.

Without this resourcefulness and flexibility, a newcomer was not apt to be happy, especially during his first years. About this Antonio Gallenga, an Italian visitor, wrote: "The man who aspires to make his way in a new country should be hampered with no recollections or aspirations—no repining or hankering after the things he may have left behind in the old one. He must start with a stout determination to be a settler among settlers; he must be ready to do in America as the Americans do."

9

Italy's national hero, Giuseppe Garibaldi, had similar thoughts: "This is a land in which man forgets his native country. He acquires a new home and different interests." As a free spirit Garibaldi, who worked for a time making candles on Staten Island, never became an American citizen; yet he claimed that he was one. Much later, Eric Hoffer, that cheery and loosely idealistic voice of American manual labor, would maintain that an indispensable motif of the immigrant experience was accommodation to the environment: "They came here," he wrote, "with the ardent desire to shed their old world identity and be reborn to a new life; and they were automatically equipped with an unbounded capacity to imitate and adopt the new. The strangeness of the new country attracted rather than repelled them. They craved a new identity. . . . To have to learn to speak a new language enhanced the illusion of being born anew."

One response was to act out the dominant success ethic on the surface but to retreat more deeply into oneself, to dissemble, to conceal anxieties. Other defenses involved attempts to manipulate the environment and the significant authority figures within it. A Mediterranean peasant mentality shrewdly exploited the limitations of personal power, masked by a screen of verbal effusiveness. The operatic stereotype of Italian buffoonery sometimes troweled over feelings of malaise and inferiority. In psychiatric terms, this was isolation of affect (emotion or feeling).

Without substantial and overt renunciation of the past it was not going to be easy to escape the lower social status that was the unlettered immigrant's lot. To cling to old mores and to vowel-ending names was to court criticism of inflexibility, of valuing the safety of a form of ignorance rather than accepting new challenges. Consequently, most Italians, at least superficially, came to abandon *le vie vecchie*, those old ways that cut them off from new neighbors in a terra incognita.

To claim that all immigrants were even outwardly in harmony with the American environment is of course ridiculous. When asked how he liked life in the brash new country, one newcomer paused for a moment, grinned out of two rows of tobacco-stained teeth, and said: "Italy is for us whoever gives us bread." He spoke as if the question had been asked about some strange land he had never seen. Another new resident put it this way: "It is foolish to tell any Italian to forget Italy . . . for me, as for others, Italy is the little village where I was raised." A lonely south Italian argued that "if one lives away from Naples, the heart is broken!"

What seemed most natural was to distrust the unfamiliar. An intense privatism acted as a barrier, expressed in various proverbs: "Whoever walks alone is well off" and "The man who plays a lone hand never loses." Yet, newcomers had to develop some sense of trust, despite another adage to the contrary: *Fidati era un buon uomo—non ti fidare era meglio di lui* ("Trust was a good man—Don't Trust was better than he"). The stresses and contradictions of the peasant past led to a layering of suspicion, summed up in the maxim "A friend to everyone can be loyal to no one." Yet another south Italian saying ran: *Meglio solo che mal'accompagnato* ("Better to be alone than to be poorly accompanied"). One other proverb perhaps best captures a primitive wariness of all strangers: "He who loves you makes you cry. He who hates you makes you laugh."

Rebellious feelings were awakened in workers by *padroni*, the ethnic brokers who peddled immigrant flesh to factory, mill, and mine owners. Unmarried males sought to escape *padrone* contracts and stashed away money enough for the return passage home. I will discuss these "birds of passage" later.

One ought not to overlook how a form of mental transiency gradually became part of the immigrant's way of thinking. Diomede Carito recalled this phrase: "Doctor, we brought to America only our brains and our arms. Our hearts stayed there in the little house in the beautiful fields of our Italy." Nostalgia and sentiment had effectively blocked out the misery of the past and a form of denial set in early.

Those who felt a callousness in the new country's tempo of life would have agreed with D.H. Lawrence: "When you are actually in America, America hurts." D'Angelo remarked that he could not "understand these people in America and their cold ways. They

11

will go to the funeral of their best friend and keep a straight face. I believe they feel ashamed if in a moment of fortrightness they've turned to look at a flower or beautiful sunset." He wrote of passing a florist shop where he saw a glorious display of color: "It seemed as if these cold people made it a silly point of honor not to stop or glance."

Pavese, in his novel *La luna e i falo*, has an immigrant say: "I went to bed with many women, one of them I almost married, and I never found out where they had their father and mother and their land." Pavese's character speaks of American women "who came from who knows where." He doubted whether he could settle down with women in such a culture: "I often thought of what race of children would have come out of us two—out of those smooth hard flanks, out of that blond belly nourished on milk and orange juice, and out of me, out of my thick blood." These women stood in sharp contrast to those of Sicily's villages, overstocked with shrunken widows and diffident madonnas. Immigrants tried to reconcile such contradictory sexual patterns. Alongside the warmth of their previous family life there had been the ambivalence of attraction and repulsion. Letters home did not feature such delicate matters. But they did reflect how the dominant culture demanded passivity and dependence while exalting individual enterprise.

The American assimilationist attitude, sanctioned semiofficially, has done much to limit the infusion of ethnic values into our society. Immigrants had to gain the approval of both their peers in Italy and of their new neighbors. This encouraged a divided self-image and strange personal improvisations.

An observer from the old country saw America as driving its newcomers slightly mad: "The Italian immigrant who does not become a delinquent or crazy—is a saint. No immigrant is normal. America is a land of immigrants who do not speak the original tongue, nor follow its religion . . . full of the abnormal."[3]

In order to fathom the mysteries of American life, the foreign born took refuge in status illusions and material achievements. Because the rewards of work were at first trivial, exaggeration and braggadocio helped make one's fantasies a bit truer. Letters to fellow villagers seldom mentioned the cracks and seams of poverty. In justifying their rejection of the old country, immigrants could hardly admit the inevitable setbacks. Actually, they were being remade by America. For the benefit of those back home, however, they sought to portray the New World as it had always been known to Europe's peasants. Thus, frequently not mentioned were the negative aspects of American life—the appalling overcrowding in the slums, the dismal life on the streets, the overflowing spittoons in public buildings, the open gutters and sewers filled with rotting garbage, the illnesses that resulted from poor sanitation and malnutrition, and the stresses of having to conform to new circumstances.

Conflicting emotions festered in the unconscious mind—that elusive and symbolic instrument by which we obscure our innermost fears and wishes. There is, furthermore, evidence that depressive emotions were repressed and unconsciously converted. "Hysteria" and "neurasthenia" were the terms used before the turn of the century to describe the breakdown of persons diagnosed as having "overworked" themselves. The great white plague of the lower east side of New York was tuberculosis, the origin of which was still not understood. Another mysterious disease, asthma, seemed to accompany being choked off from average attainable expectations. Suicide further marred the abrasive life of the ghettoes.

A psychiatrist who over a period of twelve years examined almost two hundred Italian American patients recorded the following impressions:

> The first generation was characterized more by multiple somatic complaints, a tendency of seeing their psychiatric problem as based on physical causes, that is, physical illness, or on the action of unfriendly people outside the family. . . . The second generation complained of more typical neurotic or psychotic symptoms, was more accessible to psychotherapy and psychodynamically was characterized by a sense of guilt toward the parents. . . . The third generation tended to distinguish itself for acting-out behavior, often of sociopathic type.[4]

Even the psychologically untutored historian ought to be able to discern "identity diffusion" in the immigrants he studies. These foreigners found it difficult to know where to put their angry feelings. We can see in the immigrant record that link between emotional disorders and their autonomic discharge in the form of ulcerative colitis, peptic and duodenal ulcers, rheumatoid arthritis, and other psychoneurotic ailments. The displacement of anxiety also surfaced as overeating (leading to obesity) and stealing (kleptomania). I shall examine these symptoms and their effects throughout the book.

I should make it quite clear, however, that countless immigrant parents—the major influencers of child behavior—were not disturbed. They showed tenderness and healthy strength in support of their progeny. Others were less generous, sometimes because of their own emotional fragility. Still others were ruthless, pushing their children toward lives of desperation. The Mafia, although it replaced poverty, provided a violent, cruel, psychically squalid alternative to family life. Brutality was endemic among those who chose that route in search of a place to belong.

Persons who cannot get rid of anxiety feelings sometimes act upon them. Irritable, tense, and jumpy, they lose control over their emotions. By saying or doing *something*, which they may later regret, they add guilt to their anxiety.

Crowding and physical confusion contributed to both mental and somatic illness. Forced into the decaying neighborhoods of the cities, crowds of gesticulating, animated foreigners competed with one another for decrepit tenement housing. Greeks, Jews, and Italians attempted to preserve human dignity in an atmosphere of vice and filth that made their native European villages look attractive. Although the poverty, ignorance, and intolerance of the present had replaced that of the past, it seemed best not to shatter the illusions of loved ones left behind. Also, one must never admit defeat or error. It was important to avoid being "talked badly of" (*sparlati*) back home. For all these reasons America's streets remained paved with gold, at least in letters to the old country.

Meanwhile the memory of village life grew hazy. The images were distorted. In order to exalt the America they had chosen, some remembered even beautiful places as dank, retrograde, or downright evil. Pasquale D'Angelo sought to explain this phenomenon: "Something had grown in me during my stay in America. Something was keeping me," he wrote, "in this wonderful perilous land where I had suffered so much and where I had so much more to suffer . . . somewhere I would strike the light." He continued: "Without realizing it, I had learned the great lesson of America: I had learned to have faith in the future. No matter how bad things were, a turn would inevitably come—as long as I did not give up."

"God grant me a landfall," Columbus had written in his ship's log. Materialism dominated the hopes of his successors as much as did idealism. Immigrants valued practicality over philosophic contemplation. Few were psychologically introspective. More accepting than resentful, they denied the very past that had shaped them. Like children, they sought to please the new land in which they now placed their faith.

The passage of time has allowed historians to trace with greater accuracy those steps by which the immigrant confrontation with America occurred. The first phase involved obvious cultural shock. This is the phase dwelt upon most by novelists and historians. Frightened, disorganized, and poor, immigrants had indeed been overwhelmed by what they initially encountered in the New World. Survival at that stage was their central concern. Then came an emerging self-consciousness—that working up the ladder of success which has become such a cliché. As pride in their attainments increased, the most talented moved closer to the mainstream of America's national life. Still later came more self-affirmation and even occasional militance about their status. Not until the second and third generations could most of them afford to become disillusioned. This so-called practicality, really a disguised form of repression, helped them to move out across America and determined the places they would live in and the kinds of lives they would lead.

II

DISPERSAL

EMIGRATION HAS BEEN Italy's traditional safety valve. One Italian in ten departs, usually either to other European countries or to the Americas. Were it not for this exodus, Italy's population today could well number not 56 million persons but 80 million.

Prior to the arrival of most Italians, thousands of Germans, Scandinavians, and persons of English stock had settled in the United States. The railroads had spread westward in large measure by dint of Irish and Chinese brawn. Now another nationality entered the scene. "The wop on the track gang" also became a familiar figure. He, alas, faced both the Irish and the English who, despite their past rivalries, closed ranks against competing *braccianti* from Calabria or Sicily. Some of the Irish were Catholics, like the Italians, but they froze these Mediterraneans out of jobs. Only superficially did Latins (including the Spanish and Portuguese) feel any sense of attachment to one another on the hiring line.

Unfortunately for the Italians, their migration was a late one. Most of them arrived long after the American civil war had ended. From 1860 to 1870 only 12,000 Italians left their homeland for the United States. Italy's agricultural depression of 1887, however, made unemployment acute. The year 1894 saw a massive peasant uprising against Sicily's fossilized aristocracy. A decreasing need for farm labor in Italy also stepped up expatriation. By the turn of the century Italy had an excess of births over deaths of 350,000 persons a year. Most Italian emigrants arrived in the United States in the years from 1880 to 1924, during one of the greatest waves of immigration of all times. In 1889 there were, for the first time, more immigrants from Italy than from any other land. That year twice as many Italians as Britons arrived. In 1901 alone half a million persons left Italy. The pattern of European migration to the United States was so well established by the turn of the century that one-third of the nation consisted of foreign-born residents or their children. For years the annual number of arrivals into the United States passed the million mark. A peak was reached in 1907, when 1,285,000 foreigners arrived.

By 1910, the federal census counted 1,343,000 Italians— mostly poor, ill-educated, unable to speak English, and lacking in technical skills. With native-born children they numbered well over two million. In the following decade another 1,109,524 appeared. Six million persons of Italian origin would ultimately forge a living link between their homeland and America.

Over the years, American immigration laws were passed to stem what one writer called a "tide of scum and ignorance." In 1882, Congress excluded paupers, criminals, and other undesirables. Three years later foreign contract labor was shut out, as were additional "bad risks." By 1917, a literacy test was required of adult immigrants. These restrictions represented an economic and social reaction to the tremendous increase in immigration and to the shift in its origins toward south-central and eastern Europe. From 1911 to 1915 almost 70 percent of America's immigrants came from these areas. In 1921, following a slackening during World War I, the United States drastically restricted immigration, establishing an emergency national quota. Then, in 1924, a permanent quota policy of restriction, demanded by

American labor organizations, virtually stopped the flow of cheap manpower.

Over 70 percent of these immigrants settled within the ethnic patches of the eastern United States. There, factories and mines fueled America's new industrialism. Its barometer was steel, transformed by the blast furnaces of the Bessemer process into a low-cost commodity from which thousands of items from railroad rails to barbed wire could be fashioned.

Though Henry Bessemer and Andrew Carnegie, whose names became synonymous with the steel industry, were themselves immigrants, no Italian of their generation would grow so affluent. Old photographs record long rows of foreign laborers, with drooping mustaches, muscled like athletes and ready for years of hard labor. The wop had arrived on the track gang. As prospective miners who had never been below the surface of the ground spilled off the trains at Pittsburgh, little did they know that they would spend whole lives furrowing its pits and tending its furnaces. These willing *braccianti* joined Serbs and Croatians in Lackawanna, New York, as well as Polish and Welsh laborers in Passaic, New Jersey, and Slovenes and Bulgarians in the Pennsylvania coal and iron mines at Steelton. By 1910 almost 85 percent of Passaic's 55,000 inhabitants were either first or second-generation immigrants; of its more than 28,000 foreign born, three of every four were so-called new immigrants.

The coal- and oil-bearing lands that lay along the banks of the scrofulous Monongahela and Allegheny rivers kindled one's need to escape from such a meager existence. The blast furnaces of America's steel mills lit up the nights, posing a sharp contrast to the mountain villages of the Apennines, with their goats, olive and walnut trees, and half-ruined monasteries.

It was natural to recoil from the baffling steel and concrete cities of the east coast, to seek a psychological defense against the fragmentation of one's soul. The callous new society, however, made it hard to create a personal island in its midst. Rather than to cringe, foreigners and natives alike were expected to scatter pieces of themselves, figuratively, over the American landscape, to surrender personal values and attitudes to a greater whole.

In another book I have written about how foreigners who traveled beyond the hundredth meridian escaped into an experience different from that available on the east coast. Fiorello La Guardia, the son of an army bandmaster, paid tribute to the emancipative forces of Arizona, which started him on a career that ultimately made him the greatest mayor of America's greatest city. National stereotypes have obscured the life patterns of others who also successfully penetrated the Yankee world out west. In 1913, for example, Columbus and Carmel Giragi took over the *Tombstone Epitaph,* one of the most conspicuous Anglo newspapers in the American West. They were the sons of Sicilian immigrants who had come to the Arizona territory in the 1880s to work in the Tombstone silver mines. Columbus Giragi became the owner of a string of newspapers and a prominent Arizona figure. He reminds one of A. P. Giannini, founder of California's Bank of America, and countless other persons of Italian origin who "made it" big in western America.

Not all those who went west encountered the sprawling prairies and rich forests described in European accounts of America's interior. Sometimes dusty squalor and ugliness replaced what they had sought to escape. The unfamiliar landmarks of the West did not quiet feelings of malaise about the future. Beyond the Mississippi, except for San Francisco and New Orleans, the towns had a ramshackle, almost anti-European, look to them. Only those who made it to California would discover a relatively familiar Mediterranean shoreline and climate. Even that resemblance was hardly a substitute for life in the piazza at Agrigento or Siena.

Mining towns like Butte, Montana, seemed almost to poison themselves by fumes from copper refineries. El Paso, Texas, was a brush-strewn desert crossroads, loaded with sand fleas and cheap Mexican labor. In the coal-bearing foothills of the Rocky Mountains immigrants became involved in serious labor strife, including

Colorado's great Coalfield War. Too many Italians lost their lives in that state's Ludlow Massacre during 1914.

On the Pacific slope, where immigrants seemed quickly to prosper, the percentage of foreigners remained high. Not only did the European resident population grow; so did colonies of Japanese and Chinese. In 1870 California's Irish constituted one in four of its immigrant residents. Ten years later Nevada's foreign born made up 41.2 percent of its population and in 1880 that state's Eureka County consisted of 59 percent foreign-born folk. Remote and isolated Nevada attracted a larger per capita foreign population than did any other American state or territory.

At San Francisco during 1880, out of a population of 233,959 persons 104,244 had been born abroad. By 1900 that city, with a foreign-born populace of close to 40 percent, was a major cosmopolitan center, along with New York and Chicago. San Francisco was peopled by more Italians than any other foreign group. In fact, it bore the name of their favorite saint, Francis of Assisi.

The Italians, as did other immigrants, sought social acceptance and *rispetto*. More than two-thirds of them had once lived close to the Italian countryside, and they did well in farm settings when they were allowed to commingle with the "better people." Merle Curti's study of late nineteenth-century Trempeleau County, Wisconsin, stresses the unity of races in a rural environment; "Whether foreign-born or native Americans," their social gatherings "brought most elements of the population together on an equal and entirely democratic basis."

Except for the Chicago area, the mid-Atlantic states, however, attracted the largest number of immigrants. In 1900 New York City contained more Jews than did Warsaw, more Italians than did Florence, and more Irish than did Dublin. In fact, it housed more foreign-born persons than any other city in the world. By 1920, when first-generation Italians in California reached only about 80,000, and those of a state like Texas 8,000, over 500,000 Italians lived in New York, some 200,000 in Pennsylvania, and more than 300,000 in Rhode Island. The immigration law of 1924 reduced the annual Italian quota to only 5,500 persons, and it remained at that level for many years.

Immigrants were everywhere—on ranches, in mines, and in construction work of all sorts. Did the West offer greater acceptance because of its diversity? It is still an open question whether a rural environment helps to equalize differences among nationalities. Do urban settings exaggerate separateness?

A study of the social atmosphere in Minnesota's mining towns has suggested that the assimilation of immigrants is a theme that should continue to be stressed alongside that of alienation. Although immigrants who settled in the Mesabi and Vermillion ranges encountered small-town "cultural islands" of nationalism, these rural centers could not withstand "the assimilating effects of shared experience." Smaller communities encouraged bonds of unity, reducing the stigma of being a foreigner. Immigrant women, traditionally more sheltered from life on the streets than were their menfolk, felt freer out west to shop in stores where English was used. All of this led to an "astonishingly rapid adjustment of all groups to prevailing American folkways" that extended to school children, civic activities, and recreation. The growing number of immigrants who married outside their national group also exercised "a mediating role among newcomers of the father's nationality." In the small towns of Minnesota, religious life also became markedly interethnic, even in Roman Catholic congregations.

In Arizona of the 1870s, although loneliness faced immigrants at every turn, three out of ten westerners had been born abroad. Nearly 60 percent of Arizona's population was foreign born. In that year more than half of the men aged twenty-one and over in Utah, Nevada, Arizona, Idaho, and California had been born abroad. St. Louis, Denver, and Salt Lake City were full of foreigners.

For those who stayed behind, the eastern urban areas offered cohesion. Congestion, however, produced unhealthy slums crammed with decaying brick buildings. As many as ten or twelve boarders slept in three-room cold-water flats. Rows of tenements

21

housed thousands of persons who threw their garbage and slop out onto back alleys that teemed with rats and children. Laundry hung over the alleys, the sagging clotheslines supported by wooden poles. The smell of stale urine blew off the damp bed sheets and the rancid odors of garbage and of horse manure further offended the senses. Under these conditions the memory of one's mountain village seemed sweet, despite the marsh fevers of Campania and the vulcanism of Mount Stromboli.

In those early years before the advent of medical insurance, a young wife and mother who came down with tuberculosis imperiled the very future of her husband and children. This "immigrant's disease" was especially contagious among children. Milk contamination was a precipitating cause, which too long remained unknown. As we shall see, children were crucial to the maintenance of urban ethnic families. A child's work, whether as a mill hand or as a newsboy on city streets, provided income that might be lost if he fell ill. Yet relatively few children, as in Dickensian England, had to search an American city's ashbins for half-burnt cinders to take home to their mother's stove. Furthermore, it was not unusual for peasant children in Italy to scoop up manure droppings behind a horse, later to be used as fertilizer. Each of the two worlds—European and American—had its shortcomings.

Competition in the new land remained fierce. Evan Hunter's novel *Streets of Gold* (1974) portrays an America in which wop fights mick until the blood flows. Digging New York's BMT subway tunnels, brawling immigrants found their bosses to be ruthless, consuming both brawn and sweat recklessly. One could be buried alive in a cave-in. The myth of America's twenty-carat streets had not, furthermore, included warnings to newcomers at Ellis Island that they were entering a guinea ghetto in which your brother might put his hand in your pocket.

It was a relief to get home at the end of the day even though immigrant walk-up flats were bare of all but the essentials. Sparsely furnished rooms might include a wooden table, a chair or two, and a hard bed, with no rugs on the floor or curtains to cover the windows. The ambiance was not so squalid as plain. There is no need to stress only the depressive effects or to sentimentalize it all, as Oscar Handlin did in his rather maudlin book *The Uprooted* (1952).

To save money for "Dago Red" wine, men cut their big, strong Tuscan cigars in two, smoking them half at a time. The women filled soup kettles with backyard green vegetables that took the place of meat. Immigrants cooked "pasta fazool" (Neapolitan for *pasta e fagioli*) three or four times a week. This mixture of pasta and beans was cheap yet nutritious. The alternative for north Italians was *polenta*, a cornmeal mush combined with sausage or tripe in tomato sauce. *Bagna cauda*, vegetables dipped in hot olive oil, was another inexpensive staple. Homemakers used newspapers in place of a tablecloth and rolled them up as a substitute for firewood. These frugalities may seem chic or even cute today. But they were essential among foreigners.

However, slum families rather quickly got beyond hand-me-down clothes, the rule in the peasant villages of Italy. These were replaced by brand-new American dresses, coats, and trousers bought in stores. Soon gone, too, were the memories of fighting off rats with one hand while filling in correspondence course forms with the other.

The promised subways, electric lights, and flush toilets did not come soon enough for tenement dwellers. The Italian American novelist Lucas Longo portrayed one of the characters in his *Family on Vendetta Street* as grossly dissatisfied with life in an eastern ghetto:

> One summer afternoon while teaching me the finer points of boccie in our back yard, he stopped to wipe his brow. "I should never have come to New York. Never. This damn city. Filthy. A dirty hell. I should have done the right thing. I should have saved more money and taken a boat for California. That's the place for human beings. Farmland. Sun. Space. They say the land is so beautiful there. And that the earth brings forth lovely things. Here what happens? What happens in this filthy hell? Here I plant my lettuce and your mother's stupid cat lifts her stupid rear and wets it.". . . I offered to get him a glass of water, which always helped. As I was leaving, he called after me, "Let it run. Let it run quite a while." Then he cursed the city and its rotten plumbing.[1]

By the turn of the century Harlem, formerly a prosperous theater community—with attractive restaurants, bands, an opera house, and a philharmonic orchestra—became a commuting point for downtown Manhattan. Elegant brownstones deteriorated into tenements that housed thousands of immigrants. The Italians settled in east Harlem, the Jews farther west, and the Germans to the south of the Italians. Still later the Puerto Ricans squeezed themselves in between the Germans and the Italians (and pushed out both groups).

On the lower east side of Manhattan yet another Italian community, Mulberry Bend, took shape. It comes alive today in the angry stills taken by Jacob Riis, who documented the dismal living and working conditions in Manhattan's ghettoes. We can see the peddlers' carts in the chaotic streets and almost hear the babel of tongues. Those who had mastered a few words of English began to call later comers in their Old World clothes (and clinging customs) "greenhorns," a word that became part of the American language. The inner-core neighborhood of Mulberry Bend and Hester Street (mostly Jewish), with its dirty alleys, open sewers, and rows of brick tenement houses, provided a dank environment in which to rear one's children.

On the east side of New York 200,000 immigrants lived in a territory less than one square mile in size. In this city within a city as many as five thousand persons were crowded onto one street, fifteen to a four-room flat, and four hundred in tenement buildings intended for fifty persons. Congestion, with poverty, disease, and crime, made the east side a noisy miniature Europe, a polyglot boardinghouse for breadwinners from every land. Today crowded remnants of that ghetto remain intact. The ten blocks from Houston to Canal streets are a clutter of aging flats and boarded-up shops in disrepair and decay.

Why did the Italians stay on in Mulberry Bend? Was it to bury there the village hatreds of the past? Did the bustle of the ghetto provide at least a superficial sense of security? Making it in America was a complex matter. Coming of age there involved absorbing life's daily humiliations—for which one had to possess strong inner resources. Mulberry Bend may have been the necessary halfway house at which unsettled and apprehensive persons remained as long as they could.

In 1900 the 290,000 persons per square mile who lived in the lower east side stood in contrast to the nearby communities outside the city. These were only sparsely settled by Italians. An immigrant shack on the outskirts of greater New York somehow seemed less desirable than a ghetto room surrounded by one's kin. Like bees in a hive, most immigrants were gregarious. America's suburbs could, furthermore, scarcely mount such spectacles as Mulberry Street's week-long *Festa di San Gennaro*. Gradually other nationalities crowded in, too. As at San Francisco's North Beach, in New York the boisterous Chinese replaced the once teeming Italian community centered upon Mulberry Bend.

Although the Bend was metropolitan, its possibilities for alienation were no less real than those that other communities offered. Inside the Bend's tenement houses were close relatives, newly acquired friends, and mutual reinforcement. Outside lay the anonymity of America's mean streets. We also know, however, that slums and poverty alone do not produce lives of horror. The ghetto by itself does not induce crime. Nor do the suburbs promote mental health. The child nurtured in a slum family can grow up as secure as someone reared in a mansion. But the environment must be a facilitating one. The psychohistorian ought not to be concerned only with degrees of poverty. Also important is the quality of nurturing, really another form of wealth. Although cycles of economic disadvantage undoubtedly exist, poverty-stricken persons do succeed in breaking out. We need to know more about how such escape occurs.

Beneath the surface of American society lay forces as authoritarian as the emancipation that had been overly advertised throughout the world. The poorly ventilated tenements, windowless factories, and smelly gasworks were only the symbols of an environment in which the immigrant seemed trapped. But, as Baudelaire reminded us, life is a forest of symbols.

In the midst of the country's greatest city, Mulberry Bend

became the main outpost for Italians in a land larger than Europe itself. That settlement, and others of its type, provided a sheltering and a rooting that in places like Boston's well-known north end, became permanent. Two other predominantly Italian neighborhoods in New York—Arthur Avenue in the Bronx and the Carroll Gardens section of South Brooklyn—have also substantially resisted pressures for change. The former remains an enclave, some four or five blocks deep by three or four blocks, in the north-central Bronx immediately to the south of Pelham Parkway. It is surrounded by formerly Jewish, now predominantly black, tenements. Arthur Avenue is the commercial spine of the neighborhood. Its businesses are uncompromisingly Italian; most of them are food stores, but there is a sprinkling of travel agents and knicknack shops. The architecture is vintage mid-Bronx—an old-fashioned mixture of tenements, along with a small number of one-family houses boasting small attached gardens. It is, like the surrounding area, solidly working-class and seems to have survived as an ethnic enclave for a number of reasons. First, because Arthur Avenue is close to Pelham Parkway, surburban outsiders may relatively easily drive in from nearby Westchester County to buy fresh food in its markets—virtually impossible to get in the washed-out suburbs; second, because it has always been aloof from the neighboring Jewish community, Arthur Avenue has felt a less immediate impact from the heavy black in-migration around it than have superficially similar enclaves; third, because it continues to attract immigrants from Italy, the drifting away from the neighborhood is offset; and fourth, its working-class inhabitants simply do not want to leave.

In Brooklyn, Carroll Gardens is the remnant of what was the much larger Italian ghetto of Red Hook and South Brooklyn. This character-filled area is quite extensive—some five or six blocks across and eight or nine blocks deep. It is cut off on two sides by an expressway built in the 1950s and on the third side by water. This imposed isolation helped protect Carroll Gardens from the decay that overtook much of nineteenth-century and downtown Brooklyn. And, as it is open by land to only well-to-do Brooklyn

Heights to the north and as Carroll Gardens consists almost entirely of brownstones, with very few tenement buildings, gentrification is spreading slowly southward into the area, which, while it remains largely Italian, is no longer exclusively so. Its shops are, of course, all Italian; and there is a substantial commuter population into Manhattan.

Over the years such ethnic neighborhoods have helped to form attitudes that are neither Italian nor American. There were, of course, wanderers not content to stay behind in these ghettoes. For them the portals of the east coast led to a wider existence elsewhere. Yet, life within the ghetto had already provided a partial emancipation from European folkways.

III
SEEKING SHELTER

THE MAJOR TRAUMAS and fears came in the earliest years. What a strange world America must have seemed to immigrants from rocky, remote villages high in the Apennines or from the arid reaches of Calabria who settled in the crowded Bronx or the north end of Boston. Nevertheless, they all felt the lure of America. The immigrant writer Mary Antin once described the foreign born as people who missed the *Mayflower* and came over on the first boat they could find. It made a big difference, however, if that particular vessel was named *Fior di Maggio*. Its load of swarthy passengers stood little chance of ever becoming Boston Brahmins. Yet immigrants scarcely came to the New World because they sought assimilation in a melting pot. To be washed out into tasteless uniformity is not a human goal.

The disruptive changes that were occurring in American life ravaged the authority of the immigrant family. Even the family-centered kinship pattern was hard to keep intact. Limited in controlling the environment, some heads of families maintained the illusion that they had greater control over their destiny (*destino*) than was actually true. Through a compulsion to work one could overcome distressful feelings at the same time that healthy goals were materializing. The skill of A.P. Giannini, founder of the Bank of America, and the cautious workmanship of the vintner Louis Martini, for example, made them great successes in faraway California.

Wherever they settled, to sing a song of defensiveness about their Italian past was unseemly. Better to keep a stiff upper lip, to follow the "American way." But not everyone could be so compliant. These cursed America's woes in a phrase that few cared to utter: *Managgia l'America!* ("Damn America!").

The ways in which the immigrant and his children acted out their frustrations have remained veiled. We scarcely remember that it was Gaetano Bresci of Paterson, New Jersey, who traveled to Italy with a pistol in his pocket in order to kill King Humbert I. The assassin of the fierce anti-Fascist Giacomo Matteoti was Amerigo Dunini, born in St. Louis, Missouri. Edmondo Rossoni, one of the major protagonists of Italian fascism, was, before 1914, a leader of the I.W.W. movement; he also was an advocate of using dynamite in order to advance anarchist-syndicalist causes. Yet, only the rare immigrant actively participated in labor strife, despite what some ethnic interpreters may tell us today. Even those who outwardly rebelled usually did so alongside non-ethnic laborers.

Foreigners from a country in which property was scarce would do almost anything to acquire a plot of land or a small business of their own. In order to feed large families they would work nights pressing pants in a nearby town or dig coal in a mine or bag cement. Many held down two jobs at once, sometimes crossing over the hazy line between blue-collar and white-collar work. The success ethic, of course, followed the dominant Horatio Alger mythology that a poor boy could rise from rags to riches. This myth promised success but not happiness. So one learned to hide stress, to disguise anxieties, and to act as though such repression was good. What was a fantasy became a reality. Meanwhile, the immigrant would be rewarded by displaying the traits of diligence, industry, and sobriety.

The twists and turns of joining the in-group meant acceptance of the harsh masculinity that pervaded the dominant society. This made it seem wise to reject sentimental, soft, or feminine feelings as unworthy or weak. One had best erase memories of fishermen from Sorrento singing *"O mia Italia adorata!"* Hard-headed materialism was looked upon as the clearest means by which to achieve progress, so-called. *Braccianti* thus took on those strong and efficient Yankee patterns by which farmers and merchants alike were accumulating worldly goods. The Americans obviously valued optimistic tough-mindedness over somber peasant ruminations about *il destino*. At times it seemed as though life were becoming a daily violation of one's best concepts concerning oneself.

Yet, America's fear of strangers dictated the need to conform, at least outwardly. The Greek term "xenophobia" reminds us that animals and humans alike distrust the outlander. How well foreigners are tolerated depends partly upon whether they seem troublesome or not. In the United States, before immigrants could qualify as "our kind of people," various shades of differentness had to be reconciled. This involved personal and family names, language, and appearance. In addition to skin color and body smell, garlic-scented breath and malodorous Toscano cigars hardly furthered the respectability of the "spaghetti benders." Accordingly, newcomers who did not appear capable of absorbing the new culture were labeled bad. Assimilation was, furthermore, a one-way process. For the natives, the "best" values and insights did not come from abroad.

The term "adjustment" became crucial for immigrants. The Marxist critic Theodor Adorno, who was himself foreign born, saw the willingness of "persecuted people" to adjust as vital to any nationality. They were expected to prove themselves and "not to be so haughty as to insist stubbornly on remaining what they had been before." This necessity for accommodation is summed up in an Italian maxim: *Avere la legittimità dalla propria: e il modo con cui si stabilizzano le rivoluzioni e si tengono le donne* ("Make sure accepted customs are on your side: that is the way to settle revolutions or to keep women").

In seeking acceptability, families often stood divided. The instant assimilation that immigrant children hungered for had not been a part of their parents' experience. In Italy the peasant mentality had resisted quick changes in status. Furthermore, it proved tiring to wear down America's resistance to foreigners. It seemed easiest simply to block out the cultural milieu from which a family had come, especially to delete the word "Italian." Quite commonly immigrant children would describe their background as Piedmontese or Roman or Venetian, instead. This separation from one's past, however, did involve a devaluing of selfhood. whether the immigrants knew it or not.

The ability to speak English without an accent became one of the first tangible means to acceptance. Hence, the most ambitious immigrants felt a genuine discomfort whenever one of their countrymen insisted upon speaking proper Italian rather than the patois spawned in America. To be reminded that one had given up one's original language required repression of a sense of loss. What psychoanalysts call "identification with the aggressor" took the form of boasting that the superiority of the New World made it worthwhile to sacrifice one's past ties and loyalties and to endure abuse. This self-justification was itself a disguised form of denial, as the immigrant exalted such material values as "better" American housing, clothing, and transportation. Recourse to the Italian past only kept one swimming upstream.

In rural Italy "do not create envy" had been an unstated rule. A poor peasant felt so vulnerable to thieves that he did not dare divulge possession of valuables. Some slick city invader might take away one's riches. Hoarding and secrecy about one's attainments would guard against loss. Indeed, if a person grew too rich he might be abused by others more powerful than oneself. The strategy of countless peasant generations, therefore, had been to keep the invader at bay, to minimize one's status in life, to keep a low profile. America, however, called for a reversal of such attitudes, for Americans measured worth by the display of property and position.

Children pushed their families toward greater material achievements. The home one's parents were able to buy and the furniture they placed inside it were criteria by which a child compared himself with other children. A sort of achievement glue fastened together status and success.

In America it was also difficult to insist that children avoid social climbing. The immigrant family faced some touchy challenges that arose from the greater personal freedom available to the young. Reduction in the authority of both father and mother and increased class mobility also led to sharp contradictions with the Italian past. The rigidity of old ways had to give way to plasticity and adaptability.

Yet, family roots are necessary in order to nourish a sense of self. In Robert Canzoneri's *A Highly Ramified Tree* (1976) we can see how one immigrant child felt bifurcated. Part of his personal root system was in Sicily and another in his new Mississippi home. Canzoneri came to see his family "roots and branches not only as a means of nourishment, but as what each of us diverges into."[1] The Sicily of his father's boyhood hardly helped Canzoneri to fuse two markedly different and confusing life-styles.

Retreat into the past proved impossible for immigrant children. It was painful for their parents to keep persons one loved from vanishing forever from memory. Anaïs Nin (who was not Italian) described both the wrench of separation from the Old World and the callousness of Americans: "They do not reveal themselves, they do not even seem present." It was the newcomer's place to establish himself, not America's. This could be done only by changing past values.

Within the immigrant family there was an intense need for love and approval. Competition among children centered around the fear that parental affection would be withdrawn. A rigid parent might award love according to such matters as whether a child sat at the table properly, ate his spaghetti neatly, or spilled red wine on his First Communion suit.

The wish for more "normal American parents" was frequently expressed by members of the second generation. I discuss their storms of adolescence later, a singularly difficult time for sons who sought to revolt against their fathers by bringing into the family the values of the outside world.

As the children of immigrants moved into adulthood, they were forced to mature more rapidly than were those of non-foreigners. They dressed, talked, and thought like persons a generation or two older than themselves. Accordingly, they could not be fully responsive to the authoritarian values of their own fathers. This problem trapped them between destructive hypocrisies and contradictions that were bottled up defensively within themselves.

Inside the family, children were taught that strangers would let one down. Indeed, outsiders who got too close aroused the old peasant images of dependency and vindictiveness, as well as fears that had blackened the quality of life in remote Italian villages.

Memories of the old country cast a shadow across the generations. The poverty and the brutalities of remote villages could scarcely be forgotten. In America, uneducated day laborers continued to work in a back-bending and sweaty ethnic isolation. Immigrant declarations of self-satisfaction masked defensiveness about personal honor and dignity. Upward mobility hardly guaranteed self-respect.

Furthermore, America had already set up the rules by which the game was played. The majority dictated the terms, conditions, and rewards. At times it looked like none but Anglos could win. The emergence of these stereotypes, substituted for one's own values, led foreigners toward ego impoverishment.

Parents ˙were exasperated by an inability to control their children. Not all of their feelings were respectful either. Pietro di Donato, who grew up in West Hoboken, New Jersey, recounted the story (in his book *Three Circles of Light*) of how his mother sought to protect him from the inroads of American life. He quoted her as saying to his Italian employer:

> I beg you, Signore Pellegrini, help me to save my first-born masculine from the savage manners of the braying Americans who consume parents, respect not Christians, nor revere the humility of gentle Christ. My son will obey you as keenly as the razor's edge. . . . Otherwise I'll ring his noggin like a bell.[2]

All immigrants, not only the Italians, used a variety of maneuvers to defend themselves against the fear of being personally invaded. They sought inwardly not to succumb completely to the commanding society; yet they outwardly avowed that America was marvelous. Sublimation and isolation both of one's person and feelings were ways to overcome pressing anxieties. In the privacy of home it was possible to keep the past alive by listening to treasured operatic recordings by the tenors Enrico Caruso or Beniamino Gigli. In the 1930s others tuned in their radios, covertly, to the speeches of the Italian dictator Mussolini or to the interpretations of his American Fascist apologist Giuseppe Cardellini. There was a furtive aspect to these isolating activities.

On occasion, anxiety spilled over into eccentricity. This was the case with Baldasare Forestiere, who had migrated to Boston in 1902 from Messina, Sicily, at the age of twenty-three. Renouncing the life of a subway worker, he moved to Fresno, California, where he sought refuge underground. In 1906 he began digging living quarters, including a kitchen and a bedroom, then a chamber where he made wine, and a subterranean vault where he aged cheese and cured meats. Next he built a chapel, then grottoes, and a series of tunnels. One of these led to an auditorium or dance hall 100 feet long, 50 feet wide, and 25 feet high. In the roofs of other rooms he dug skylights out of the hard bedrock for which he fashioned glass covers.

Forestiere's subterranean refuge resembled the ventilated tunneling by harassed Chinese immigrants under the soil of Eureka, Nevada. Forestiere's strange maze of subsurface structures perplexed his neighbors. He became known as the "Human Mole" as he constructed his ten-acre underground network.

Forestiere's galleries, which took thirty-one years to dig, suggested that he liked living away from the world he saw above ground. He filled his underground world with graceful archways that covered aesthetic nooks and planted orange, tangerine, grapefruit, lemon, and lime trees in underground courtyards. The trees flourish to this day, producing fruit each season, their branches reaching to the surface out of deep holes. His nephew Ricardo remembered:

When I was much younger and Uncle Baldasare was still alive, my father would worry after not seeing him for several days. Dad and I would go into my uncle's underground maze and start looking for him. It was easy to get lost. We would look with a lantern. Father would holler out his name—"Balde, Balde."

"Hey, over here," Uncle Baldasare would shout back. And we would find him busy at work late at night.

There were many stories all over Fresno that my uncle had buried a fortune in money somewhere in the tunnels or in one of the rooms.

To this day people claim my uncle buried anywhere from $100,000 to $500,000 in cash somewhere down here underground.[3]

Forestiere's family had tried to stop the digging, for he was ridiculed by perplexed neighbors. When he died in 1946 these same relatives wanted to destroy the more than one hundred caverns he had created. "Uncle Baldasare and his underground diggings were an embarrassment to them," his nephew recalled. "My father did not understand his brother's obsession, but he admired his work. The relatives gladly let my father have his ten acres of diggings."[4] For, upon his death at age sixty-seven, Forestiere left behind more than a thousand acres of rich California farmland, along with "Forestiere's Underground Gardens," as they are known to tourists.

One mile outside Julesburg, Colorado, there labored another Italian tunnel builder. But we know less about Umberto Gabello. He also sought underground a place where he would not be disturbed by outsiders. Gabello left behind what has become known as the "Italian's Cave." A miner who had made a small fortune in the gold fields at Cripple Creek, Gabello was considered crazy by his neighbors. He lived like a hermit in his house-cavern, avoiding all contact, even with persons who dwelled nearby. Upon his death, mysterious carvings were found in Gabello's cave that seemed to suggest that he considered the place to be his monument to the sun.

Better known are the "Watts Towers" of Simone Rodia (Rodilla) in Los Angeles, California. He fashioned these out of bits of junk—glass, cup handles, corn cobs. Because he had no building permit, Rodia was in constant dispute with city officials over safety. And Rodia's neighbors thought he was crazy:

fastened to the towers by a window-washer's belt, he would sing Italian operatic arias while he cemented tile or bits of glass high above the ground.

Rodia was born in a village near Naples in 1879. He emigrated as a child. His explanation of the thirty-three years that he spent on the towers was that he "wanted to do something for the United States because there are nice people in this country." This seems almost too pat an explanation.

If we travel to the Los Angeles suburb of Watts we see a flat and dry landscape of desolate bungalows, today a black ghetto. It is as boring and undistinguished as many towns in the American Midwest. Watts is bypassed and overwhelmed by a vast system of freeways that link downtown Los Angeles with the city's beaches and harbor. In the 1920s, however, the waving palm trees and the cheap land probably appealed to Rodia. The Mediterranean climate of southern California made it possible to live comfortably enough on little money.

As one drives along the rusting railroad tracks on 107th Street, Rodia's mosaic-encrusted spires jut into the sky. He may have needed to project outward on unsettling inner feeling for beauty, rusticated in steel mesh, mortar, and rubble. The largest tower is nearly a hundred feet tall, giving these structures which break up the bleakness of the surrounding plane, a sense of abstract power and force.

Rodia seems not to have been a fanatic. But he may have felt oppressed by the middle-class sterility of Protestant southern California. Perhaps he wished to combat aridity, both within and outside himself. He hardly could have built the towers if he was only a fanatic. Yet this is the most common explanation for his construction of a monument once called "a pile of junk."

The towers were almost demolished in 1959 by a bumbling Building and Safety Department of the city of Los Angeles. Five years before, Rodia had simply walked away from his masterpiece, deeding his property to a neighbor. A stress test established that he had built his towers well; they withstood a 10,000-pound pull load (the equivalent of the force exerted by a seventy-mile-per-hour wind blowing for five minutes).

Rodia's beloved towers are now recognized as a major achievement of twentieth-century folk art. We need not berate those who could not appreciate his creations. Nor should we canonize Rodia for his artistry with broken bottles, cement, and seashells. We might, however, seek to understand this Italian immigrant and his productions. For the towers are more than the protest that art critics see them as. The towers in fact do not seem to express outrage such as one finds in much modern art.

Rodia's eccentricity reminds us of that of other obscure individualists such as Ferdinand Pavel, a French postman who built an ornate mausoleum that has been compared to the curious art nouveau of the Catalonian Antonio Gaudi. (It was once rumored that Rodia had buried his wife under one of the towers, but his towers are not a mausoleum.) One thinks also of Gutzon Borglum (the son of Danish immigrants), who created his own national park in the monumental sculpturing of Mount Rushmore, South Dakota. In Rodia's case, he used the by-products of an affluent society. The obsessive personality is often compelled to control the environment, to shape his surroundings, to achieve mastery over inner anxiety by material works.

Is eccentricity enigmatic? These immigrant social isolates bring to mind the character of Old Jules, that indomitable and strange father of Mari Sandoz, the Nebraska frontier writer. She has well described his rough and tough, brawling aggressiveness, acted out amidst the sod houses of a primitive and elemental prairie existence. Her father's way of coping with malaise was to project it outward as anger.

Were primitive immigrant productions a tangible way by which neurotic anxieties could be displaced and acted out? Were Rodia's phallic towers really a projection of inner turmoil? To answer these questions we would have to know more about the early lives of Forestiere, Gabello, and Rodia. Their eccentricities might not have been fully related to alienation. One does wonder whether they sought escape from a squalid world on the surface of the earth by burrowing below or building above it. Whatever their motives, these immigrants became compulsive social isolates. Each built enduring monuments: Rodia's bizarre towers of mortar, steel, and rubble are now a historical structure protected by the city fathers of Los Angeles; Forestiere's and Gabello's labyrinthine earthworks also endure.

It is too much to believe that these complex persons were unconsciously acting out their feelings of helplessness? Whereas Forestiere and Gabello buried their feelings underground, members of the Mafia created a distorted system of subterranean justice. Indeed, it is my belief that immigrants concealed their resentments through a form of self-burial, but that anger had to be defended against by passivity and conformity. These defenses, in turn, required denial of affect (feeling). Isolation of helpless feelings produced further resentment; the classic anxiety-reaction cycle resulted.

The need to be loved in a strange land took concealed forms. By submerging their rage immigrants hoped to avoid rejection. The hiding of anger made it possible to play things safe. To deflect their inner hurts immigrants employed defense mechanisms learned in childhood, and repeated later in life—among them denial, undoing, and the ritualization of daily life. These behavior patterns are understandable: they seek to protect the ego.

Those *contadini* who became "urban villagers," a term first used by Herbert Gans to describe displaced *agricoltori*, maintained some odd attitudes toward self-preservation. One of these, cruelty toward animals (and sometimes children), sprang from a poverty-stricken past in which non-workers were treated intolerantly. A primitive practicality became prized. Just as fruit trees were favored over ornamental ones, draft animals took precedence over dogs and cats. And unwanted children stood in the way of the wife's laboring alongside her husband. Extra mouths to feed were a liability.

As I have said, cruelty toward animals and children occurred within some immigrant families. Control of our sadistic impulses is particularly difficult when we are anxious, as many immigrant parents were. So, occasionally, the immigrant father kicked the dog, the cat, or the whining child. Related to this displacement were hostile feelings toward nature itself. The Italian culture lacks a strong tradition of love for the out-of-doors. In America persons who had spent their lives in stone villages, whether in Liguria or along the crowded cement blocks of an American city, might eventually grow to appreciate the countryside; but more important than its preservation was self-preservation.

The loss of one's self was nowhere more obvious than in the adoption of a new language. Immigrant children went to public schools, whether their parents were miners in the Mesabi Range or fruit pickers at San Jose. They read the same books that their non-immigrant schoolmates read. Only in certain cities, such as San Francisco, could immigrant children attend parochial schools where their parent's tongue was spoken. Following the passage of a relatively few years, afterschool classes in Italian became harder to find. In the public schools the nationalistic *McGuffey Readers*, Portia's "Speech on Mercy," and Scott's *Ivanhoe*—assigned reading for all—had a part in making immigrants look upon English, not Italian, as their major inheritance. And because some members of the first generation knew only a local dialect, English was the first *common* language among Italian immigrants.

Italian immigrants also picked up a quasi-English (immigrant American) from Poles on the lower east side of New York, from Chinese storekeepers in San Francisco, and from Jewish garment workers in Brooklyn. The foreigner's use of language resembled his job situation: he filled in the gaps with work and words far removed from what he had been trained to do or say in the old country.

Uneducated persons tranformed English words: for instance, bum got an "Italian" plural, *bummi*. Rag, bar, and car became *raggo*, *barro*, and *carro*. Job, basket, shop, and mortar were changed to *jobba*, *basketta*, *shoppa*, and *mata*; grocery to *grosseria* and customer to *cos-tu-me*. Business is hardly recognizable as *bi-zi-ne*. No one could guess that *Bokeen*, *stracinosa*, *sediolo*, *rai-ro-de*, and *elettricosa* stand for Hoboken, station house, city hall, railroad, and electric cars.

H. L. Mencken, whose book *The American Language* discusses this tranposition of words, pointed out that the "new language" the immigrants created was of real value to them. Many spoke only local dialects, some mutually unintelligible, so that persons from the same region tended to flock together. Their "American-Italian" jargon usually included terms unfamiliar in the homeland. Among these were *visco* for whiskey, *ghenga* for gang, *loffari* for loafers, *blacco enze* for black hand, *grinoni* for greenhorns, *roffu* for roof, and *gliarda* for yard. The word fight became *faitare, faiti, faitava, faito,* and *faitasse.* The Italians of the West used *ranchio* for ranch, a word seldom heard in the East. You bet became *you betcha;* a son-of-a-gun was a *sanemagogna;* job was transformed into *giobba,* along with lynch into *linciare* (the latter term was one that no immigrant cared to utter loosely).

Persons seeking entry into American life could not afford nostalgic retreat into *Italianità,* cherishing memories of Neapolitan songs, Bolognese pasta, or Venetian gondolas. Language and other patterns of behavior, including dress, formed part of a ticket without which rising to the top was impossible.

Pressure to change family names by eliminating vowels or shortening them also grew. Some anglicized both first and last names. Tomassini became Thomas and Lombardi was changed to Lombard. Like almost everything else about the immigrant experience, the changing of one's name involved hidden complexities. Some few emigrants, before boarding steamships bound for New York, instructed friends in overseas registry offices to enter substitute surnames in the records. Sometimes such names were randomly picked from the most recent annual list of Italians decedents. In this way, one could go to America with a clean record, based upon the name of a dead person. Countless draft dodgers, and not a few criminals too, made it over through such a strategy.

In other cases feckless rubber-stamping clerks on Ellis Island simply assigned entrants different names, for the sake of simplicity. Names were frequently anglicized by bureaucrats, or by immigrants themselves, for ease of pronunciation. There was a passivity about the way in which immigrants allowed these things to be done. On the surface they seemed happy about their new names, but the circumvention process was not like passing an heirloom down through untold generations.

An immigrant father, waving his hands in the air for emphasis, once told his son that there were three things he should never change: his name, his religion, and his wife. For that old man it was as though the change of one's family name represented the final cutting away of roots in the past.

This attitude of impending cultural death is portrayed in the Italo-American novelist Lucas Longo's *Family on Vendetta Street*, which gives us a glimpse of an Italian American doctor who changed his name from Bentolinardo to Bentley when he received his medical degree:

> Doctor Bentolinardo. How many years his father had waited for his son to gain that title. All his life he had worked with one firm, Feliciani & McGinley, building contractors. He used to arrive early on the job, a half hour before, so that the bosses would never find fault, never fire him, and always send him out on the new jobs. He needed the money to pay for his son's medical education. Sacrifice was his daily bread—but he did it willingly, to work to save a few pennies. Some on the job—not Italians—seeing the olive oil seeping through the brown paper bag, called it dago grease. . . .
> Bentley. When the old man saw that gold-lettered shingle hanging out off the building on Prospect Park Terrace, his whole being buckled. Dr. Bentley. He couldn't read English, but that betrayal he could read. All the letters weren't there. . . . He wept like a baby and called his son a traitor. He returned to our street still crying. Some, trying to ease his ache, lied, saying, "The printer is to blame . . . the stupid printer who made that sign is to blame . . . not your boy . . . your boy, the doctor, he loves you . . . but that printer how does he know to spell these long involved Italian names?" During all this time, his son, Dr. Bentley, busy curing so many, never came to see him. One day the doctor called on a patient who lived on our street. He felt he had to declare himself: "I don't want to hurt my father. But he's unreasonable. I can't explain to him my feelings. . . . I had to change my name to feel right and different. I know he's my father, but I can't live the way he has lived."
> He didn't trust anyone any more, that poor old man. He ripped his name out of the mail box. His physical appearance became deplorable. He never opened a window. Missed Mass. Refused to throw out garbage. Did not care what happened to his money. Shut himself off completely.
> "Sick I went to work. With fever. I saved. Every penny. For him. My Ralph. And how does the traitor pay me back? With a new name. I am Bentolinardo. This new Bentley—who knows him? God, do you?" Then, overwhelmed by frustration, unable to understand the betrayal,

he fell to the ground, where, like a demented fool, he pounded the concrete with both fists. He tore at his clothing. He was about to bang his head against the pavement when friends ran to him, picked him up, carried him home.

The name change to which Dr. Bentolinardo's father objected so strenuously calls to mind Shakespeare's couplet:

> He was a Kinde of Nothinge
> Until he forged himself a name.

In America dark-skinned persons have been forced to reassert their human worth. Paradoxically, this sometimes has led to rejection of one's self. Only with difficulty can self-hatred be replaced by self-acceptance. If, by denial, one could gain status, an old peasant proverb forecasts acceptance by one and all: *Chi ha denaro ed amicizia va nel culo della giustizia* ("He who has money and friends fucks justice in her ass"). This notion, once again, can be related to some other Shakespearean lines:

> But he that filches me my good name
> Robs me of that which not enriches him,
> And makes me poor indeed.

Unlike Dr. Bentolinardo, not all foreigners anglicized their names or gave up their accents. For some older, strangely sullen persons, the breakdown in *Italianità* scarcely occurred. They clung to the symbol of Columbus and his discovery of 1492, much as French migrants still bask in the memory of Lafayette's participation in the American Revolution. Such folk simply did not participate in expediency, refusing to hide what and whom they were. Most immigrants, however, joined the battle to rid themselves of damaging stereotypes.

Although expansiveness is not the possession of any one national group, the Italians had a reputation for coping with life by dramatic overstatement. The words "dago" and "wop" led less vituperative persons to turn their hurts inward. Others, like New York's future secretary of state Mario Cuomo, felt childhood constraints that could be acknowledged only many years later:

I can cry now when I think about the time when I was fourteen years old and embarrassed to bring my father to St. John's Preparatory School to meet the teachers and other parents because he didn't speak English well. Looking back now, and feeling the anguish of that recollection teaches me all I need to know about the ethnic self-hate and the melting pot myth and what it means to deny a heritage.[5]

A substantial number of immigrants hardly seemed conscious of giving up any part of their past. Some even denied they were victims of prejudice. They felt that the United States was treating them with a generosity that required reciprocation. They loyally accepted their underdog status as temporary and saw their own dignity as the quality that would live on after they were gone. It was the talent they contributed to the new society that mattered, not what they took out of it.

Looking back on their record, the psychohistorian could easily see these persons as cowed by American life. We could say their very souls seemed seared. A kind of stasis did set in among them, as intimacy posed problems related to identity. Freud's *Civilization and Its Discontents* reminds us that all cultures exact a conformist, repressive price of the individual.

If we look at the German and Polish experiences in America, we see these nationalities as having had, like the south Europeans, to withstand the demands of the American life-style. The Germans did, however, show a certain brittle strength in resisting the tug of Americanization. In Kansas, German Mennonites settled in closed communities and fought to maintain native-language schools, German customs, and their national churches. In Texas, too, the Germans resisted change. Whenever cultural patterns they could not respect were thrust upon them—by legislation or intimidation or boycott—the Germans spurned ideas suited to life in America. Conversely, Italians were rarely critical, aloof, or superior in attitude. They felt in no position to push for the dubious benefits of foreign identification as opposed to the orthodoxy of Americanization. Unlike the Poles, who continued to smart over the division of their home country between Germans and Russians, the Italians had little desire to keep nationalism alive in America. At most, they listened to the echo of folk traditions within the walls of their homes.

The Italian minority experience can also be compared with that of modern blacks. America's black community has produced a store of poetry and other literary efforts by which former slaves once worked through their emotional conflicts. Blacks cultivated patience, and even apathy, in the face of abuse, aided by music and folklore. Although European immigrants overcame social and economic prejudice more rapidly than did blacks, there is no large body of first-generation poetry, novels, or folk songs among the Italians that might have helped tide them over their times of trouble.

As we have seen, some Italians fled the ghettoes, changed their names, and gave up their language and folkways. The Italians had also to abandon a number of props: mutual aid societies, patriotic lodges, and national churches—all signs of the immigrant's alienism.

During Prohibition even wine had to vanish from the family table. In America a sterile Victorian code irrationally linked respectability with abstinence. So, at least during the 1920s, a few immigrants once again swallowed their pride and abandoned drinking wine. Others kept on nursing their Zinfandel, California's alternative to Florentine Chianti. As Merle Curti pointed out in his study of a Wisconsin county, there was a strong sentiment for temperance in America, and "the immigrant was expected to do things the way the old stock specified." In *The Paesanos*, Jo Pagano had one of his characters say: "By God, what a country! Make a goddam criminal out of you joost to take a glass of healthy wine!"

Few Italians participated in temperance societies, as did Scandinavian and English immigrants. Yet, they stood in sharp contrast to whiskey-imbibing native Americans. In quiet defiance of the Prohibition laws some went on brewing both beer and wine. Youngsters skipped many a Saturday evening bath because the family tub was filled with fermenting alcoholic beverages. Most Italians kept wine in their cellars throughout the bleak Prohibition era. Under the shade of a grape arbor, they enjoyed the conviviality that accompanies washing down pasta with what Americans called Dago Red.

Wine usually was drunk at meals or relaxed amusements such as Sunday afternoon *boccie* matches. These were played on almost any level plot of land available. *Boccie* players were often lonely older men. Yet the games were conducted in a vociferous manner. Players wagered money, a shot of *grappa*, (a kind of brandy) or a bottle of wine on the outcome of a match. They fascinated their American neighbors with the intricacies of the game. Each player was allowed two wooden or steel balls, known as *boccies*. The leadoff player rolled a smaller ball, the jack, down the smoothed dirt alley. Noisy contestants tried to hit this moving target and to knock their opponents' balls away from the jack. The proud winner was the person who came the closest to the jack ball. San Francisco's Bocci Ball Restaurant catered to customers who played the game and to opera buffs who came to hear "La donna è mobile" or "Un bel di" and to sip poncino (coffee laced with brandy). The boccie game was both a symbol of the past and an indication that the immigrant could afford to relax.

The tenor of immigrant life gradually improved. Whereas village women once wore black dresses to avoid laundering, in America their clothing changed to brighter colors. Bare feet took on shiny shoes. Old clothes gave way to new ones. Each Christmas, tons of rarities, bought with money buried in backyard Mason jars, were sent off to relatives and friends in Italy.

At week's end a worker who had worn rough laboring clothes was eager to change into a white shirt with collar, new necktie, and patent leather shoes. He invested in upholstered parlor furniture, carpets, electric lights, and flush toilets—all evidence of his newfound wealth. Yet, the more he indulged in such amenities, the more the immigrant grew similar to his American neighbors.

Immigration historians face some odd contradictions. On the one hand they have to appraise the horrific sacrifices and discrimination to which I have alluded. Yet, there is increasing evidence of rapid upward mobility, as recorded in Humbert Nelli's history of the Italians in Chicago and Thomas Kessner's *The Golden Door*, which examines the interaction of Jews and Italians in New York.

There is a curious Italianate resilience that has been described by John Horne Burns, an American of Boston Irish stock who was in Naples during World War II: "Unlike the Irish who stayed hurt all their lives, the Italians had a bounce-back in them." This, even when harsh discrimination stared them in the face and although (for the first few years at least) America's Italians seemed destined to live on the margin of urban life—when they faced an uncertain future as ragpickers, peddlers, short-order cooks, or garbage collectors.

One premise of the melting pot ideal had been to reduce everyone, regardless of background, to sameness. But the immigrant experience was not constant. Merely a few arrived with values resembling those of the American middle class. Even in Europe there had been regional, as well as rural and urban, variations. Discrimination arose from the immigrant's differentness. He did not share the stabilizing formative background of his neighbors. Yet, only a few foreigners "got stuck," neurotically, as they sought to shift from one society's values to another's.

IV
BIRDS OF PASSAGE

FEW PERSONS who have seen Alfred Stieglitz's famous photograph "The Steerage" realize that it depicts immigrants *leaving* America. Our dreams of triumph have so swamped reality that most Americans scarcely consider that America's woebegone newcomers could ever have wished to return home.

It is true that the majority of immigrants never returned to Italy. But some were unable to take root away from the mean little villages where they had been born. For these "birds of passage," or *golondrinas*, a full rooting never occurred. Their transplanting did not work, and some laborers returned to a life close to that of a beast of burden high in the Apennines or to indigence in their native Naples or Taranto. There is much to be learned about why these persons placed such value upon life back home.

There were some good emotional causes for this return to *la miseria*, to illiteracy, to poverty, to a society dominated by the rich, to a decaying system of government sunk in Byzantine inefficiency. Deeply felt matters of heart and soul pulled certain immigrants back toward their pastoral and patriarchal past—where the feudal baron, or *marchese*, who lived in the *castelleto* on the hill commanded their destiny. The tug of the familiar, the need for a resting place called home, the sleepiness of the ages gnawed at their center.

The return from America was also an escape from a disquieting world that appeared orderless. Although one might be wretched and desperate back in Italy, fear of the future seemed to be reduced there. Even unscrupulous and cunning officials, like the local mayor or prefect, were excused for their corruption. Although one might be robbed of personal rights, life felt more comfortable on home grounds. Irrational as these causes may seem today, certain repatriates needed to retrace their childhood origins. This phenomenon was not to occur again until the third generation of immigrants who stayed on had fully taken root in the New World.

The process of remigration was complex. Some laborers merely commuted back and forth to Liguria or Piedmont, looking for endless summers and good pay, whether in the Argentine or California. Others went home permanently, to report that America's stars were not their own. Between 1900 and 1910, 2,045,877 Italians came to the United States. But 1,154,322 of these returned to Italy.

Some visitors, wherever they may travel, find it impossible to forget their homeland. The letters they send home resemble those of refugees rather than those of immigrants. These torn souls begin to lament their departure almost before they leave. Their accounts drip with sentiment about *la terra vecchia* and are filled with whining complaints. A few, to paraphrase Angelo Pellegrini, might be called roving parasites. Still others are disagreeably inflexible and rather graceless folk, hardly willing to give a new land a chance.

Malcontents among immigrants linked poor health to their burning desire for a passage back to their relatives. Their inability to adjust to the new society was also economic. The ups and downs of the business cycle led to unemployment during the depression years 1893, 1907, 1921, and 1929–1933. However, it was hard to return to the low wages of one's home village. In 1905, for example, the pay of the best stonemasons at Como was five lire per day; their assistants received one to two lire daily, depending on age and strength. Dollar equivalents would be numbered in pennies, especially within poor agrotowns in the foothills of the Alps or Appenines.

A surprising number of returnees were women who claimed that they found the adjustment to life in the United States simply impossible. The martyred and wronged wife-mother is a familiar figure in immigrant literature. Such *donne beate* had subserviently followed their husbands to America, weeping in secret over loved ones left behind. They dressed in black, as if to mourn the death of their once happy lives. There was a peculiar convergence between the color black and their desire to return home. It was as though their stay in America represented a retreat with grace (*garbo*). Black clothing was a carry-over from the old country, an exclusively female practice with powerful symbolism. It connoted self-sacrifice, misery, but also determination. The woman who dressed in black was a consolation to her very self. She vicariously sought the peace that might one day come to her among the olive trees and gray stones of her native village.

In America, women forced by economic circumstances to take in boarders encountered immigrant males who were frequently coarse, their speech laden with obscenities. Usually young, virile, and lonely, and without female companions, these working-class men seemed to be spilling over with a libidinal potency, which they exhibited toward their landladies in peculiarly offensive ways. (Neurologically, the old-fashioned term "libido" can be labeled "hunger.") Furthermore, such male tenants seldom showed proper appreciation for the washing, cooking, and mending that turned some immigrant women into nags and drudges. Among these were women who had barely known their future husbands and who had married because of economic or family pressures. Disgruntled and frustrated, a few came to act like *strege*, or witches.

Others were sensitive and intelligent, like the mother of Edward Corsi (who became President Franklin Roosevelt's commissioner of immigration). Signora Corsi hated the dingy tenement house in Harlem into which her husband took her to live. It stood in such contrast to the verdant fields outside her Italian village. From her arrival in America to her departure, she was despondent. Finally, she abandoned her family and returned to her native land, "in desperation to die," according to Corsi. He wrote about his family's experience in his candid *In the Shadow of Liberty:*

> Such dreams as I had had of the land of promise were well-nigh shattered by the grim reality of what I had been forced to undergo. Long before my mother had gone back to Italy both she and my stepfather had realized the futility of their adventure. America had failed to offer its pot of gold. It had offered instead suffering, privations, and defeat. My stepfather's bondage in the piano factory literally crushed him for the rest of his life.

Corsi recalled that his mother never overcame the repulsion she felt in a land where people were judged by how much money they earned:

> She loved quiet, and hated noise and confusion. Here she never left the house unless she had to. She spent her days, and the waking hours of the nights, sitting at one outside window staring up at the little patch of sky above the tenements. She was never happy here and, though she tried, could not adjust herself to the poverty and despair in which she had to live.[1]

During the 1920s the mother of young Luigi Barzini (who became, like his father, a prominent journalist) also felt the sting of American prejudice. Like Signora Corsi, Barzini and his mother saw Americans as "odd and unpredictable," as well as "often inordinately stubborn." Yet, Yankees were not to be contradicted, even when they spoke against foreigners. Signora Barzini "never felt happy in the United States. . . . What disturbed her about the Americans . . . was their lack of interest in . . . books, poetry, history, and . . . their indifference to the virtues she cultivated: Moderation, discipline, skepticism, prudence, thrift, patience, and understanding."[2]

Just before World War II Barzini's family left behind an America that his mother viewed as "an incomprehensible and practically uninhabitable country." Barzini did not fully relish returning to Italy, but he bitterly described how he felt no full chance to succeed "at a time when ordinary Italians were looked upon in the United States as barely human." For the Barzini and Corsi families it was an affront to suggest that success in America depended upon birth and status values that they were sealed off from, with full acceptance denied.

Defensive and ill at ease, some foreigners complained that Americans were habitually disrespectful. An intelligent Pied-montese woman, Antonia Pola, wrote that for twenty-three years she endured humiliations that included the terms "ignorant dago, dirty wop, and greaseball." She resented the supercilious ways of store clerks who treated her differently because of her foreign accent. She claimed that dentists, members of a local ladies social club, and even neighbors kept her from loving her adopted country without reserve: "I ought to be happy and satisfied. I am not." She spoke of having buried one child in the new land and of others still alive: "If it wasn't for those children of mine, I would sell everything and go back to Nuvale." There no one would laugh at or ridicule a person "for speaking a broken English, talking too loudly, and gesturing with their hands."[3]

A young immigrant who settled in California's Napa valley provides an example of how one immigrant handled the emotional tie to Italy. He was Franco Mortarotti. First hired as a cleanup helper in a winery, he advanced to master keg maker. Dissatisfied, however, with his courtship of a local vintner's daughter—because she was "too American"—he broke off the relationship. Employing a go-between, he next contracted for a bride from his native village. He used up a year's savings in order to return to Italy for the marriage ceremony. For Mortarotti's new wife, life in the Napa valley soon proved too raw. She fell ill and he feared she might die; so he spent another year's savings to send her home. Each winter, for fifteen years, he traveled the ten thousand miles back to Italy in order to be with his wife. Although he brought

51

three sons to America, he would not allow his two daughters to leave their mother alone in Italy. Nor would he give up his profitable employment in California.

Returnees, with their imitation leather suitcases, became familiar figures in the Italian villages. They dressed expensively, often in poor taste. The men wore coats that were too long, ties that were gaudy and wide, Panama hats, and heavy gold watch chains. Along with costly Havana cigars, gold objects were de rigueur. The returnees formed a study in gold: gold cigarette cases, gold tiepins, and showy imitation gold rings. Above all, one's front teeth must be faced with gold. Women who had left their native villages with black scarves on their heads returned wearing bulky hats, their black patent leather purses stuffed with dollar bills. The immigrant's showy materialism aroused envy. The good-hearted among them, however, helped their native villages by building a new water fountain, buying the local church a new clock, or giving money to expand the town cemetery.

Some males had the misfortune to return during 1935, when the dictator Benito Mussolini launched the Ethiopian war. Those who had not become United States citizens were liable for military service under Italian law. These returnees were to curse the day they left America's shores. Furthermore, they came to feel that a new and different harshness had settled over an Italy bent upon conquering an African empire.

In those tense years immigrants encountered a strange reception at times. Upon landing at Genoa, one good-natured returnee slipped an American cigar into the breast pocket of a customs inspector. He was quickly rebuffed by the touchy official, who blurted out angrily: "Il Fascismo non si vende." ("Fascism is not for sale.")

If returnees planned to stay on, it was best that they relearn the traditional Italian *arte di arrangiarsi*—the skill of making do, of adjusting to any circumstances. A few had mistakenly been lured back by promises of higher wages than they had once known at home. Others were pressured by relatives to stay on after too short a family reunion. Still others met local spouses, settled down, and promptly forgot their broken English. Sometimes prestige came to these because they were the only villagers able to afford two-story homes with balconies and brass doorknobs and new Fiat autos.

Some exasperated immigrants looked upon the return home as a psychological cure. An Italian American psychiatrist recalled that, in taking the personal histories of immigrants, "I have heard of attempts by Italian Americans to cure themselves, or members of their families, of symptomatic distress by taking trips to the home town in Italy."[4]

Back in Europe, the tug of Americanization sometimes collided with the pull from the past. One returnee found Naples to be "the most kaleidoscopically animated city in the world," a place where "commotion is king and tumult is queen," a city in motion:

> People, horses, wagons, carriages, bicycles, donkeys, autos, hearses, wheelbarrows, flower carts, fruit carts, vegetable carts, pass as if on a revolving stage. Everybody is talking, gesticulating, singing, laughing, as though there was just so much action to be gotten out of life, and this was the last day. It is all contagious, electrifying.[5]

Returnees introduced American ideas and methods into their homeland and sometimes the industry and thrift of such "model immigrants" were admired. Yankeefied Italians were eager to recount the wonders of the New World to all who would listen, as if to confirm the truth of the letters they had sent home.

Thornton Wilder once reflected upon the changes that overtook returning immigrants:

> They had invested their savings in the diamonds on their fingers, and their eyes were not less bright with anticipation of a family reunion. One foresaw their parents staring at them, unable to understand the change whereby their sons had lost the charm the Italian soil bestows upon the humblest of its children, noting only that they have come back with bulbous features, employing barbarous idioms and bereft forever of the witty psychological intuition of their race. Ahead of them lay sleepless nights above their mother's soil floors and muttering poultry.[6]

Various factors kept immigrants from going back in large numbers. Distance, in an age before the airplane, was one of these. Investments in businesses, machinery, vineyards, and orchards kept successful persons deeply involved in the new country. As family responsibilities grew, the yearning to repatriate diminished. Those who did not return sent home dollar remittances. (In the year 1907 alone these amounted to $85 million.)

Others could no longer quite understand the old country. Reidentity is a problem raised in Angelo Pellegrini's book *Immigrant's Return* (1961). Pellegrini, who had become a university professor, visited his homeland and was startled to realize how Americanized he had become. The limitations of the Old World dampened his former loyalties. Pellegrini's fulfillments had occurred not in Europe but on the other side of the Atlantic. The immigrant, revisiting the scenes of his youth, felt but could not quite explain the changes that had come over him. When he came back to Seattle it was with a new sympathy. Now the "pick and shovel days" of brawn and sweat were surely over.

Jerre Mangione has recorded how Sicily became a magnet for him, how "for all my faith in the American Way of Life and the Lucky Break, the Sicilian Way began to obsess me." Upon his return to Palermo he experienced a surge of joy, "a miracle of sorts that left me euphoric . . . my senses were overwhelmed with the emotion of being a fullblooded Sicilian in direct touch with his life source."[7]

Some returnees remained ambivalent about their homeland. Mangione's Uncle Vincenzo talked to him about his years in New York State, where he had felt like a foreigner. But, when he returned to Sicily, he came to feel much more foreign there. He urged his brother "to stay where he is. Things have changed here. . . . The neighborhood in Rochester where I lived is far from beautiful, but I would rather be there. . . . I curse the day when I decided to come back to this benighted land."[8]

For recent immigrants the conveniences of life in America have made the return home even more difficult. Furthermore, this hegira, especially for members of the second and third generations, has often been misguided. Some returnees have gone looking for parts of themselves that stayed behind in Europe, but they could not find those pieces of their personal puzzle. Only shadows lived on—as in a childhood nursery—replaying past scenes that never advanced toward completion.

A contemporary novelist has succeeded in portraying the feelings of the *trapiantato*, the transplanted person who tries to rediscover his homeland:

> You see my friend, you come back to your own land after almost forty years, and how do they treat you? Like a dog. They almost tell you you're not Italian any more. And over there they tell you you're not American. So you are nothing. Believe me, if you leave your country for more than five years, you're lost. You don't belong anywhere.[9]

Yet the attraction that Italy offers is undeniable. The 1950s saw the emergence of a democratic Italy, and a passion for things Italian—Necchi sewing machines, the movies of Sophia Loren, Italian sports cars, and women's knits—suddenly made Italianity fashionable. The Rome of Pope John XXIII was an appealing place for Americans and Italo-Americans alike to visit. Although Italy's disorder was confusing, the antiquity, colorful countryside, and lingering family associations did attract. Returnees soon grew restless for America, however. The novelist Jo Pagano has one of them say: "I longed with a fierce, almost panic-stricken desire for the familiar noise of America, the clang of street-cars, the hum of machines, all the raucous clatter that was for me associated with home."

A New York reporter, standing before the house in which his Abruzzian father had been born, experienced these feelings:

> I didn't cry. My heart didn't beat faster. But I was very glad I came. For the house, like the town and even Italy in general, confirmed my suspicions. I wasn't underneath *really* Italian. Neither was I just another good old red-blooded American. I was an Italian-American—a unique breed, an identity in itself.[10]

Despite the family root systems they discovered in Italy, the materialistic children of immigrants clamored for America. They yearned for the breakfast ham and eggs with buttered toast and jam, hamburgers, milk shakes, and filtered cigarettes. Travel-worn clothes that needed dry-cleaning were impractical in primitive villages, and flush toilets sometimes nonexistent. Nostalgia be damned; it was the plumbing they missed.

V

THE ROOTS
OF DISCRIMINATION

ON OCCASION THE PEASANTS who came to America had actually
been their own beasts of burden. They had pulled ploughs over
rough mountain slopes where no animal could gain a sure footing.
How might they now be certain of what was really underfoot,
along the paved streets of an entirely new country? The road to
success was wearisome and harsh. As the foreigner went in search
of respectability he was stereotyped on all sides. These damaging
generalizations were usually based upon only a kernel of ethnic
reality. Such clichés, for example, linked fair-haired English, Irish,
or Scandinavian stock with democratic institutions. Obviously,
the swarthier south Europeans would have to be weaned away
from their danker instincts. Greeks, Serbo-Croatians, and
Sicilians were considered especially wild. Poles were high-strung.
Italians were primitive and disposed toward crime, dirtiness, and
poverty. Government immigration hearings produced official
reports filled with such pseudoscientific labels, which were utilized into the 1920s by immigration restriction leaders.

Ethnic stereotypes were also employed by immigrants themselves. They repeated generalizations about Italians concerning their low rate of literacy, emotionalism, talent for intrigue, excessive frolicsomeness, and laziness (despite their obvious ingeniousness as laborers). Italians long continued to be portrayed as short of stature, dark in complexion, cruel, and shifty. They were prone to carry knives and were seen as having a theatrical nature, confirmed by Italy's strutting opera singers and organ grinders.

Scots were known for stinginess. Blacks were considered brawny, athletic, and not too bright. The Jews allegedly had a high percentage of hook-nosed merchants and conniving pawnbrokers in their ghettoes. The Irish were viewed as heavy drinkers who libations were presided over by tough saloon keepers, usually named Duffy. As for the English, Italian immigrants belived they were self-righteous, snobbish, and aloof. As to food, blacks feasted on watermelon, possum, and chicken. Italians were vegetable freaks and "spaghetti benders" who guzzled second-pressing wine and smoked killing Di Nobili cheroots. Russians could not live without borscht and caviar. The Chinese relished smelly bird's nest soup, swallowed rotten eggs, and ate raw dogs.

It was difficult for immigrants to counter stereotypes against them, for these were based upon the unconscious needs of their accusers. Intolerance and prejudice provided a means by which WASPs (a term then unknown) could project internal angers onto foreigners. Sometimes deep-seated anxieties could thus be allayed via a pecking order of intolerance. By depreciating helpless newcomers, ghettoes were perpetuated, forcing the exclusion of tenement dwellers from better neighborhoods and jobs.

In the eighteenth century, the stereotypes had at least been mixed. Jefferson and Madison could admire the Florentine patriot leader Philip Mazzei. America then seemed confident of its ability to change the immigrant and to adopt him into the traditional community. Titanic forces, however—the Civil War, industrialization, and westward expansion—seemed eventually to weaken the grip of the dominant culture, some of whose members loathed the hordes of immigrants who stepped ashore on Ellis Island. According to an immigrant slogan: "America beckons, but Americans repel." Nativists not only feared that the flood of cheap labor into the United States would lower the standard of living, they also dreaded the power of foreign priests and rabbis.

Although nativism is not unique to the United States, the historian is bound to record that its heritage of bitterness and distrust has scarcely ennobled our history. Anti-foreign movements, from the early Know-Nothing party onward, have wrought negative results in the name of preserving what we promote as the American way of life.

In the nineteenth century even the most educated engaged in racist pronunciamentos. Henry James complained bitterly that Boston Commons was overcrowded with strangers who "spoke a rude form of Italian, and others some outland dialect unknown to me." Foreigners came, in James's words, to be "in serene and triumphant possession" of Boston. For him the immigrant threatened to destroy traditional New England culture. The only alternative was a struggle to keep the penniless at bay as long as possible.

Anxiety about the future of the United States, and a desire to guard its ideals, long continued to concern the dominant classes. Edith Wharton's novels, so reflective of upper-class values, recorded the snobbish diffidence of New York society toward this human spillage at the waterfront. Both her *House of Mirth* and *Age of Innocence* dwelled upon proper people who made their fortunes outside the range of immigrant life. Wharton's heroes and heroines resented the "little Jews" trying to edge their way into high society. She pictured such "new people" as growing in upward mobility but as barely housebroken socially.

True, the Jeffersons and the Madisons, admiring Mediterranean culture, had modeled homes and public buildings upon Roman and Greek architecture. But this Latinate adulation did not extend to modern-day Italy, which exported destitute, garlic-reeking pasta eaters. North America's literary nourishment had come by way of England. Only a slight intellectual substratum supported contact with Italy. Mark Twain, Edith Wharton, and other American literati showed themselves to be anti-immigrant.

In 1864, in part because of the labor shortage during the Civil War, Congress had passed an act to entice immigrant workers. Although this legislation was rescinded four years later, there was no enforceable prohibition against recruiting labor in foreign countries. Agents sent manpower until 1885, when the importation of contract laborers was ended by congressional statute.

Newspapers of the 1880s were filled with appehension concerning the hordes of peasants being dumped on the shores of the United States. Southern and eastern Europeans were portrayed as especially disposed toward brigandage. The *New York Times* of July 9, 1881, described the horrifying activities of one Giuseppe Randazzo, "a genuine Italian bandit, black-eyed, swarthy, and wicked, with rings in his ears, a fellow who has actually robbed and murdered, held travelers for ransom, and cut off their ears when the ransom was not forthcoming." He was finally "captured by a New York detective on a peaceful Mississippi River watermelon sloop." The *Times* regretted that so many romantic young women had their imaginations fired by reading in the public library about such dark villains. Even the corner peanut vendor had become "transfigured in their eyes, so much does the romantic nature crave something Southern, Latin, and intense."

Scapegoating, a psychological device that allows racists to project their own hatreds outward, continued to infect the literary establishment. After the turn of the century the novelist Kenneth Roberts wrote in the *Saturday Evening Post* that immigration restriction was necessary to exclude "a hybrid race of good for nothing Mongrels." Frederick Lewis Allen, son-in-law of the financier J. P. Morgan, pointed out how successive immigrant groups—the Irish, Italians, and Slavs—"tended to form a proletarian level under the previous one." As each group lifted itself out of poverty, its place was filled, at the lowest economic base, by newer immigrants.

One could say that the cities of America suffered from a species of immigrant indigestion. They had to absorb waves of people who were profoundly different from the native stock. Down below Fourteenth Street, where the Roosevelts and the Tildens once lived, hoards of foreigners chattered away in odd languages that New York's Four Hundred could scarcely be expected to understand. Streets made to accommodate the carriages of the rich were suddenly filled with pushcarts, rag peddlers, and banana vendors. No wonder the presence of the immigrants caused consternation among America's elite.

As the unemployed filled in the slums of factory towns, they kept wages depressed. In a sense, condescension toward foreigners was understandable. Because native-born Americans mainly saw poor and ill-kempt common laborers who spoke incomprehensible languages, they scorned dagos or kikes or Polacks or Hunkies. These terms were in bad taste in the Anglo world; but, oddly, they became acceptable among foreigners themselves. It was as though, masochistically, to uplift oneself meant to give up ethnic pride—to become less Italian, Slavic, or Greek.

In a convoluted way this process, however, played into the hands of immigrant critics. Violence among foreign-born persons also lent itself to fevered headlines, be it a knifing in some basement along Mulberry Street or a vendetta on Boston's north end. Italians were believed to be lacking in scruples, and they were suspected of constant intrigues. This reputation for deceitfulness stemmed from the days of the scheming Machiavelli and the swindling Count Cagliostro. In the deception of women one could add the name of Giacomo Casanova, yet another scoundrel. Innocent Americans seemed well advised to be on their guard against foreign wastrels. At best, they would become little more than hod carriers. Americans could hardly forsee the time when the San Francisco banker A. P. Giannini would belie the notion that all Italians achieved their goals illicitly. In California also, the toughness and obstinacy of a major vintner, Louis Martini, doubtless helped some Italians to overcome their feelings of being outsiders.

Whereas intolerance seemed less pronounced in the West than back east, it was rampant down south. Not only did the natives hurl insults at foreigners, but immigrants there seemed at the mercy of forces beyond their control. Exploitation of foreign laborers was common. In the 1890s, to entice cheap labor southward, cotton mills paid commissions of $25.00 for each immigrant family brought to a company town or plantation. Wages of $.50 were paid a mother or her children for an entire day's work—little better than what was then available in Italy. Workers down south earned as little as $.15 for thirteen hours of backbreaking labor under unhygienic conditions. Large and small growers alike abused foreign workers: one of the most important planters in the South, O. B. Crittenden, was once arrested for mistreating his Italian cotton-pickers.

Ignorant whites and blacks, with whom Italians had to compete, proved to be no more tolerant toward immigrant newcomers than were southern employers. Field hands hated the idea of an Italian family working from sunup to sundown—long into the night, when the moon lit up the landscape.

Discrimination also accompanied the *padrone* system of work control, begun in the Mediterranean world. This resembled the seventeenth-century practice of indentured servitude practiced along America's eastern tidewater. One can also liken the *padrone* system to feudal serfdom, a phenomenon with a non-American connotation, unlike the respectable—because American—indentured servitude.

Padroni were supposed to act as friends, to smoothe one's path in unfamiliar circumstances. Instead, they often were bloodsucking brokers of immigrant labor, human leeches depicted in a peasant saying: "A friend who hurts you is worse than an enemy who leaves you alone." The *padrone* negotiated a contract for men working under him, whether they were miners, railroad workers, or field hands. These contractors, taking advantage of illiteracy, particularly in southern Italy, sent peasants accustomed to meager fare and hard work to New York, Boston, and Philadelphia.

In collusion with contractors, the *padrone* drew up agreements binding workers for one to seven years; he furnished transportation to the place of work; he was the middleman who represented the workers to the employer and the employer to laborers. Corrupt *padroni* hired the immigrant at a fixed rate and expected to profit from whatever wage they obtained for him above that rate. The *padrone* not only demanded commissions from both laborers and employers but also made money out of furnishing immigrants food; he could even exact a commission from wages sent back to Europe; he might also demand a cut out of the steamship passage.

Hawk-eyed *padroni* posed as protectors of befuddled immigrants, who were sometimes fleeced of their worldly possessions, even by fellow countrymen. Hotel keepers, stationmasters, cabbies, baggage handlers, and restaurant owners charged these travelers exorbitant prices. People would give them false directions, cheating them out of precious savings. An immigrant traveling through a terminal city like Chicago, St. Louis, or Omaha was well advised to stay away from saloons, billiard parlors, or houses of ill repute.

There would have been some logic to keeping the *padroni*, rather than the immigrants, out of the country. *Padroni* not only repudiated employment contracts but also pocketed fees after leading workers to far-off places where, jobless, they remained abandoned.

A few *padroni* armed guards with Winchester rifles to prevent laborers from running away. Like a government, they could fine workers or punish them for resistance to authority. On Sunday, contractors could keep them at work and one was known to tax his men in order to buy a birthday present for his wife. "A feudal Lord would not have expected more from his vassals," one contemporary account complained.

The number of immigrants who needed work strengthened the padrone's power over them. But, once foreign workers had lived with their own kind awhile, mutual courage grew among them. When they learned that contracts signed in Europe were unenforceable in American courts, they tore up these documents, to which they had agreed only in order to gain steamship passage. Workers who signed contracts after landing in the United States sometimes ran away when labor conditions grew unendurable.

The 1890s were years of horrendous working conditions for all immigrants. During 1893, the Chicago National Gas Pipe Company crammed together its workmen, near Logansport, Indiana, into a flimsy shack. The shack was blown down by a windstorm and several Italians were killed. Neither the number nor the names of the dead were ever made known. These foreign laborers were designated only by figures.

Immigrants formed mutual aid societies and travelers' aid groups in order to prorate the risks of illness or to share the expenses of death. The Italian government subsidized these organizations and also set up "immigration bureaus." The government sought to reduce swindling of its emigrants, stipulating that no one could recruit or sell them steamship tickets without a license. By 1885, labor brokers had to deposit $1,000 security and sign an agreement to protect immigrants from exploitation. The Italian government gave the Society for Italian Immigrants, located in New York City, thousands of dollars and instructed its consulates in the United States to offer immigrants their good offices.

Partly as a result of these moves, the *padrone* gradually lost his ability to exact tribute. Ultimately the *padrone* came to be relied upon by only the most illiterate. Increasingly, foreign workers joined American labor unions. A survey of Italian workmen in Chicago in 1896 showed that they worked for *padroni* an average of only eleven weeks and four days after reaching America.

Yet another device existed by which employers could, however, bilk immigrants. This was the company store, or commissary, located close to the foreigner's place of work. Debt-ridden immigrants were forced to use the contractor's "pluck-me store," where laborers sometimes even had to purchase the "straw on which they sleep." Prices for food staples ran as high as 100 percent above the cost of the goods to the seller, with the quality as bad as the price was high. The commissary system amounted to a form of peonage.

Higher wages and free transportation were used to entice workers to remote labor camps. On the eve of World War I, Giuseppe D'Angelo (uncle of the author) was lured from New York to Florida by such promises. The living conditions and food were abominable but D'Angelo had no money and so could not escape. For eight months he was guarded by blacks who were told (according to him) to use their guns "at the least excuse." As he sank evermore deeply into debt to the company store, D'Angelo received virtually no wages. After quarreling with his fellow immigrants, he escaped their misery, fleeing back to the North in search of another job.

Added to a serious agricultural slump in the 1880s, demographic, economic, and psychological factors altered the south Italian love of homeland, fear of travel, and ties to a patriarchal, agricultural way of life. Southern Italy had, furthermore, become an exploited colony of a northern industrial complex, which intensified emigration out of the Italian south. From Sicily, the Abruzzi, Calabria, and Campania came a new flood into the United States.

When hordes of south Europeans threatened the legendary monopoly of Irish workmen and the police, outbreaks among immigrants mounted. Tension plagued the relations between New York's German and Polish Jews. In the Pennsylvania mines, riots among Hungarians, Swedes, Italians, and Irish broke out.

The age-old quarrel between north and south Italians did not disappear either, even in the New World. Whereas the Italian north had evolved within the European cultural mainstream, southern Italy had been shaped by centuries of misery. Persons from north Italy enjoyed a more industrialized, cosmopolitan environment in closer contact with Switzerland, France, and Germany. North Italians, who had provided the leadership of Garibaldi, Mazzini, and Cavour during Italy's unification (Risorgimento), assumed a stance of superiority toward southern

Italians. Many Piedmontese, Lombards, and Venetians, furthermore, arrived in the United States before the Calabrians, Neapolitans, or Sicilians. Until 1876, northern Italy had accounted for 85 percent of the country's immigrants annually.

In the decade after 1900, United States government reports indicated that three times as many arriving north Italians as south Italians were professionally trained laborers. Only 11.4 percent of the northerners were illiterate, as compared to 57.3 percent of the southerners. The north Italians, with more money in their pockets, gave *padroni* the most trouble, demanding higher wages. Despite their aggressiveness, they met easier acceptance. An old immigrant from southern Italy once told me: "When you are ignorant there is no respect."

In 1901, one study noted, 63.14 percent of the Italians who reached California were from northern Italy. By 1904, some 73 percent of them came from the Italian north. Southerners tended to settle along the east coast of the United States. Whereas only 2 percent of the Italians who went to the western states in 1901 were south Italians, 88 percent of those who reached the north Atlantic states that year were from the Italian south.

A *pizza* versus *polenta* rivalry extended beyond food. North Italian immigrants resented the fact that swarthier, short-statured southerners represented the "typical Italian" in the American mind. They also disliked the adverse impact of these southern folk. North Italians looked down their noses at southerners, who in turn saw northerners as "tight" and "mean," a bit like shrewd but graceless Yankees. South Italians saw the enterprising northerners as a juiceless lot. With good cause the southerners resented the distinction made between them and their northern compatriots.

In the United States, employers also contributed to north-south stereotyping. Straw bosses saw the northerners as sober and work oriented—in contrast to greasily rhetorical, operatic south Italians. The American critic William Dean Howells differentiated between Italians born in the north and in the south. The first was said to have an appealing "lightness of temper." The second was

65

from only a "half-civilized stock," which, however, sometimes produced "real artists and men of genius." Henry Cabot Lodge, Boston Brahmin that he was, excluded from his ethnic stereotypes the northern, or "Teutonic," Italian, who had Germanic blood and who belonged "to a people of Western civilization." Other racists found the south Italian too slow to abandon the ways of his forefathers. Forgetful of the quarrelsome and vindictive Visconti and Sforza families of northern Italy, Americans thought of the southerner as more violent, addicted to stiletto and revolver, quarrelsome, feuding, even murderous.

All of this overlooked the fact that Italian anarchists were frequently northerners. Both Nicola Sacco and Bartolomeo Vanzetti were Piedmontese. (Sacco was born in Turin, Vanzetti at Villafaletto, Cuneo). Labor disturbances at Paterson, New Jersey, and Barre, Vermont, were attributed to volatile south Italians. These outbursts, however, stood in contrast to the freedom from strife at colonies in Hammonton, New Jersey, Bryan, Texas, and Canastota, New York, and in the vineyards of California's Napa valley.

"Anarchism" was a terrfying word in an age when European-born radicals became instigators of labor unrest. Yet, in Italy this phenomenon was not exceptional; generations of clandestine conspirators had organized insurrections against invaders. In the United States, calls for the deportation of undesirables and for restriction of immigration were based partly on a nebulous association of the immigrant with political assassination and Machiavellian poisonings.

Discrimination against foreigners waxed and waned. During the panic of 1893 immigrants were blamed for city slums and corruption, unemployment, and the way in which the times seemed out of joint. A new wave of nativism, not to be equaled until after World War I, featured anti-foreign labor upheavals and resentment of immigrant parochial schools. The little red schoolhouse, that symbol of patriotism, was being undermined.

During eras of fervent nationalism, American organized labor came out in favor of literacy tests for immigrants and made sharp distinctions between the "new" and the "old" immigration. The American Protective Association blamed industrial depression on papal subversion and even circulated bogus encyclicals. New Englanders unfurled the flag of Anglo-Saxon superiority and supported literacy tests to restrict Latin and Slavic immigration. "Southern Europeans" and "international Jews" were the new fifth column in the minds of nativists who had once regarded the Irish as the greatest threat to the Republic.

In the 1890s nativists turned to Darwin to support racism, categorizing immigrants as Aryan or non-Aryan. Racists showed little confidence in America's ability to assimilate its newcomers. Tired of refugees who mended and remended their ragged clothes, bigots demanded that America's golden door be closed.

Foreigners, fresh from the corruption of Europe, were seen as carriers of a major contagion: class conflict. The influence of the Catholic church—to which Italians belonged in large numbers—was pernicious, especially as viewed from the Bible Belt of the American South. Leaders of the American Protective Association, founded at Clinton, Iowa, in 1887, smelled a Jesuit conspiracy to take over the United States. The association, seeking to safeguard the Protestant character of the country, lashed out at foreignism of every sort. At first a secret organization directed against "Romanism," the association had its members take an oath never to vote for a Catholic or to employ one in place of a Protestant. Dissident members of the Knights of Labor who considered themselves in competition with Italians and Jews supported the A.P.A. After 1893 this society skillfully used political parties to foment distrust of Catholics. Scandinavian and English immigrants who felt themselves superior to Irish Catholics joined the organization, whose newspapers bannered religious hatred from Seattle to Boston.

The racist assumptions of such exclusionists as the Boston Anti-Immigration League were absorbed by historians of the nineteenth century, as well as by the general public, via anti-immigrant diatribes in the daily press. The Anglo-Saxon cult of superiority flavored the writings of at least two major chroniclers.

The American frontier's most important interpreter, Frederick Jackson Turner, showed ethnic prejudices, as did west coast historian Hubert Howe Bancroft, whose writings described a great Aryan march to the Pacific coast. Neither Turner nor Bancroft knew quite how to tell the immigrant story in their writings. More sympathetic interpreters might have blended the immigrants' search for opportunity on the frontier with abandonment of Europe's feudal background. Owen Lattimore, who has studied frontiers in other parts of the world, has argued that the immigrant himself (rather than "the West") demolished ideas about aristocracy and its notions of a hereditary landed gentry.

For the West continued to show its prejudices, as easterners did. Reuben Gold Thwaites, a chronicler who ventured into the Ohio valley at the turn of the century, observed an example of discrimination in the Middle West. He encountered a "tall, raw-boned, loose-jointed young man, with a dirty, buttonless flannel shirt which revealed a hairy breast." This individual, unemployed as a result of the influx of foreigners into local coal mines, was vociferously anti-immigrant: "I tell ye, sir, the Italians and Hungarians is spoil'n' this yere country fur white men; 'n' I do'n see no prospect for hits be'n' better till they get shoved out uv't!" Thwaites, however, felt that this critic was projecting other anxieties onto foreigners in general and wrote: "What new fortune will befall my friend when he gets the Italians and Hungarians 'shoved out,' and 'things pick up a bit,' I cannot conceive."

The western states, lenient in granting aliens the right to vote after declaring their intent to become citizens, gradually restricted such privileges. In 1899 the Dakotas were the last states to grant aliens full suffrage. By the turn of the century only half of those states that had previously extended this privilege retained it.

The Spanish-American War saw some dilution of national prejudice. In the name of patriotism, all citizens were exhorted to pull together against the common enemy. In fact, the American Protective Association was a casualty of the war. But, with the war over, racists felt threatened anew by the continuing avalanche of foreign laborers.

An alternate attitude toward immigrants arose. This was "hyphenated Americanism," so deplored by President Theodore Roosevelt in one of his speeches:

> When I refer to hyphenated Americans, I do not refer to naturalized Americans. Some of the very best Americans I have ever known were naturalized Americans, Americans born abroad. But a hyphenated American is not an American at all. The one absolute certain way of bringing this nation to ruin—would be to permit it to become a tangle of squabbling nationalities, an intricate knot of German-Americans, Irish-Americans, French-Americans, Scandinavian-Americans, or Italian-Americans, each preserving its separate nationality, each at heart feeling more sympathy with Europeans of that nationality than with other citizens of the American Republic.

Roosevelt's emphasis upon Americanization was reflected in the handbooks of social workers who dealt with immigrants, as well as in the popular literature. A well-known weakness of the Progressive movement was its insensitivity toward race. Even the most progressive journals of Roosevelt's era, *Munsey's Review* and *Outlook*, paid scant attention to the values of the immigrant past.

The failure of public leadership toward the whole subject of immigration had mixed effects upon American labor. Americans could never quite make up their minds about immigrant involvement in unionism. Some writers averred that immigrants shied away from union membership. Quite the opposite was true. Trade unions had existed in Italy since the 1840s, but not many workers had been able to join them.

In America fear that foreign workers would bring unemployment and violence led Illinois, Wyoming, and Idaho in 1889 to prohibit corporations from hiring any alien who had not declared his intention to become a citizen. Meanwhile, immigrants awkwardly became involved in disputes not of their own making. In 1898 they were among laborers organized by the United Mine Workers. (That union won its first big strike at Virden, Illinois, by confronting armed company guards and strikebreakers with rifles, shotguns, and revolvers.)

Locked out of some unions, immigrants admittedly undercut

domestic labor. During the 1880s New York's Italian Labor Bureau offered men for hire at $.50 to $.60 per day. In 1900 investigators for the Federal Bureau of Labor found Italian unskilled laborers in Chicago who earned as little as $4.37 per week. These workers were excluded from the American Federation of Labor (which adopted a literacy test for members in 1897). Sheer physical strength was no guarantee of security, no protection against exploitation, especially for illiterates.

During the years of heavy Italian immigration violence between management and labor was supported by foreign-born ideologues who followed the teachings of Mazzini, Bakunin, and Sorel. One of these was a disgruntled socialist agitator, Carlo Tresca. He came from the Abruzzi region, where his parents, paradoxically, were wealthy landlords. A radical champion of the peasants, Tresca left for the United States when he heard that Italian immigrants were being exploited by American capitalists.

The year was 1904, and Tresca became a labor agitator among the steel workers and coal miners of Pennsylvania. He was virtually a one-man socialist party who constantly urged restive immigrants to organize against company mill and mining town owners. A huge, angry man with menacing brown eyes, he participated in some of the great strikes early in this century. Among these were the 1912 strike of the textile workers in Lawrence, Massachusetts, and Paterson, New Jersey, as well as the Mesabi iron range strike of 1916. Three years later he founded *Il Martello*, a journal devoted to exposing management abuses. After a lifetime of fighting against social injustice in all forms, Tresca became an enemy of the Italian dictator Benito Mussolini. He was also an anti-Stalinist. In 1941 he was shot to death by an unknown assassin. One of the suspects was Carmine Galante, whose criminal record was well established.

The early labor struggles seemed to be inescapably linked with immigrant violence. A frustrated and angry Paterson, New Jersey, silk worker named Gaetano Bresci returned to Italy in 1900 in order to assassinate King Humbert I. To what extent was this a displacement of his anxieties onto a hated authority figure? A year later Bresci's desperate act inspired Leon Czolgosz (the disgruntled son of immigrant parents) to shoot President William McKinley. Again, a despised father figure was eliminated by blazing fire from a pistol barrel. How much did both assassins act out their frustrations? Bresci testified at his trial:

> I wished to avenge myself, as I was forced, after having lived a very hard life, to emigrate. When in Paterson I read of the events in Milan, where they even used cannons. I wept with rage and prepared myself for vengeance.

Bresci and Czolgosz, although unknown, by their irrational acts gained revenge against deeply resented internal hurts. And their names, incidentally, came to be recorded in books like this one.

Some neglected unskilled workers were drawn toward the Industrial Workers of the World (I.W.W.), a radical union with a reputation for violence. According to a United States government report published after the turn of the century, trade unionism among north Italians was nearly three times as high as among native Americans. In 1907, an Italian "Wobbly," Joseph Ettor, organized a lumber mill strike in Portland, Oregon, which swept the Pacific Northwest. In punishing foreigners convicted of violence during such outbreaks, judges frequently handed down severe sentences.

Ruthless mine operators virtually forced Italian miners to join in the Minnesota iron strikes of 1907 and 1918. These were organized by the Western Federation of Miners (as were various Montana mining outbreaks from 1912 to 1914). Italians were caught up in serious labor disputes all along the crests of the Rocky Mountains. These altercations began with the 1904 Cripple Creek strike and continued until the tragic Ludlow Massacre ten years later. At the Rockefeller-owned Colorado Fuel and Iron Works near Pueblo, an immigrant tent colony became embroiled in a demonstration over wages, hours, and working conditions. After a heated battle with the mine operators broke out, the state militia was called upon to quell the strikers. Troopers raked them with machine guns and burned the entire Ludlow tent camp to the ground. Since two Italian women and thirteen children were

71

burned to death, President Wilson finally interceded. The state of Colorado ultimately paid damages to the survivors, also admitting partial responsibility for the deaths.

During periods of unemployment, competition among poorly organized minorities itself increased, aggravated by a hostile press. Almost like animals, immigrants seemed to establish a pecking order of aggression against their own kind. Boston's Irish and Italians repeatedly reached a point of violence that had characterized the early rivalry between the Irish and the Chinese who built the transcontinental railroad.[1] The San Francisco anti-Chinese movement of the 1870s was fanned by an Irish labor boss, Denis Kearney. In New York, meanwhile, German Jews discriminated against Polish Jews, while in St. Louis newly arrived Germans drew the ire of their more established compatriots. Factional struggle and backbiting also occurred among immigrants who colonized a wholly germanized New Braunfels, Texas.

Paradoxically, a major sponsor of strict immigration was California's Anthony Caminetti, one of the first Italian Americans (1890-1895) elected to the United States House of Representatives. He actively lobbied for Oriental exclusion. While Caminetti, as President Wilson's commissioner of immigration, turned the force of his office toward restriction, in the Pacific Northwest two Norwegians, Haakon Langoe and Olaf Tveitmoe, became leaders of a post–World War I Americanization movement.

After the war ended, and with no further need to mollify America's wartime ally, Italy, her nationals came under the same sort of criticism as was directed against Germans and Hungarians. The 1920s witnessed a frenzy of xenophobia. A postwar deportation delirium, directed against "anarchists, troublemakers, and revolutionists" by Attorney General A. Mitchell Palmer, stained the last days of President Wilson's administration. Even Italian war veterans felt it necessary to take refuge by joining American Legion posts and the patriotic lodges of the Veterans of Foreign Wars.

During this great Red scare nativists roamed through ethnic neighborhoods seeking out subversives even on tenement roofs.

When a young Italian anarchist, Carlo Valdioce, got blown up by a bomb that exploded in front of Palmer's house, the vigilante hunt for alleged Bolsheviks was on in earnest. Valdioce, like Bresci, came from Paterson, New Jersey. During the so-called Palmer raids of 1920, six thousand immigrants were arrested and incarcerated. Some five hundred alleged subversives were deported. The raids accompanied the crushing of national strikes, among them the "big steel strike" of 1919.

Within the shadow of Plymouth Rock, in an atmosphere of suspicion, there occurred the famous Sacco-Vanzetti affair. Both men had emigrated to America in 1908 but did not meet until 1917, when they spent time in Mexico to avoid being drafted into the American armed forces. On May 5, 1920, they were arrested in a streetcar at Brockton, Massachusetts, charged with having murdered the paymaster of a Massachusetts shoe factory. Their unspoken crime, however, was to have voiced anarchist criticisms of American society. The Sacco and Vanzetti case, tried in Dedham, a suburb of Boston, was to drag on from 1920 to 1927. Intellectuals of the time, among them Theodore Dreiser, Sinclair Lewis, Walter Lippman, and Felix Frankfurter, joined in protesting the verdict of guilty. Reminding us of this miscarriage of justice are Upton Sinclair's *Boston* and Edna St. Vincent Millay's poem "Fear" in her *Wine From These Grapes*. The actions of these literati stand in contrast to the prejudices of Wharton and James earlier.

The novelist John Dos Passos was sure that Vanzetti was innocent. About Sacco he wrote in his memoir, *The Best Times*, that "it seemed barely possible that he might have convinced himself that seizing money from a capitalist paymaster, to be for the defense of his persecuted comrades, was a justifiable act in the class war."

What can the psychohistorian add to an understanding of the motives of Sacco the cobbler and Vanzetti the fishmonger? Beyond the technical evidence of whether they were guilty or innocent (evidence that by now has hardened into dogma), one encounters a special climate inside the storm of the Sacco-Vanzetti case. Because of the strain that both men had to endure, each was for a time admitted to a mental hospital. Did they also live in an inner world made up of childish fears that came to be expressed as outward heroism? Would the records of the psychiatrists who admitted Sacco and Vanzetti give us a clue to their internal difficulties? Freud believed that revolutionaries seek to replace traditional authority by another form of control, which they project onto a society.

It is conjecture, but both Sacco and Vanzetti may have harbored a vague dream (which would have been supported by Christian tradition) that the dawning industrial world could be made less brutal and more fair. Certainly such men as they had tried to escape changeless native villages and the roles of cobbler and fishmonger. Like other immigrants, they had sought a justice (*giustizia*) based upon the prospect of new equalities. But America, the place for finding the lost dreams of childhood, had let them down. This new mother country, with its sweatshops and exploitative labor bosses, was hardly the nourishing and redemptive new *madre* that they, and Carlo Tresca, too, had envisioned, that place where past injustices could be set aright. Revolution in a new missionary field was their response to the internal hurts of the past. This way of thinking, however, led to a great confusion of reality. Actually, America has never been friendly to its radicals. In his 1927 essay, entitled *Facing the Chair*, Dos Passos described how "many Italians planted the perfect city of their imagination in America." But America had, for Dos Passos, murdered those who would not let Back Bay Bostonians forget the dream promised by the words engraved on the base of the Statue of Liberty.

For Sacco and Vanzetti, opposition to authority seemed as much a part of their nature as the rhythm of one's heartbeat. Ethnic prejudices coursed through the rigid Yankee society that they encountered. Sacco viewed anarchists, including his volatile friend Carlo Tresca, as more than wild-eyed bomb throwers: instead, they were all men of "extravagant ideas" who seemed "generous, self-sacrificing, warmhearted. . . . They were fanatics, of course, but there was humanity in their fanaticism."

Yet these idealists did not hesitate to advocate destruction of a social system that they deemed reprehensible. Anarchists might murder, steal, or destroy to further their beliefs, Sociopaths exhibit similar defenses when frustrated. But anarchists showed little practical ability to shape organizational goals, for they were often themselves fragmented persons.

Sacco and Vanzetti represented a radical fringe and were not typical immigrant workers. Immigrants were actually best recruited by conservative unions rather than by revolutionary groups. As early as 1919, Italians who had joined the Industrial Workers of the World began to abandon that organization.

Like other workers, unemployed immigrants stood in soup lines for hours, with their tin pails and glass jars, hoping to carry away food dished out by the Salvation Army. They also got caught in street fights as labor scabs or as strikers on picket lines. But these activities hardly made them radicals. Despite the weakness of the immigrant's position, a racial mystique of Anglo-Saxonism continued to dominate the nation. An obsession with the idea of superior ("old-stock" immigrants) versus inferior "races" led even educated Americans to elevate Teutonic peoples over new immigrants of darker complexion.

As we have seen, among the earliest achievements of the Italians was the creation of neighborhoods with solid roots. Why, then, did they suffer silently the hectoring of a bad press? Their passive response was related to keeping a low profile in the hope that the bad times would pass. Their passivity to abuse, in marked contrast to the attitude of the Irish, may also be explained by a self-image that they came partly to believe and to accept. The racist myth of the superiority of Nordic peoples was widely embraced in Europe, fostered by an atmosphere in which competition for jobs was sometimes intense. Escape from the resultant stereotype of the swarthy, distrustful, inferior Italian became difficult.

Discrimination led to the assigning of dangerous jobs to the Italians. Pietro di Donato's *Christ in Concrete* (1939) portrays, in frightful detail, how his father, a construction worker, was buried alive under a stream of mortar at a building site collapse. Because the father had been given such dangerous work, Pietro, at age thirteen, became the sole support of his family. This terrifying event reminds one of how hundreds of other immigrant workers were maimed or killed in industrial accidents. Laborers who lived out their lives as cripples stormed against exploitative employers.

Americans showed a limited capacity to identify with immigrant beliefs and attitudes. The European's sense of tragedy had no counterpart in a culture wherein crises seemed to come and go like the seasons. Few had the patience to listen to cynical political or religious views. As late as 1940 a relatively sophisticated historian, Carl Wittke (in his *We Who Built America*), would see only the liabilities even of Italian religious holidays. Their "great religious festivals," he wrote, "not only involved the expenditure of money and time that might well have been used for other purposes, but impressed American observers as manifestations of Medieval superstition." Disdain for foreign folkways led social workers to try (not very successfully) to change even the eating habits and mores of newly arrived peasants.

But was xenophobia typical of the average American? Was the intolerance shown by the Native Sons of the Golden West really comparable to the goodwill of less prejudiced Americans toward newcomers? There had always been a few critics of intolerance in America. As early as 1849, Melville's *Redburn* called for an America that would be not merely a "narrow tribe of men" but a land whose "blood is as the flood of the Amazon, made up of a thousand noble currents all pouring into one." Roosevelt's melting pot, with Nordic overtones, still celebrated the superiority of Aryans but mildly defended immigration as an enriching national policy. A 1903 article in *Outlook* put it this way: "This Italian, this Slovak, this Jew is different from the Yankee. Suppose he does not become a Yankee all at once? Is that any ground for contempt or fear of him? Is not a character that is a bit firmer than wax worthy of respect?"

Boston's Immigration Restriction League—in the 1890s the epicenter of an Anglo-Saxon cult—eventually faded; so did the A.P.A. Barrett Wendell's racist ideas of an America whose democracy depended upon an inherited Anglo genius gave way to the predictions of Ralph Waldo Emerson, who foresaw a national melting pot. Guilt may have increased Yankee tolerance, which helped the growing political strength of those immigrants who learned to use the ballot in order to dislodge the older stock from entrenched positions of power. Whenever individual status was threatened, however, nativism won back persons who called themselves tolerant. For xenophobia thrives on economic and political dislocation, as well as on the threat posed by changes in the social system.

The economic depression of the 1930s once more increased competition for jobs. Suspicions again arose that there was something unstable and sinister in the Italian character. One sees a residue of midwestern bigotry in a remark attributed to Glenn Miller, the leader of the most successful popular band of the next decade. While interviewing a saxophonist named Jimmy Abato, Miller said: "Kid, I like your playing but I don't know whether to hire you because I don't like to hire Italians and Jews. They're troublemakers."

Only slowly would foreigners escape from prejudice. As for the Italians, acceptance was further complicated by the link repeatedly suggested between them and organized crime, my next topic.

VI

A TOUCH
OF THE GUTTER:
La Mafia and Crime

IN AMERICA, that new land where both good and evil could take root in the immigrant soul, one false step might lead to ruin. As we have seen, labor agitation and anti-foreignism came to be linked with crime. The Mafia, usually described as a sinister and secret "international terrorist organization," has allegedly been behind much criminal activity in the United States.

In western Sicily there were perfectly sensible reasons for the spread of a Mafia. The backwardness of rural life and of entrenched bad governments ruled the island for centuries. Law enforcement was spotty, indeed chaotic. Hence some of the leading families formed loose coalitions among themselves, known as *cosche*. The word *cosca* literally means the heart of an artichoke. Incidentally, the leaves of the Italian variety sport protective spines, unlike the bland American version. Sicily's human *cosche* consisted of families who protected their estates against intruders and competitors.

If agreements as to land boundaries were infringed, feuds might begin that could last over several generations. In the cities too there were *cosche* which derived from ancient and degenerated urban guilds. These regulated vegetable, meat, or flour markets by fixing prices, discouraging competition, and exacting tribute. Spain's Bourbon invaders, long the rulers of the Italian south, considered such carryings-on as banditry, which they tried brutally to exterminate. This only toughened the resolve of local *Mafiosi* to *farsi rispettare*, to demand respect—whether by threats, hijackings, kidnapping, or even murder. In the cities or countryside the *cosche* controlled the basics of life, whether marriages between families, contracts for vital foodstuffs, or public works, even the election of local bureaucrats. Terror was the Mafia's not so hidden weapon.

Fear and power came to be commingled within the word "Mafia." In Italy (and later throughout the world) it became a misunderstood generic term that gave great offense to the American Italians. There were also local, non-Mafia organizations such as the Unione Siciliana, an American creation, and Calabria's Onorata Società, as well as the Neapolitan Camorra. These groups ultimately turned to crime on a large scale as chagrined governments were unable to control their secret family crime systems.

Those *Mafiosi* who have planned tha Mafia's worldwide operations have not ordinarily been viewed as psychological deviants. Instead, criminologists and popular writers more often depict the Mafia as a clandestine society run by leaders who call themselves "men of respect." According to a Mafioso, Vincent Teresa, these "dons" insist that they are "men of honor":

> Most people don't understand what a don is. First of all, the name, don, is a title given to a Mafioso who has earned special respect for his wisdom and fairness. A don is like your father and mother and God all rolled into one. He is your life. He is the head of your family. You owe him everything. You owe him the breath out of your lungs, your life, your soul, your religion.

How much did such omnipotence lead young ethnic hoodlums to

commit horrendous street crimes under the Mafia's cloak of immunity?

Their parents, terrorized by threats of retribution, concealed how *Mafiosi* preyed upon those merchants who refused to pay for "protection." Bakers, fruit dealers, and cobblers were regularly beaten up or their businesses set afire if they refused to yield to extortion.

The Mafia was originally regulatory—designed to punish wrongdoers who had escaped the law. Some of the "best" Sicilian families became involved with the organization, in which land, money, power, and the ways to wield it were major concerns. Sicilians most involved preferred to call themselves *amici* ("friends"). A sacred duty, or *omertà*, makes it dishonorable to turn toward the police in order to right a wrong. To do so is to court punishment, even death in the middle of the night by "unknown assailants."

In Sicily there is an old and a new Mafia, a rural and an urban Mafia. Originally considered an "honorable society," the old Mafia grew out of distrust of a foreign rule that lasted for twenty-five centuries. This distrust has expressed itself in the organization's obvious sullenness; Sicilians, furthermore, do not act like mainland Italians. Their strong disrespect for government developed over the years into a resistance movement against established law.

There are sharp differences between the old and the new Mafia. The old organization was not originally criminal. Despite occasional violence, it was capable of restraint, even gallantry. Frequently, the foremost Sicilian provincials were its leaders. The new Mafia exhibits pure gangsterism.

Toward the turn of the century the Mafia, in its American form, seemed almost as remote from Italy as Americanized Tong warfare in China was outside that country's tradition. The so-called Black Hand (*Mano Nera*), indeed, probably originated in America's urban crime jungles. In 1889[1] the American writer Ernest Schuyler pointed out that Italian laws forbade the departure of persons accused of ciminal activity from Italy. He added: "I have now lived for over three years on the outskirts of Alassio, a town of six thousand inhabitants, about half way between Nice and Genoa. Theft here is rare, burglary unknown, so that we have slept for weeks with doors unlocked and even open. . . . A murder has not been known here for fifty years . . . crimes produced by lust are almost unknown."

Yet, in America, where the Mafia was blackening the reputations of countless Italians, the average native remained unaware that the incidence of criminal convictions among Italian immigrants was approximately the same as that for other foreign-language groups and was even lower than that of native-born persons. Italian homicides received especially heavy attention in the press. Southern Italians were portrayed as dramatically vicious in committing gangland crimes. This evoked the bugaboo of the avenging, bloodthirsty Italian—a persistent image. In the early years of this century, headlines in metropolitan newspapers stressed "Italian crimes of passion"—stabbings, murders, and assaults—and intrigues.

In the United States the Mafia became massively corrupted by second-generation criminals reared in the slums of rotting American cities. About this Luigi Barzini wrote: "The theory of an international Mafia with headquarters in Sicily and branches in the United States is comforting and plausible. It helps explain mysterious events, accounts for strange loyalties and alliances, and sometimes justifies the impotence of the police." These displaced suppositions are supported more by folklore and reputation than by firm evidence.

This is not, however, to say that links between American criminals and gangsters living abroad (especially family members) do not exist. The Mafia as a formal organization cannot be traced; there are no headquarters, no offices. The Mafia has no written statutes, no lists of members, no fixed rules. The question of who becomes a leader is a matter of family prestige, influenced by personality and force, never the result of balloting. The Mafia can be defined as a coalition of individuals and groups working independently in local situations but cooperating to control a share of the economic life of an area. There is, thus, not one organization but an endless network.

Italian crime and discrimination came to be linked in the American South even before its appearance in the East and Midwest. Strong nativist prejudice down south had weakened cosmopolitanism in that area—a by-product of French and Spanish colonization of the lower Mississippi valley. By the 1890s the Italians unwittingly got in the way of white demagogy. Unschooled in the racial prejudices of the South, they sometimes refused to interfere in attempts to hold down blacks. Instead, they were attracted to southern populism, which proposed "that both whites and Negroes look with less prejudice at their mutual problem of making a living."

In this little known conflict between Italians and nativists, the naive conduct of Louisiana's Italian Americans in matters of race did not please white supremacists. The Italians, themselves unassimilated into southern culture, had no reason to look with nostalgia toward the antebellum past. They seemed impervious to anti-black feeling at a time when the Knights of the White Camellia and the White League were flourishing. Indeed, when the Populists threatened the southern Democratic party structure, the Italians unwisely joined groups that opposed anti-black discrimination. They thereby obstructed the political objectives of southern Democrats who wanted to rally whites around the cause of white supremacy. Eventually Italian ignorance of the depth of southern racial feeling helped incite mob violence against them.

In 1890 the New Orleans press set the scene for identification of the Italians as criminals. The *Times-Picayune*, pointing out how deeply involved they were in fish and fruit trading, at first congratulated them on their "progress." But it soon became clear that the Italians controlled the city's Caribbean fruit import market. By their pro-black views they risked the hatred of racial bigots. Soon a foreign outbreak at New Orleans would assume the proportions of an international episode.

A series of "Sicilian crimes" there, some of them vendettas, occurred during 1890. These were related to envy over interference in the local fruit trade of various Mafia chieftains (*capi mafiosi*) belonging to the secret Black Hand (*Mano Nera*) society. These avaricious Sicilians allegedly levied tribute on every banana freighter that came into the harbor. Italian competitors who tried to muscle into this lucrative traffic were dumped into canals with their throats cut. Others became the victims of mysterious bombings, gunnings, and knifings.

A number of Mafia suspects were tried for these crimes. None was convicted, which led the public to believe that bribery had impeded justice. An even greater shock then occurred. On October 15, 1890, while investigating criminal charges against New Orleans Italians, Chief of Police David Hennessy was murdered. Asked who "did him in" he reportedly answered, "Dagoes," as he lay dying. Sicilian flags were seen hoisted above the Stars and Stripes, which flew over the fruit and oyster schooners anchored offshore. A dragnet ordered by the mayor followed these instructions: "Scour the whole neighborhood! Arrest every Italian you come across." A mob brought in dozens of Italians, as the mayor openly acknowledged his prejudices against them to the sensationalist New Orleans press.

A supremacist committee, out to "suppress the Mafia," uncovered flimsy evidence that two rival Sicilian dockworking gangs were involved in Hennessy's murder. Toting shotguns and rifles, this vigilante group brought nine suspects to trial. When six of these were acquitted, a larger mob assembled, charging that there had been a miscarriage of justice, which included threats to members of the jury. After a mistrial was declared for the other three suspects, the *New Orleans Times-Picayune* maintained that the Sicilians cowering in the city jail were involved in the slaying of Chief Hennessy. This jingoism inflamed public opinion. On March 15, 1891, the mob advanced on the jail, seized eleven Sicilians, shot nine of them, and hanged two others.

This lynching was rationalized by stereotypes that are still used to describe Italians. Even the distant *New York Times* wrote: "Our rattlesnakes are as good citizens as they; our own murderers are men of feeling and nobility compared to them." The *Times-Picayune* congratulated the mob, moralizing that "desperate diseases require desperate measures." The paper reported proudly that when the mob left the parish prison, eight culprits lay dead on its blood-stained floors and "behind the crumbling walls of the gloomy old prison another lay dying on a stretcher near where he had been shot." The police ultimately arrested more than a hundred Italians in an anti-foreign delirium that swept New Orleans.

When news of the lynchings and arrests reached Italy, its government demanded punishment and an indemnity. Secretary of State James G. Blaine explained that the lynchings had received public approbation in New Orleans, which included the approval of law-abiding Italians. For this reason indemnification would be difficult. Nevertheless, President Benjamin Harrison apologized and described the affair as "an offense against law and humanity."

In 1896 there was yet another lynching of Italians in the town of Hahnville, St. Charles Parish, Louisiana. Once again the United States government paid an indemnity ($6,000) to the survivors of three "subjects of Italy's King Humbert." Whenever the Italian government learned of discrimination against its nationals, as in still another lynching of five Italians at Tallaluh, Louisiana, in 1899, it tried to discourage emigration.

In 1912 the Italian ambassador to the United States reported a lingering American prejudice, particularly against Sicilians: "To hear these gentlemen, all our Sicilians are ostensibly affiliated with secret societies, all are ready to commit havoc because of hatred or a vendetta spirit. They would, furthermore, use any means including firearms, stilettos, and even poison." In his volume on America, Vito Garretto complained that "this shameful discrimination" was designed to keep cheap labor out of the United States. He saw a Celtic-Anglo-Germanic superiority complex directed against Latins and Slavs. For the Italians, whom he portrayed as hardworking, to suffer such indignities was an intolerable situation.

In those years New Orleans, not New York, was the focus of criminal accusations against the Italians. Yet, in 1931 the United States Wickersham Commission on Law Enforcement found that in 543 homicides committed in New Orleans between 1925 and

1929, only four Italians were officially charged and concluded that "this feeling against Italians seems hardly justified." Nevertheless, sensational books continue to appear that repeat the 1891 allegations of the lynch mob leaders long since discredited. Despite all this calumny, there have been two Italian mayors of New Orleans in the past thirty years, as well as numerous judges and other public officials of Italian descent.

Today's criminologists link crime and violence to ignorance, educational deprivation, and overcrowding. All of these factors were present in the cities to which the immigrant was drawn. At Baltimore, called Mob-Town, ugly and bloody disturbances were common. During most of the nineteenth century, trouble in the crowded centers of Boston, Philadelphia, and New York had become virtually institutionalized. And the continuing flood of immigrants heightened fear of those who had already arrived and who remained unemployed or transient.

An event like Chicago's violent Haymarket Riot of 1886 produced an image of foreign-born radical agitators who were lawless and undesirable. The paranoia in American politics, identified by the historian Richard Hofstadter, reflected fears first of Latin Catholicism and later of communism. By the 1920s a mounting public hysteria demanded minority scapegoats.

In 1924 President Calvin Coolidge signed an immigration act designed to keep so-called undesirables from entering the United States. Meanwhile, Al ("Scarface") Capone had emerged as prototype of the world's most famous gangleader. Capone conjured up a vision of mobsters who left behind a trail of bullet-riddled corpses.[2]

Immigrants hardly knew how to overcome the stigma fastened upon them. Most Italians were even harsher than native Americans in condemning gangsters; they deeply resented the ill repute into which the Al Capones and the Lucky Lucianos threw them. In an interwar atmosphere of jazz and bootleg booze, the defensive immigrant was wont to condemn America's dank slums for causing the emergence of a Capone:

In place of the "Festa Campestre," (the village dance) the "Festa Patronale," (the feast of the patron saint) America offers to the Italian man the curse of the saloon, the poisonous atmosphere of cheap moving pictures, and the dangers of the slum dance hall. In Italy we know the difference between a peasant who has lived there always and one who has spent a few years in America and then gone back. The former is poorer but the latter is quite rotten.

During the interwar period, persons of Italian descent expressed rage toward the abuse heaped upon them. Some even denied that a Mafia existed. To reduce their ethnic guilt, apologists argued that hoodlums, albeit of foreign parentage, had merely entered rackets already in existence. Indeed, Italians had showed a special talent for reorganizing these enterprises along efficient lines, skillfully combining crime and politics.

The lawless decade, as the 1920s were called, produced a parade of con men and hoodlums with Italian names. At Boston, Charles ("the Great") Ponzi went from $16.00 a week as a fruit and vegetable peddler to $200,000 per day as an embezzler. He was deported to Italy in 1934. New York, too, was developing famous crime families.

In Chicago there arose a close connection between criminals of immigrant descent and local political stooges. Chicago's best known early Italian crime figure was Luigi ("Big Jim") Colosimo. He began by selling newspapers and shining shoes, got into ward politics, and became the maestro of a brothel and the owner of a swanky restaurant on Wabash Avenue. In 1920, shortly after leaving his Vernon Street mansion, he was gunned down, possibly by Johnny Torrio, one of Colosimo's own lieutenants. The funeral turnout honoring the criminal (who was to be succeeded first by Torrio and later by Al Capone) included a notable cortege. Following the body to the cemetery were three judges, eight aldermen, an assistant state attorney general, a congressman, a member of the state legislature, artists of the Chicago Opera Company, gamblers, ex-gamblers, and a number of saloon keepers. Republicans and Democrats alike were among the pallbearers who helped make the event national.

Criminals unwanted in Italy flourished in the United States

partly because American law enforcers were unfamiliar with their traditions of cohesion. Decent Italians sought to escape the resulting stereotype, but their efforts have been all but forgotten. A member of the New York Police Department, Lieutenant Joseph Petrosino, organized an "Italian Squad" to fight crime in Brooklyn. He ultimately was gunned down in Italy while pursuing an Italo-American hoodlum. After Petrosino was murdered, he became a legendary figure. Books, pamphlets, and comic-strip magazines about him gained wide circulation. Petrosino was a hero of miraculous achievements, his life portrayed by Ernest Borgnine in the Hollywood film *Pay or Die.*

An inexorable fate seemed to hang over criminals who claimed to be captured by America's ghetto streets, Yet, few of them chose to forsake the soot of the cities for cleaner vistas. Another film, *Little Caesar* (1931), was about a sneering slum dweller named Ricco who yearned "to be someone" on his own terms. But what did it mean for a disturbed person to be someone? The film starred Edward G. Robinson as an ethnic gangster, a composite of Torrio and Capone.

For criminals who had not gotten their way in childhood, a cult of toughness allowed them to defy parental ways. A disoriented bravura seemed to atrophy the consciences (superegos) of corner gang members. The gangland life became a dramatic alternative to family boredom (anger).

Juvenile hooligans appropriated even the stereotypically rasping voice of their new Mafia leaders. This characteristic, incidentally, remained a psychological mystery for me until I read a key phrase in a letter to Freud from the psychoanalyst Georg Groddeck: "People get hoarse," he wrote, "when they have got something that can only be told in whispers, a mysterious complex which, on one unconscious level, they want to communicate, while on another they struggle against it."[3]

The Mafia style was emulated in the television series *The Untouchables* (1958), and Mario Puzo's novel and film *The Godfather* (1969) helped make big-time crime virtually synonymous with Italian gangsters, sawed-off shotguns, and bulletproof limousines crashing through plate glass windows. It grew to be acceptable to glamorize Italian gangland killers who were in fact sociopaths. Albert Anastasia, for example, appears to have sabotaged the French ocean liner *Normandie* in the port of New York in order to convince the United States Navy that he could be useful in security work!

In the inter-war period, 1920–1940, a search for identity had already taken other misfits into various pursuits. Dale Carnegie's book *How to Win Friends and Influence People* (1936) stressed how much the popular culture demanded "success," of almost any sort. Members of the leftist Lincoln Brigade went to Spain, acting out the bravado of the macho Hemingway heroes by fighting on the loyalist side against the Fascist General Francisco Franco. Achievement, sometimes won at the disabling expense of what came to be known as the "nervous breakdown," inspired the neo-Freudian psychoanalyst Karen Horney to write her *Neurotic Personality of Our Time* (1937). She insisted that "status anxiety" within the dominant success culture provided the raw material for neuroses.

Some sociological studies continue to maintain that poverty and unemployment are the root causes of crime. Actually, most poor people turn out to be law-abiding, not criminals. Ethnicity is also a dubious major cause of criminality. Bad parenting would seem to be a better explanation. This does not mean that a child who always gets his way will not be a criminal. Perhaps, also, the ghetto is not an ideal environment in which to rear model children. Whatever their genetic or blood line, most people do not become even ordinary hoodlums, let alone violent criminals.

Any discussion of the Mafia has to be tied to various clichés about what people think are the root causes of crime. The liberal myth that poverty breeds criminals grossly simplifies complex psychological issues. It is a myth to believe that if you alleviate poverty, killing and robbery will be reduced. Haiti, one of the poorest of countries, is among the safest. Three of the least prosperous nations in Europe—Spain, Portugal, and Ireland—share its lowest murder rate. In America the current surge of homicides began in the peak prosperity period of the 1960s.[4]

We need to consider bad parenting and poor early identification with healthy authority figures instead of offering exclusively sociological explanations of crime. Sociologists, moreover, have failed to differentiate types of criminals. Some Italian hoodlums ran rackets to earn a good living. Indeed, they took pride in the quality of their work; as straight professionals they were rarely caught. Our knowledge of criminals has been distorted by amateur gamblers who end up in jail. Professionals, however, provide a neutral environment for such gamblers but do not themselves gamble.

Recent psychoanalytic findings concerning criminal behavior (by Samuel Yochelson and Stanton Samenow) reveal that some criminals are pursuing excitement and power. When apprehended, they offer excuses for their behavior that fit whatever theories currently are in vogue. The psychiatrist Eric Berne has argued that such criminals are playing a game called "cops and robbers."

Although the game of crime was played out in slum neighborhoods, let us distinguish between economic hurts and psychic wounds. It is childhood ego deprivation that later frees the criminal adult conscience (superego) from the restrictions of morality. Persons who seek indemnification for their low self-esteem may act out delinquently. This neurotic maneuver is also entwined with escape. In severely distorted family settings the reduction of tensions became merged with revulsion against working-class origins. Young ethnic hoods did not want to become kitchen helpers or even cooks, like their fathers or uncles. Their loyalties were so confusingly conflicted that these adolescents scarcely recognized that they were being pressured to conform to two cultures at the same time.

In *The Business of Crime*, Humbert Nelli went so far as to suggest that Italian criminals in this country were actually motivated by the American dream of success. Rather than a phenomenon characteristic of Sicily or the Old World, a new success drive, fulfilled at any price, by any means, was acted out within certain families.

Permission, furthermore, to actualize vindictive feelings—among the most primitive of emotions—came out of such families. Pietro di Donato, in his *Three Circles of Light*, noted that "when a man did grievous wrong to tradition he had to pay for it with his life. In differences of opinion this green race of Americans resorted to nose-bashing fisticuffs and name-calling. That was for children and not real men."[5]

The Sicilian and Calabrian way of working out internal problems was brutal and devious. It allowed confused second-generation youths to fill the interval between childhood and adult status by dramatic means. Children who came out of a chaotic family environment began criminal life with petty lawbreaking. This was followed by stealing objects, as if to replace that real love which their parents had failed to provide. Defiant Italian kids, drunk on red wine, hung out on street corners and picked up loose girls. Others learned to run numbers. Young make-believe hoods dealt in hot goods or trafficked in drugs. Street fights, knifings, and robberies allowed these disturbed adolescents to act out internal pressures under a cloak of adventure. Their hypomanic defenses resembled the borderline behavior of the sickest neurotics.

The career of Frank Costello helps us to understand the process of criminalization. He was born Francesco Castiglia in the Calabrian village of Lauropoli in 1891. His father, who had already migrated, called for the family to join him when Costello was four. By the age of thirteen, Costello had quit school. He openly defied his parents, joining the groups of young hoodlums who roamed the streets of Manhattan's east Harlem district. It was virtually useless for his alarmed father to ask, *"Perchè non vai lavorare?"* ("Why don't you go to work?") The son was employed only briefly in a piano factory. He found the job hard and dirty; as for the pay, it was comtemptible.

By the age of seventeen, Costello (as he now called himself) had assaulted a man with a hammer and was arrested. This was his first offense and it was explained by the "influence" of older criminals; the case was dismissed. Three years later, in 1911, he was booked on the same charges; his case was again dismissed. By

1914, when he was once more arraigned for attempted robbery, Costello had a reputation as a hardened gunman. Although sentenced to a year in jail, he was released after ten months for good behavior and because he had married and "assumed family responsibilities." In the future he was to insist upon operating secretly, usually behind the cover of successful politicians and "legitimate" businesses.

Costello, who sought excitement through danger, despised the safe routine of hard, dirty work and slow advancement. He sought out risky adventures with high stakes. Addicted to action, Costello found his particular drug to be danger itself. This behavior is characteristic of impulse-ridden sociopaths who require gratification through the discharge of tension.

For such criminals, stealing is not limited to material goods. Costello was an imitative man whose very clothing (including spats and ivory cigarette holder) and life-style were copied from others. His biographer quoted him as saying: "All I know I stole. If I saw you hold a cigaret a certain way, and I liked it, I would steal it from you."[6] A defective ego can be covered over, at least temporarily, by the accumulation of "wealth" belonging to others, including appropriation of even the identity of another person.

Costello later said that he had spit on the good parts of his life, "denying it when it was wonderful for me to live it." Gangland successes led to further risk taking until he became America's premier crime Boss. Costello remarked about this elevated status: "It isn't nice being called prime minister of the underworld. Yet what can I do?" Was this his way of expressing helplessness about a life pattern that might at any moment signal a bullet aimed at Costello's head?

In 1947, when Costello was in his mid-fifties, he suffered from depression, for which he visited a New York psychiatrist. He did this secretly, of course, not telling even his closest friends. In these sessions he revealed how he had hated his father, indeed, had despised the old man's humility and inadequacy. He had loathed how his parents were willing to settle for a life of drudgery and near poverty. (He was later to build a gigantic mausoleum for them and for himself.) Costello's psychiatric treatment lasted two years, until the newspapers found out about it. The psychiatrist, Richard Hoffman, admitted that he had been seeing Costello, which so angered his patient that he denied being treated and broke off the sessions. In fact, Costello maintained that it was Hoffman who asked his advice about other patients. The classic defense mechanism known as denial seemed all too evident.

Costello revealed also that he had been made to feel inferior because of his Italian past. Despite his wealth and accomplishments, this sense of inferiority lingered. At this stage in his life Costello was having to undergo the further embarrassment of backing down from his control of large criminal syndicate operations. Vito Genovese and Salvatore Lucania—Charles ("Lucky") Luciano—had taken over extensive portions of Costello's gambling interests. He also resented the image of violence that the press projected upon him, although "he had never killed anyone"; nor had he ever "had anything to do with heroin."[7]

Lucky Luciano's story is not dissimilar to that of Costello. Born Salvatore Lucania on November 11, 1897, at Lercara, Sicily, he was the third son in a family that numbered two sisters as well. His father, Anthony Lucania, was a mechanic who emigrated to New York in 1904. He got a job in a brass-bed factory and sent for his wife, Rosa, and the children the next year. They settled on the lower east side of Manhattan.

Whereas his father never broke a law in his life, Lucky (who had a horseshoe tattooed on his arm) was committed to the Brooklyn Truant School as early as the fifth grade. A chronic truant, he quit school at the age of fourteen. According to court records:

> During this phase of his life, the defendant was reared in an impoverished environment. . . . he was beyond the control of his parents. . . . largely conditioned by the influence of unwholesome associates, with the result that by the time he was eighteen years old he had acquired a definitely criminalistic pattern of conduct.

Like Costello, Luciano resented the menial work done by his

father. The boy's first job, as shipping clerk in a hat factory, paid $5.00 per week; at the end of two years he was making only $6.00 a week. He quit this employment saying, "If I had to be a crumb, I would rather be dead."[8]

Luciano's father appears to have been industrious and his mother strong and healthy. The son's resentment of his position in life apparently prevented orderly ego development. He was the only member of his family ever to be arrested. By 1929 he had run up a total of seventeen arrests on charges that included possession of heroin and other controlled substances, possession of illegal weapons, disorderly conduct, bootlegging, armed robbery, operation of a prostitution ring, violation of tax laws, and assault.

By 1931 Luciano had, with Costello and other younger gangsters, succeeded in getting rid of Old World crime leaders of his father's generation, among them Joe ("the Boss") Masseria and Salvatore Maranzaro. He became an arrogant and vindictive criminal who believed that he was an American success story turned upside down.

Luciano's unwillingness to work for crumbs meant that he wanted "money to spend, beautiful women to enjoy, silk underclothes and places to go in style."[9] The Five Points Gang, one of the most notorious in New York's Fourteenth Street district, was the vehicle that Luciano employed to enter this life so different from the one he had known in his parents' house. Such slum gangs, frequently related to one another, also provided a curious substitute for emotional sustenance.

With family cohesion apparently outside his defense system, Luciano assuaged his anxieties by modeling himself after criminal parental substitutes whom he later overthrew. He continued, however, to send home monthly checks to his father. Somehow, Luciano freed himself from conscience (superego) restraints. Outside his family he became an inveterate thief, liar, and perjurer. He also seemed forever anxious to even the score for past injuries. To the end of his days his nemesis was Thomas E. Dewey, the famous prosecutor who sent him and other gangland competitors into prison and exile.

93

When he was thirty-eight years old Luciano received a prison sentence of thirty to fifty years. At Sing Sing Penitentiary a psychiatrist, Dr. L. E. Kienholz, described him as of "borderline intelligence." Luciano claimed that he was a barber and asked for such employment in prison; yet he admitted that he did not know how to cut hair. By then he was addicted to drugs, he was described as "dangerous," and his prognosis was "poor."[10]

A veritable psychodrama went on in the lives of young ethnic criminals. A few of their actions were "phase specific," that is, designed to allay inner fears at a particular time. Immigrant children, as we have seen, sought a warm and empathic response from their elders to help overcome the anonymity they felt outside the family. Instead, they sometimes met within the family itself a nonavailability of their loved ones. Their anxiety became activated by parents who could not understand what was happening to their children.

Psychoanalysts know that the earliest interplay between parent and child is central to character formation. What about the parents of other notorious gangsters who also brawled their way upward, among them Vito Genovese, Joseph Masseria, Joe Adonis, Joseph Profaci, and Joseph Bonanno? How much did confused fathers and mothers unconsciously condone antisocial acting out in order to gratify their own forbidden impulses? Did they displace destructive anxieties onto their children? Or, did the children punish the parents by resorting first to truancy, then to lock picking and safe cracking, as well as petty theft, and finally to murder? We may never know with certainty how much covert parental permissiveness helped to shape the lives of young Italian hoodlums. But we do know a great deal about the effect of thrusting neurotic parents upon children. Destructive sanctions are at the heart of such sick relationships.

The neurosis of a parent may provide signals in support of a child's asocial disturbances. Anna Freud has described how certain neurotic mothers have a need to create distorted children. Parents may unwittingly encourage amoral or antisocial behavior. Such neurotic discharges sometimes grow out of the inability of the adult's environment to satisfy pressing needs. The world of the immigrants compounded stunting experiences in the parents' own disturbed childhoods. For children who feel that family life is stifling them, crime and even suicide offer escape. If one's selfhood is diminished, life does not seem quite so worth the struggle out of darkness.

Too often we stress economic handicaps encountered by slum victims. Delinquency should also be linked to anxiety, depression, and other severe personal disabilities. Hardly understood is the hidden shame that lay in the illiterate peasant past; such shame festered in the unconscious mind and infected the children of immigrants.

The young Lucianos and Costellos of America's "mean streets" demanded immediate gratification of their drives. They were not interested in the future goals for which "normal" persons wait. Poor impulse control accompanied their faulty sense of conscience (superego). Teresa has given us a view of the explosiveness of angry young mobsters:

> Mob guys aren't used to holding their tempers. They often boil with frustrations. Unlike the average guy, they can't tell the boss to go to hell and quit, and the man who tells the boss to go to hell is measuring himself for a pine box. The pressures of daily survival are so great, with danger around every corner and in every bar and restaurant, that mob guys often explode right in front of the people below them.[11]

This behavior borders on the sociopathic. The true sociopath is contemptuous of society, but he usually acts within bounds that are not psychotic. He is, however, intent upon destroying family values. The immigrant children who left their own families behind to enter Mafia-like groups could be called pseudosociopaths who hid out within the protection of a new "family" based upon fear and economic gain rather than love. True sociopathy has childhood origins that are closer to psychotic, rather than neurotic, behavior. True sociopaths, whether they murder their brother or rape their sister have no remorse; they wish to push the order of things out of shape. The Mafia weeds out true sociopaths; they are too dangerous and too destructive to group discipline. Every other cemetery headstone may well represent a deviant whose aberrant behavior had become unacceptable to some *capo* or other.

On the surface, criminalized immigrants or their children looked like winners. Young males transcended the power of their real fathers for the safety that a "godfather" could offer. The real parent could then be distanced as a forbidding and angry remnant of the past. This distancing process allowed disturbed youths to become virtual exiles from their own families. At the legal withdrawal age of fourteen, future mobsters left school and took to the streets. These dropouts acted in a way akin to their parents' metaphoric abandonment of the mother country.

The mothering process is so vital that the psychiatrist Anthony Storr has called its distortion by aggression a behavioral plea for a return to the maternal breast—rather than the seeking of immortality through bravura. With criminals it is as if they derive psychic strength via omnipotence over the environment in order to compensate for the motherly care they lacked.

A major reason why a child reaches outside the family for affection may lie in the parents' incapacity to give. An immigrant mother or father's consuming anxieties were bound to affect children who grew up in conflict between dependency on parents and resentment of their mysteriously hard and cold ways. Both parents and children were also frightened by the harshness of alien neighbors. Each came to view the outer world as dangerous. At times each felt unwanted, cruelly rejected, wounded, hurt. Children victimized by emotionally exhausted parents who beat them grew up expecting evil in strangers. The repression of angry feelings led to further anxiety. Feelings of helplessness and of being endangered were hard to disguise, as was envy of more fortunate rivals.

If one could somehow develop a compensating protective power (Mafia), one might reduce an imagined enemy's capacity to hurt. By this process the former underdog became top dog. Power-driven Mafiosi models, furthermore, garnered admiration. Indeed, the Mafia chieftains displayed a need to be respected, to dominate, to humiliate their foes. Their hostility actually covered a deeper-seated fear.

We could also look at joining the Mafia as a form of sexuality gone astray. Disturbed youths left hostile family settings to form a symbiosis with a predominantly male society. Was this a homosexual projection of anger, screened by camaraderie and secrecy? Mechanical conformity formed part of a process of fusion with another family outside one's real family. This new fantasy fraternity offered the narcissistic support that the disintegrating immigrant family could not provide.

Disposal of emotional sewage is difficult. In the immigrant child who became criminalized we can see how important are those psychosocial forces that elicit individual and mass hostility. For the disturbed child, criminal activity becomes a flight from troubled life situations and stress. This leads to a kind of self-murder that takes the place of love. Otherwise, emotional familial impoverishment might be castrative.

The south Italian family structure encouraged deviousness. Only with difficulty could non-foreign Americans reconcile the ingrained Sicilian attitude toward honor with the covert hypocrisy practiced within the family. Illegal acts were troweled over by sanctimony and duplicity. The result was a massive confusion of mores in the mind of the Italo-American child. Unable to satisfy either the American social system or the code of the family, youngsters responded to their loss of autonomy by adventurous misbehavior.

Back in Sicily there were two types of criminals—the quick and the dead. The quick stayed within the protection of their families. In America the archaic familial order, however, came to be defied. Tempted by the new "kill or be killed" environment, a child like Frank Costello resented being treated like a piece of property that had to be kept in working order for the benefit of the family. One sees him struggling against a pervasive sense of hollowness. He acts out his turmoil in an atmosphere of social disintegration and rebellion against the parents. Their strictures become unacceptable. So, he projects his most disturbing, even murderous, thoughts outward onto society rather than keep them bottled up.

Confused youths, seeking to avoid a guilt-laden image of themselves, seemed almost to wish for punishment as they withdrew from the decaying authoritarian family circle. The unconscious desire to be caught in criminal acts is related to groping for protection against committing even worse offenses. Who knows whether the gangland followers of Al Capone may not have repressed an unconscious wish to die by police gunshots?

For them an exciting new way of life had opened up a defense against their parents. Acts of bravado beyond the authority of home and law became an elated primitive escape, with hypomanic overtones. The whole process defended angry delinquents against something they dreaded worst of all—the threat of personal annihilation, of never being fully validated as persons. Personal depression was set aside while the stormy developmental crises of independence were acted out.

One cannot, however, say that confused parenting alone caused criminal character disorders. In the Italian family early oral deprivation (a frequent cause of childhood disabilities) did not typically occur. In fact, overindulgence of the son by the mother was often the case. To what extent this prematurely eroticized and confused the male child is another matter. An outward impertinence veiled the wish to escape from the suffocating indulgence of the mother. With homosexuality strongly tabooed in the Italian culture, criminal aggressiveness alleviated pent-up resentments against authoritarian family ties. Adolescents seeking identity may find that crime offers a sense of uniqueness. The child psychoanalyst Erik Erikson has described how important it is to achieve early personhood in his *Young Man Luther* and *Childhood and Society*.

For Al Capone and Johnny Torrio, depreciation of their parents discharged an underlying unresolved childhood rage. It is as though such immigrant children were born with latent consitutional defects and vulnerabilities. These fault lines, under stress, may crack open underlying character defects. The ghetto environment also fostered criminality. Certain children were expelled from dank and forbidding homes into pestilential, high-risk environments.

Denial became their way of fitting into this new world. Capone frequently said: "I'm no Italian. I was born in Brooklyn." A ruthless butcher, he carried a business card that read: "A. Capone. Antiques." He called himself "a second-hand furniture dealer."

One way to approach what seems to have been going on within these criminals is to examine the career of a lesser known figure. The story of Johnny Lazia, crime king of Kansas City, lies all but forgotten. Lazia grew up in an underworld of racketeers and hoodlums harbored within the city's Italian district. By the 1930s this soft-spoken, dapper young man became virtual political boss of its north side. He ruthlessly eliminated the city's Irish strongman, Michael Ross. Kansas City's Italians, with little political organization, had been unable to escape satellite status under Irish bosses. Once the north side Democratic Club came under Lazia's control, he made an alliance with the Thomas J. Pendergast political machine, which dominated Kansas City. Pendergast (whose sister Mary had married an Italian, William C. Costello) grew fond of Lazia.

The mild-mannered Lazia, wearing rimless glasses and spats and carrying cane and gloves, was deceptive in appearance. He spoke good English, chewed gum incessantly, told humorous stories, and was superficially modest and polite. Lazia kept criminals from Chicago and St. Paul "in line" for Pendergast. He dumped visiting gangland victims along Jackson County's roadsides. Not surprisingly, Lazia used a chauffered bulletproof car and a personal bodyguard named "Big Charley" Carollo.

Lazia had never advanced beyond the eighth grade. He, however, studied law on his own and seemed headed for a legal career when, at the age of eighteen, he was caught in a robbery attempt. Sentenced to fifteen years in the Missouri Penitentiary, Lazia served less than a year. He was released in 1917 partly because of intervention by local businessmen and partly because of the temporary wartime atmosphere of clemency toward America's ally, Italy. Lazia next turned to lending money to friends, keeping youngsters out of jail, trading real estate, and managing gambling and bootlegging enterprises. Nicknamed "Brother John," he robbed the rich, supported local charities, gave money to down-and-out panhandlers, and ingratiated himself with "Boss" Pendergast. Although he was once indicted in a liquor conspiracy, he obtained freedom when his bodyguard took the rap. During 1928, Lazia led Kansas City's Italian community in a successful election campaign against the Irish machine. By using force, charm, and unusual organizational abilities, Lazia built up a strong political following. Soon he had a voice in naming men to the Kansas City Police Department, from which there flowed gambling and liquor concessions, as well as police tolerance of organized vice.

Lazia's power derived indirectly from Kansas City's Italian community, crowded into a relatively small area east of Market Square. By 1929, 85 percent of the residents in the Little Italy district were of Sicilian origin. Some fifteen thousand persons of Italian descent lived there, squeezed between the blacks and the Irish, in an atmosphere of racial antagonism.

In 1934, Lazia was thirty-seven years old and at the peak of his power. Mussolini had recently bestowed the Order of the Crown of Italy upon Lazia's protector, Pendergast. As one dictator rewarded another, Pendergast had derived strength from a political alliance forged with Lazia as boss of Kansas City's north side. Just as the Confederate "bushwhacker," Quantrill and the James Boys once ruled the countryside around that city, Pendergast and Lazia now ran it internally. Because federal authorities investigated income tax evasion charges against Lazia, Pendergast had written to Postmaster General James Farley on his behalf.

Then, on a sticky July day, Lazia was machine-gunned by unknown assailants. Among the key figures who attended his funeral were Pendergast, the city's police director, and even Mike

Ross, whom Lazia had unseated. Lazia's murder was never officially solved, but was probably the work of a rival gang.

Whether in Kansas City or New York, the processes of gang formation were much the same. Lodges like Brooklyn's old Unione Siciliana were based upon *fratellanze*, or brotherhoods. These were loose confederations, often of Sicilian Americans, some of whose members became criminalized. The old "Mustache Petes" among them gave way to second-generation criminal achievers, who transformed the selling of insurance into protection rackets and extortion rings. Italian lotteries, sometimes organized with the blessing of a local church, grew into loan shark operations. *Ziganetta*, a card game much like poker, was converted into big-time betting. Gambling rings used their earnings to produce illegal alcohol in stills hidden behind legitimate business fronts.

A specialized vocabulary drawn from their clanlike Sicilian past developed to describe the hierarchy of Italian American crime leaders. These included the titles "boss" (*capo*); "underboss" (*sotto capo*); "counselor" (*consigliere*); "captain" (*caporegime*); and finally "soldier" (*soldato*), the lowest member of the hierarchy.

Extortion rackets, kickback schemes, and bootlegging became so profitable that even murder grew justifiable among gang members. In the 1930s the so-called Castellamarese War was fought in New York between insurgent second-generation members and the older Mustache Petes. Originally from near Corleone in Sicily, they dressed conservatively and were ill at ease outside Italian Brooklyn. Passing the torch of power from one generation to another led to more ferocious gunfights between rival gangs, whose bosses sought to organize crime along syndicalist lines.

There was an almost complusive character to gangland slayings, a kind of acting out. The psychoanalyst Wilhelm Stekel once described a compulsion as an act that must be carried out in order to counteract anxiety. In Freudian terms, criminals can reduce anxiety and tension by doing away with other criminals. As his aggressiveness is allayed, the assassin experiences a measure of calmness.

Mario Puzo's novel *The Godfather* (1969) recreated the Mafia underworld in New York, with its rage, violence, lust, and terror. "The Godfather," Vito Corleone, was superficially a benevolent despot whose cravings for power and "justice" led him to "right wrongs," even by the use of murder. In his admixture of family loyalty and predatory instinct Puzo portrayed a vast underground empire, partly a product of popular imagination. This empire was controlled by Mafia subchieftains deeply involved in a variety of rackets—gambling, bookmaking, and union irregularities. Puzo depicted the Corleone family as perfecters of terroristic gangsterism.

Both criminalized fathers and sons had escaped their blue-collar origins in the ghettoes of America. But the media portrayed them as sadomasochistically fixated at an adolescent stage of emotional development. In the public mind they became symbols of amoral power with a talent for chaos. Depicted as violent, treacherous, and cowardly, the gangster gave rise to a stereotype that hardly promoted ethnic understanding. Puzo's popular book also reflected the type of newspaper headlines with which the 1960s closed—featuring the involvement of criminal elements in corporations, chain stores, and other fronts. The annual take of the underground octopus called the Mafia was reputedly in the billions of dollars.

Mafia operations in Italy remain even more clandestine than those in the United States. Today large corporations like Alfa Romeo (now government owned) complain of gangland pressure regarding the choice of new automobile factory sites. In 1979 it became known that the Mafia was instrumental in selecting construction firms to build a steel mill at Gioia Tauro in Calabria. Its adherents have also become involved in building a harbor in the same area, as well as tourist centers throughout southern Italy. (These are, incidentally, said to be run more efficiently than are competing facilities.)

Whether in Italy or America, Mafiosi loan sharks penetrate

neighborhoods where cash is short and where traditional scams can be perpetrated. In immigrant America after the turn of the century it was impossible to stop such abuses. *Omertà*, the code of silence unto death, is still practiced in criminal circles, Mafia or otherwise.

Political cover-ups, bribery, and immunity are words frequently used in the Italian press. Criminals who stay above the law, thanks to local politicians, are hard to nail. These shield the Mafia, which in some parts of the Italian south controls the construction trade. Official corruption all too often flourishes and uncooperative potential witnesses stand a chance of winding up in cement. Such are the unsavory ingredients out of which the perversion of justice is made in any country.

In the 1960s, when Puzo's portrayal of the Mafia made his book a best-seller, social turbulence was rocking the American scene. These were the years in which youth groups joined blacks and other minorities in demonstrations against discrimination. By 1970 demands grew stronger among Americans of Italian descent that they be dissociated from the Mafia's awesome stigma. On June 29 of that year tens of thousands of Italian Americans held a rally in New York to assert that the Mafia was a figment of public imagination. The mass demonstration on Italian Unity Day was climaxed by a march to the headquarters of the Federal Bureau of Investigation, which the Italian Americans accused of persecuting them.

For six weeks they demonstrated outside F.B.I. headquarters in New York. The protests were instigated by Joseph Colombo, Sr., arrested later by the F.B.I. on charges of operating a multi-million-dollar policy racket in the Brooklyn underworld. Colombo (who had never gone to high school) had emerged as a robust leader and favorite son of New York's Italian American community. Responding to repeated shouts of "We want Joe," he climbed up on a parkside rostrum as the band played "For He's a Jolly Good Fellow." He sped the marchers toward F.B.I. headquarters with his blessing: "Show them they can't take us apart." Colombo and his son Anthony next climbed on top of a police van and, through a microphone, urged the crowd to go home peacefully. Most of the demonstrators complied, although some shook their fists at foot and mounted police. Two policemen were stabbed; yet police were relieved that there was no worse violence.

At this rally, hand-painted banners proclaimed: *"Basta con la Mafia"* ("Enough of the Mafia") and "Just because we have Italian names, it doesn't mean we are criminals." The demonstration took place beneath a statue of Christopher Columbus, draped in the Italian national colors—green, white, and red. Demonstrators carried thousands of Italian and American flags. Officials estimated the attendance first at forty thousand and then at half a million. Most Italian shops in New York were closed; there were threats against Italian shopkeepers unwilling to lose the day's business. In Brooklyn, a bomb exploded in an Italian-owned factory that had not closed. New York's docks were virtually idle, as Italian dockworkers took the day off to attend the rally.

On June 28, 1971, at another New York rally of the American Civil Rights League, Joseph Colombo, Sr., was shot. For weeks he lingered between life and death. He was widely believed to head a loose coalition of six Mafia families running waterfront rackets, along with gambling and usurious moneylending operations. Such men represented a new generation of Mafiosi of the gray-flannel suit variety. They seemed determined to achieve respectability and were touchy about any invasion of their privacy.

As if to reply to Colombo, the United States Justice Department officially dropped the words "Mafia" and "Cosa Nostra" from its vocabulary. In a 1970 memorandum for circulation among department officials, Attorney General John N. Mitchell said "that many good Americans of Italian descent are offended by the use of the terms in news reports dealing with organized crime. Accordingly, I am requesting that we discontinue their use in news releases, speeches or other public statements."

Joseph Valachi, a mobster who turned informer at a 1963 Senate hearing, had made the terms "Mafia" and "Cosa Nostra" popular. He had allegedly broken a blood oath by disclosing the inner workings of these criminal organizations. Serving a life sentence for murder, Valachi through his testimony reputedly led gangsters to put a $100,000 price on his head. Closely guarded when he appeared at several grand jury hearings, Valachi, the son of an immigrant, died in a federal prison in 1971.

That year the Italian-American Civil Rights League persuaded the producer of *The Godfather* to eliminate references to the Mafia and the Cosa Nostra from the film. The league picketed the newspaper offices of the *Staten Island Advance* to protest that journal's use of the two offensive terms. At Los Angeles, Unico National, a service club comprised of business and professional leaders of Italian extraction, denounced the film. The organization recommended that Italian Americans boycott or picket it in theaters across the country.

Puzo's *The Godfather* was to influence the image of the Italians in America in ways that could not have been imagined prior to the book's filming. Protests against its negative imagery continued. In 1975 Massachusetts's highest court overturned the murder convictions of two Italian immigrants because the prosecutor in addressing the jury had compared the two men to characters in *The Godfather*. The court found language used during their trial inflammatory and prejudicial. Thus, the Italians could use this case as a precedent against likening ethnic defendants to underworld characters in novels or films.

East and west, the Italian Americans have continued to combat their stereotypic connection with the underworld. In California crime has remained notably unconnected with the Italian community. Indeed, one could make a case for A. P. Giannini's powerful Bank of America as having headed off criminality among Italians there. Capitalism seemed to overwhelm crime in San Francisco's North Beach. A variety of businesses and merchants owed their success to the loans that Giannini and his bank made available to them. In this way potential gangsters were kept at bay if not in line. Only after World War II did one hear of eastern Mafia syndicates invading the Far West, with Las Vegas a focal point for their gambling and extortion activities.

The anti-defamation campaign that gathered momentum in the late 1960s reflected the detestation of the Mafia by Italian Americans. They resented the equating of one national group with crime. Italians called attention to F.B.I. and police reports that debased immigrants who had sought the protection proclaimed by the Statue of Liberty.

Some Italians were desperate to escape the stigma of association with crime. The journalist Alex Rocco has written: "When the family name is Rocco, what do you name the heirs if you don't want them to sound like they control Newark? I like names such as Frank and Pete, but if you put them together with Rocco, it sounds like you're raising a hit man. So we named our boys Mark and Lucien, and they can go legit if they want to."

As we have seen, not all ethnics remained defensive. The black power movement of the 1960s made minority groups conscious of scapegoating and group re-identification. By 1972 a coalition of Italian American organizations gave the Shell Oil Company ten days during which to include Italian Americans in its "Great Americans" game or face an economic boycott. The coalition threatened the mass return of credit cards, refusal to buy gasoline, and the urging of union members not to deliver to Shell stations: "We are serious about this thing and are definitely going to move," said D. Anthony Attisani, chairman of New Rochelle's United Society of Italian-Americans. "We have decided to notify Shell and give them a final opportunity to correct the inequity in their 'Great Americans' game." A company spokesman said the omission was "strictly an oversight." Twenty years earlier such a protest by the Italian community would not have occurred.

In 1975 two more examples of Italo-American remonstrance against prejudice took place. Secretary of the Treasury William Simon was forced to order the destruction of 350 copies of a government film entitled *Uncle Sam Caper.* Designed to sell United States savings bonds, the film provoked an uproar over the implication that organized crime was the sole province of Italians in America. New York television station WOR also found itself engaged in a bitter dispute with the Italian community over its reruns of a television series entitled *The Untouchables*, which depicted Italians as gangsters. Unification among Italian American groups seeking relief from discrimination represented a strengthening of the collective ego by a once despised minority.

Although America's Italians have been set on edge by accusations of criminality, organized crime here was dominated first by the Irish. Later, Jews moved in, followed by inner-city Mafia crime families, now slowly being replaced by black, Cuban, and Puerto Rican criminals.

The increase of crime among youthful slum dwellers can be related to their desire to escape crowded homes. Exposed to the temptations of store windows, they steal money to buy coveted goods or to support drug habits. Greed encourages deception and violence. For the sociopath, morality is an indefinite, sliding affair. Devoid of strict ego boundaries, such persons rationalize their dishonesty. They find it easy to label brutish activities moral and just, that is, performed in the name of a good cause (reaction formation). For these delinquents, crime becomes a way to control anxiety.

This maneuver was partly and covertly encouraged by immigrant parents. Or, to put the matter differently, truancy and criminality sometimes resulted from a power struggle with early authority figures. Such defiance continues to be acted out on the mean streets of wretched inner-city ghettoes all over America. The result is a euphoric, if temporary, release of tension.

It is, thus, too easy to explain criminality and delinquency as a natural response to discrimination. The key to understanding such behavior, ethnic or otherwise, lies in the exploration of unconscious mental processes, as we have seen. Consciously, Sicilians created the Mafia out of a need to band together against enemies. But this explanation fails to account for the violent delinquency that has resulted. William Fairbairn, one of the most talented contemporary object-relations psychoanalysts, has described aggression as a reaction to frustration. Whereas delinquency on the surface seemed to provide a way to win out over deprivation, it personally degraded the children of immigrants

107

and slandered the entire Italian minority. Guilt and self-hatred ensued.

Sometimes conflicting cultural backgrounds contributed to moral disorientation, clearly a psychohygienic factor in the lives of ethnic delinquents. This approach to character disorder comes close to the view of "general systems" theoreticians, who see mental illness as essentially a disturbance of systems functions within the psychophysical organism. Social integration in a healthy cultural framework simply did not occur among troubled immigrant juveniles.

Some ethnic gangsters exhibited a peculiar mixture of ruthlessness and sentimentality. After Sam Giancana—a Chicago gangster who built an empire on gambling, loan sharking, prostitution, and extortion—died in 1976, his estate was auctioned off. In addition to diamond rings and pink Cadillacs, his most prized possessions inluded antique porcelain figurines, delicate music boxes, and Meissen dinnerware. One daughter, who could barely hold back her tears at the auction, whispered: "Just look at these beautiful things. They show what a warm, sensitive person my father was." Two other daughters remarked: "He's not our father. We're here strictly as collectors."

Obsessive Mafiosi have been known to keep as much as a million dollars in small bills packed in shoe boxes stacked from floor to ceiling in the closets of Manhattan apartments.

Via the mechanism of splitting, Mafia leaders have cultivated an outward image of respectability while laundering illegally earned money through such business fronts as pizza parlors, jukebox companies, and restaurants. Behind the scenes, family members are rigidly insulated from underworld activities of all sorts. Well-kept mistresses, too, form part of the dichotomy between a real inner world and the flashy front that enormous sums of money make possible.

As time passed, the sheer power of the Mafia made some persons of Italian descent oddly proud of this network. Youthful city hoods began to dress like actors in the TV show *The Untouchables*. A strong sense of identity flowed from the Mafia image established all across America. It was as though the black shirts, white ties, and Borsalino hats symbolized that missing sense of person which ghetto children had never quite found. The impulse to imitate the Mafia's power was great.

Other disaffected groups also sprang up. Joseph Sorrentino, a onetime gang member who became a municipal court judge, recalled:

> I worked during the day as a chicken plucker, scraping up droppings. But at night I was a "Condor." I'd put on this shimmering satinette jacket and strut down the street. . . . We created this heroic make-believe image of ourselves. As individuals we weren't anybody. But when we became Condors, we made the newspapers: "Condors Wreck Bowling Alley," or "Condors Shoot Up School." It made us feel important.

In the 1970s an estimated five thousand men in twenty-four crime families influenced life in many ethnic communities in paradoxical ways. Patricia Battaglia remembered growing up in a Brooklyn neighborhood made safe by the Mafia: "I could walk down the street at any hour of night and know that nothing was going to happen." The New York City police force now includes five thousand Italian American officers, banded together in the department's Columbia Association.

A public obsession with Mafia folklore culminated in *The Godfather* (possibly the best gangster film ever made). It seemed tragic that such a traditionally individualistic people as the Italians should be publicly associated with either the Mafia or the police.

Francis Ianni has described organized criminality as a way station on the road to respectability in American society. Crime in America has become a style of life for non-ethnics, as well as foreigners. Here Sicilians, WASPs, Jews, and blacks (though separate socially) have come to be joined in both crime and political corruption. By the 1970s Americans saw the extent of a rottenness that went beyond ethnics. Was it, however, the Mafia that infected almost every level of Sicilian life and exported its contempt for law to America? This perverted attitude is summed up in a Sicilian proverb: *Fatta la legge nasce l'inganno* ("When the law is made, fraud comes forth").

VII

LA FAMIGLIA:
Defending the Old Ways

FINDING THE RIGHT NICHE in America included confronting poverty, hunger for success, feelings of exclusion, and all those internal hatreds directed against one's foreignness. These disabilities were reflected in clashes within the immigrant family that appear and reappear in the writings of Italo-American novelists.

Children cannot mature properly if resentment rules their lives. We have already looked at how the Mafia families came to be infected by rage and hate. More normal immigrant households were also caught up with apprehension over their future. Such fear had evoked the Sicilian proverb *"Chi lascia la via vecchia per la nuova sa quel che perde e non sa quel che trova"* ("He who gives up the old ways for the new knows what he has lost but not what lies ahead"). *La via vecchia* meant life within the family.

The struggle to make it in America was first played out within a self-contained setting. The immigrant's home was his sanctuary, his retreat from the harshness of life. Ideally, family and work should remain divided. Inside the household there existed a protective coloration, indeed flocking behavior. This quasi-animalistic unity called for loyalty to *parenti* (a large number of extended kin), as well as to father and mother. The rule of the parents, especially father, was law.

Freud believed that humans are overly impressed with the power of their parents. This sense of awe was especially characteristic of immigrant children. Long after the parents were dead, their offspring recited stories of severe discipline in childhood. Non-immigrants could scarcely appreciate the conservatism of a tightly knit unit that demanded such allegiance of all its members and that acted as a carrier of rigid social beliefs. At first the Italian American family allowed little room for innovation and adventure. If the transgenerational flow of commonly held ideals broke down, family unity might be lost.

The Latin cultures, overwhelmed by a masculine mystique, assigned a strange role to women within the shelter of family life. Remnants of Mariolatry surround Latin males on all sides. Whereas men cultivate traits of aggressiveness, the women assume subordinate, nonerotic roles. They are expected to show fealty to male values. Yet, Mary, the mother of Christ, occupies a special place of honor not only in every Catholic church but also in those niches tucked away behind burning candles so familiar in Italian middle-class dwellings. Women, remindful of Christ's virgin birth, are to be both worshipped and dominated. The Madonna had been a mother but scarcely a wife. Accordingly, the Italian woman has historically reduced the power and importance of sexuality by accepting a *mater dolorosa* role. Repudiation of erotic impulses has led women toward lives spent waiting upon men, including their sons. Some wives iron shirts, shine shoes, clean, mend, and cook almost constantly. In all this work they seem to be both exalted and demeaned.

In Italy the woman's role was summed up in a cruel proverb:

> *Like a good weapon she should be cared for properly.*
> *Like a hat she should be kept straight.*
> *Like a mule, she should be given plenty of work and*
> *occasional beatings.*
> *Above all, she should be kept in her place as a subordinate.*

111

Not all women, of course, stayed helpless. An immigrant child, Rita Poleri, explained:

> The concept that the Italian family was a patriarchal one is in part a myth. The women came from family origins in which they had no real closeness with a father. So, her husband remained a stranger who usually failed to meet her infantile dependency needs. She turned to her sons, overdoing for them in order to bind these spoiled males to her forever by infantalizing them.[1]

Such male children were prevented from becoming independent. Often the first daughter was selected to serve the mother's need—to hear her everyday complaints and worries and even her secret whispers about sexual dissatisfaction. The daughter also helped rear the other children and acted as a front against the frightening, alien American society.

Some of these same characteristics of submission in women and of their hidden strengths show up in other societies. For example, almost forty years ago Conrad Arensberg and Solon Kimball's *Family and Community in Ireland* (1940) reminded us that findings can be almost identical in widely separated cultures. It is difficult to distinguish what is part of a national culture and what is the product of social and economic class. Religion, too, may influence behavior between the sexes. The Irish and the Italians have, at least outwardly, been guided in their sexuality by the confining hand of the Catholic church.

In a distorted way daughters became substitute husbands, acted out the unexpressed anger of the passive-aggressive mother, and enabled her to remain the idealized madonna in the eyes of the sons. Marooned, and needing their mothers more than their fathers, eldest daughters often became trapped in a synergism that led them to remain unmarried, the guardian of aging parents.

Some mothers, as Poleri put it, "aligned the children on their side of the battlefield against the father. He remained alone and condemned. Outwardly he did appear to rule the family. In reality, the wife had a sickly power, tightening the circle of mother and children to the exclusion of the father. Within this alliance, or camp, she offered her entire being as a martyr for her children."

Few Italian children ever came home to an empty house after school. Mario Puzo recalled that although his father might be absent "there was always the smell of supper cooking. My mother was always there to greet me, sometimes with a policeman's club in her hand. But, she was always there, or her authorized deputy, my older sister."

The trouble with this odd alliance was that the children would later experience guilt if their anger toward the mother was expressed. They must continue to idealize her as a virtual saint. With these mental representations introjected, they went on to form their own peculiar families, based on a heritage of too much mother and not enough father, thus perpetuating the neurotic immigrant cycle.

Some immigrant women were caught between threatened desertion by their husbands and demands for independence by their children. Their once valued centralizing role was hard to maintain. Immigrant women, reduced to scolding their sons for coming home late and their daughters for leaving the house without authority, grew coarse and obese in old age, feeling outmoded and obsolete. No longer a household goddess, this sort of woman stood dethroned. A decaying family life produced children who superficially applauded but were confused by the father's diminished authority and the mother's weakened position.

In understanding such contradictions within the Italian family, the psychoanalyst Erik Erikson's model of the life cycle can be useful. The authority of family relationships rests upon a series of internal stages, stretching from childhood through old age. At each stage one is expected to behave in a manner acceptable to the group. Protection of the immigrant family's idealized *imago* of itself required the imposition of rigid rules and regulations that could be broken only at the risk of ostracism.

Mother centered and father dominated, the Italian family resembled a tossing ship plowing its way through the unfamiliar shoals of American life. Occasionally a bit of prow got nicked or the vessel careened as in a storm. Its passengers hoped they would survive the journey.

113

The repression imposed on the family by fathers who needed to remain outwardly dominant endangered the very structure of family life. In a permissive American setting, the school, the police, and the courts assumed the functions of the father as a mediator between the outside world and the family. These institutionalized forces made his regimentation seem outmoded and eroded his power.

In authoritarian settings much is forbidden, little encouraged. Parents from the rigid little villages of southern Italy and Sicily placed family income well ahead of personal ambition. These *meridionali* had known both *penuria* and *disastro*—abject poverty and desolation. Called *cafoni* ("lunkheads") because of their illiteracy, they flinched from the *disprezzo* ("scorn") of strangers. After centuries of oppression, one way to secure both bread and dignity was by playing it safe—within the family structure.

The alternative to family unity could prove disastrous. Troubled parents who pushed their children out onto America's mean streets deprived them of the intimacy and contact that lead to trust and care for others. True, gainful work did double, even treble, family income. Parents also worked overtime. Half a century ago work, rather than a high school diploma, was the passport to a better life. An assured income, made possible by the sacrifice of father, mother, and all their children, was the way by which the Lombardis or the Speronis could join the middle class. To achieve this upward mobility, no one must break step with the leadership provided by the parents.

Paesani (persons from the same village) might settle on the same block of a large city. And they would refuse both to admit *forestieri* ("foreigners") into their homes and to work or to intermarry with those beneath their status (ego ideal). "We had richnesses of other sorts," wrote Pietro di Donato in his *Three Circles of Light;* "we had our paesanos from Vasto, Italy, whose families had lived and died together for many centuries."[2]

He and other Italo-American writers remind us that not every foreigner wanted to become Americanized. Indeed, there was even exclusion of *gli Americani*, the immigrant's hosts:

> To my people the Americans were colorless, unsalted, baloney
> munchers and gasoline drinkers without culture, who spoke with a
> vocabulary limited to repetitive four-lettered words, listening to cater-
> wauling, imbecilic music, and all looked more or less alike. But there
> was no confusing one paesano for another and no two resembled each
> other in any respect.[3]

Compareggio, a ritualized system of godparent relationships,
stressed spiritual, rather than blood, brotherhood, family bonds
rather than direct kinship. This extended *parentela* became the
fountainhead of anecdotes, proverbs, dreams, and pronouncements of the saints—all designed to provide neophytes
safety from mysterious forces. To ward off evil spirits, older family members sometimes wore *corni*, red-colored, horned-shaped
amulets.

Ethnics who had themselves rebelled against the villages in
which all had expected them to stay resisted any rebellion on the
part of the younger generation. Family cohesiveness depended
upon keeping intact those mystic chords among godparents, sib-
lings, aunts, uncles, even distant cousins. Close relatives were the
only persons upon whom one could truly rely. Suspicion of outsiders was, therefore, normal.

In "Growing Up Sicilian," a part of his autobiography, Jerre
Mangione described having to lead a double life. One of these
lives was "among my drove of Sicilian relatives, the other in street
and at school." He identified yet "a third life," the ultimate one
that he was forced to live with himself. He saw his American
friends as "fortunate to have had parents whose roots were deeply
imbedded in American soil. . . . They had no identity problems,
none of the conflicts that gnawed at the psyche of every son and
daughter of immigrant parents to whom English was a foreign
tongue."[4]

In *Transactions*, John Spiegel presented a medical portrait of
how one immigrant family—the Tondis of north Boston—fell
"sick." Its members wallowed in generational conflict. The strain
made each child vulnerable to various illnesses. Stuttering, con-
stipation, and bed-wetting were among the first somatic forms in
which psychological strain appeared. Some children screamed in

pain when evacuating clogged bowels; others felt "black moods" or threw rocks at the neighbors; still others stammered, projected temper tantrums, or went into alcoholic rages. Volcanic quarrels flared up, followed by attempted reconciliations and restitutions for real or imagined hurts. Frustration and disappointment lurked menacingly beneath the surface of family life. Only after therapy was there a redefinition of the roles of each member of the Tondi clan. Even then, their progress in coping with conflict was slow.

Unresolved disputes led to home leavings, depressions, drinking, perversions, and, of course, criminality. As the first generation reached old age, it lamented the inability of the second to find its pleasures among the simple things of life, as in the so-called good old days.

Overpowering parents, determined to make their children feel guilty for not fulfilling the family code, helped to create neurotics. The character in Paul Mazursky's 1976 film *Next Stop Greenwich Village* uses craziness to help himself survive the onslaughts of an attacking immigrant mother. In his case, her onslaughts actually made the son tougher, via repression and denial-mechanisms for the defense of ego.

The apparent craziness of some immigrants is sometimes linked to Latin *machismo*. Actually, it can more accurately be located in an attempt to find one's roots. The films of still another ethnic director, Martin Scorsese (*Mean Streets, Taxi Driver*, and *To Forget Palermo*), illustrate the process. His characters act civilized on the surface but seem ready to shoot whoever crosses them. They have lost inner coherence.

Splitting, a more extreme means of defense, also occurred among immigrant children. Some offspring awarded a part of their intrapsychic selves to the family and another part to society. The allegiance due to each such projection made for serious internal tension. Not unusually, they had breakdowns later in life.

Erikson has described the split in second-generation family members who seek to live down a hated peasant identity. Such persons may sentimentalize a past family romance about close relations with local nobleman, and distortion occurs. Denial of the lesser aristocracy from which his family had sprung occurred in the case of the Polish-born novelist Joseph Conrad. He broke with that past by migrating to England. There, writing primarily for a British audience, he sought a new life, almost a rebirth.

At the heart of the turmoil within the Americanizing Italian family lay Freud's classic struggle between fathers and sons. Girl children, like their mothers, usually remained compliant, but a breakdown in communications among the family's males often turned the sons outward in search of understanding.

Whereas the immigrant wife maintained a tight-lipped loyalty to her husband, the children demanded more contact with the outside world. Jo Pagano described the mounting tension between the generations after a prodigal brother returned home from his wanderings. Wide-eyed brothers and sisters listened to his exciting account:

> Lou told us of the places he had been. New York and St. Louis and New Orleans. . . . We listened with all our ears—all except my father who . . . sat silently. Lou paid no attention to him. It was almost as though he was boasting about his travels to irritate my father. And you could feel the breach widening between them. It was like a wall that each passing moment built higher . . . my father had been pushed into the background. Lou was the important person in the house now, and he dominated everything that went on in it. And all of us shivered in secret delight. It was as though Lou were paying off the grievances which each of us, through the years of parental authority, had accumulated against my father, and to which we had never, until now, had any recourse.

Lou's rebellion had obviously afforded his brothers and sisters a measure of catharsis. Sometimes a son's hatred of his father matched the father's jealousy of his son. The two lived together in unresolved conflict and ambivalence. The angriest sons repudiated their parents by unconsciously seeking to be their own substitute fathers. Destructive competition and rage dissolved the love that each needed but dared not claim from the other lest their manhood be threatened through loss of face.

With the defection of his sons, the vulnerable father clung all the more firmly to old values. Fights erupted that verged upon violence. Fathers accused sons of laziness and incompetence. Sons experienced their fathers as inwardly sentimental but outwardly callous, rigid, unimaginative, and unable to share power. On and on the arguments raged about both serious and trivial matters.

The dominating father and the subservient mother paradoxically encouraged the very rebellion and anger they loathed in their children. They also helped to induce that guilt which Freud saw in those who gain a humiliating victory over their parents but who cannot discharge their shame. As for mother-son relations, we know that in every culture mothers treat their sons differently from the way they treat their daughters. In the Italian family setting, boys enjoyed a form of adulation. Yet, they were not allowed to separate easily from either the mother's or the father's control.

The immigrant father, in his surrender of power, has not been well understood. *Il padre* felt sabotaged by both outside pressure and internal dissension. As his morale diminished, he grew obstinate and resentful. Fathers attempted to recapture lost control by withholding affection. But children increasingly looked upon the father's physical punishments with disdain. With passive-aggressive pressures mobilized, a family might occasionally force a father to mellow in his chastisements.

But many fathers could not and would not yield. John Fante, in the autobiographical novel *The Brotherhood of the Grape*, has given us a poignant view of a bleak and alienated struggle by the misunderstood son of a loutish, flagrantly unfaithful father-husband. The mother is pictured as a hand-wringer lost in presuicidal masochism. Her husband, snarling in his undershirt and enraged by drink, storms about the house. While the mother discharged her anger through martyrdom, the son had no recourse but flight.

This incorrigible father lived in a California community whose major structures the old man had helped to build. Although the fire station, school, library, and even the mortuary were crafted by his hands, there was no chance that the old man would ever be honored for his lifetime of work. Meanwhile the Ford auto distributor, the town druggist, and other local businessmen were regularly honored as "Man of the Year." This father had built the town cemetery out of brick and stone—truly a work of posterity—not merely "of the year."

Fante's description of the remarkable character who dominates his book merits quotation:

> He was a hard-nosed, big-fisted mountain man from Abruzzi, short, five feet seven, wide as a door, born in a part of Italy where poverty was as spectacular as the surrounding glaciers, and any child who survived the first five years would live to eighty-five. Of course, not many reached the age of five. He and my Aunt Pepina, now eighty and living in Denver, were the only two out of thirteen who had survived. That way of life gave my father his toughness. Bread and onions, he used to boast, bread and onions—what else does a man need? That was why my whole life has been a loathing of bread and onions. He was more than the head of the family. He was judge, jury and executioner, Jehovah himself.
>
> Nobody crossed him without a battle. He disliked almost everything, particularly his wife, his children, his neighbors, his church, his priest, his town, his state, his country, and the country from which he emigrated. Nor did he give a damn for the world either, or the sun or the stars, or the universe, or heaven or hell. But he liked women.
>
> He also liked his work and half a dozen paesani who, like himself, were Italians in the dictator mold. He was a flawless craftsman whose imagination and intelligence seemed centered in his marvelously strong hands, and though he called himself a building contractor I came to regard him as a sculptor, for he could shape a rock into man or beast. He was a superb, swift, neat bricklayer as well as an excellent carpenter, plasterer and concrete builder.[5]

Nick Molise, as Fante called him, showed his rage at being treated unjustly by the community. He did so by brawling and by squandering his earnings in bars, whorehouses, pool halls, and gambling dens. Fante portrayed him as an "Abruzzi goat with poised evil horns" who turned the household into "madness, total frenzy." The old man had "great contempt for himself," overlaid by a false pride and conceit. His need to buttress a damaged ego seemed to approach the borderline of psychosis: "I believed," wrote Fante, "it was his rage at the world, his desire for triumph over the Establishment, his immigrant sense of being an outsider."

The sweaty and mean bullheads depicted in Italo-American novels slap their women around, curse, and are obsessed with avoiding loss of face (*male figura*). Emotionally they remind us of

119

hyperactive children. Studies of hyperkinesis have shown that grown men continue to manifest symptoms of this disorder. They display difficulty controlling their tempers, depression, and impulsiveness. Such persons, sometimes sociopathic or antisocial, change jobs with frequency and have trouble making friends. The fathers of the Italo-American novelists felt that they had been sold out by their sons. We find them, in retribution, turning the pictures of their children around to face the wall. Sons were supposed to suffer shame and guilt for not following their fathers' ways.

Yet it seemed impossible for the immigrant's progeny to do the squalid work their parents had been forced into. The novelist Mario Puzo recalled that his mother's highest expectation was for him to become a railroad clerk; in fact, she would have settled for less. But what immigrant child wanted to join old sewer workers, who lived with the constant threat of cave-ins and explosions of noxious gases? (In some immigrant neighborhoods, the stench was so great that residents did not open their windows.) Italians became involved with excavation work because they were more skilled at handling earth, stone, and brick than they were at sewing on shirt collars in garment factories. Work gangs frequently had a common nationality. And, as they swung their picks and dug with their shovels, sweat and brawn accompanied the unintelligible mutterings or snatches of song that few of their children appreciated. Another alternative was to operate a peanut cart or to turn the handle of a hurdy-gurdy street organ, in partnership with a leashed monkey.

Whatever impeded acceptance was resented by the younger generation. Here is a recollection of a father in another Fante novel:

> I look up at him in amazement. Is this my father? Why, look at him! Listen to him! He reads with an Italian inflection! He's wearing an Italian mustache. I have never realized it until this moment, but he looks exactly like a Wop. His suit hangs carelessly in wrinkles upon him. Why the deuce doesn't he buy a new one? And look at his tie! It's crooked. And his shoes; they need a shine. And for the Lord's sake, will you look at his pants! They're not even buttoned in front. And, oh

damn, damn, damn, you can see those dirty old suspenders that he won't throw away. Say, mister, are you really my father? You there, why you're such a little guy, such a runt, such an old looking fellow! You look exactly like one of those immigrants carrying a blanket. You can't be my father![6]

Young Fante found it difficult to attend parochial schools, where other Italian children also went. He came to loathe his family, including his grandmother:

I begin to think that my grandmother is hopelessly a Wop. She's a small stocky peasant who walks with her wrists crisscrossed on her belly, a simple old lady. . . . When in her simple way, she confronts a friend of mine and says, her old eyes smiling, "You lika go to the Seester scola?" my heart roars. *Managgia!* I'm disgraced; now they all know that I'm an Italian.[7]

A positive self-image can hardly accompany self-hatred. An Italo-American educator recalled the stereotyping that went on: "We soon got the idea that Italian meant something inferior. We were becoming Americans by learning how to be ashamed of our parents."[8] These shameful feelings of inadequacy, particularly over poor use of the English language, were painful to live with. How could terms like "wop" and "kike" make one wish anything else but to erase a past that the dominant culture obviously despised.

Jerre Mangione, in *An Ethnic at Large*, has recorded how he internalized boyhood problems of identity in the Italian district of Rochester, New York. He changed his first name from Gerlando to Jerre as a means of avoiding prejudice. His brother saw a job application torn up before his eyes by an anti-Italian recruiter, and his sister was pressured into changing her name in order to get a job teaching in public school. Jerre, having decided upon a literary career, met opposition from his parents, who viewed such a choice with abhorrence. This led him to gravitate to Greenwich Village. In his case, the struggles of ethnicity may have somehow contributed to developing strength of character and intellect. Others did not cope so successfully with their problems of immigrant identification.

Ethnic jokes with a touch of cruelness undermined positive identification within ethnic families. Without certainty about their cultural identities, irritated young Italo-Americans clawed their way up the American social pyramid. Rita F. Stein has described angry feelings and desires for revenge that became somaticized, sometimes as stuttering or other physical symptoms. The loss of love also took form as a defiant, "I don't care" attitude. In later life this might develop into depression (such as Frank Costello experienced). Outer deference merely veiled hostility to orders from above. Exhibitionism and bravura also covered a loathing of one's origins.

For disturbed ethnic children at least three major inherited symbols had been wrested away: (1) the vision of women as virginal mothers; (2) religion—whose erosion followed what was happening in American life; and (3) fatherhood, the authority of which role decayed as the emotional pressures felt by urbanized youths mounted.

Mangione, though deeply respectful of his roots, explained that "for all their wisdom, none of the Italian immigrant parents I knew grasped the dilemma of their children, who from early childhood were pulled in one direction by their parents' insistence on Old World traditions and in the opposite direction by what their teachers told them in the classroom." The result was children with "confused impressions of identity that were never resolved."[9]

Rebellious and stony-eyed children sought actively to return the hurts they suffered. They acted out disobediently against school principals, teachers, and policemen. Many a young Carlo or Luigi cultivated the tough, gutteral speech of late 1930s gangster movie heroes. Costello projected his wrath upon strangers. He hit his first robbery victim over the head with a hammer. Others became Don Juans, acting out unresolved internal rage by seducing unsatisfied wives of their parents' neighbors.

Disturbed children also employed the defense mechanism known as denial, sometimes accompanied by bravado, or what the psychoanalyst Heinz Kohut has called the "grandiose self." Membership in the Mafia allowed one to marshal bravado in order to ward off failure. Because persons striving to hide inadequacies seek to avoid feelings of depression, emotional difficulties stay buried, surfacing as physical symptoms or remaining hidden until after a breakdown.

Children who defied the Italian family system had to justify their actions. Some did so by using a mechanism which psychoanalysts (specifically, Anna Freud) call identification with the aggressor. During World War II this way of overcoming anxiety cast Jewish prisoners of the Nazis into the role of currying favor with their jailers. The children of immigrants were hardly dealing with American oppressors. Their rejection of the European past, however, led to a loss of integrity and to the piling up of unresolved guilt. Such immature individuals were responding to the will of others, which reinforced infantilization.

Erikson has described identity problems among adolescents that resemble this ethnic struggle: "The youth who is not sure of his identity shies away from interpersonal intimacy. . . . The estrangement typical for this stage is isolation, that is, the incapacity to take chances with one's identity." A sense of inferiority, even of shame, underlies the withdrawal (isolation) that Erikson described.

What seemed missing was a model of parental idealism based upon an ethic outside the one provided by the Catholic church. Thus, confused children came to live by their wits. Shrewdness often won out over ethics. Former peasants fought malevolence with cunning.

Immigrant parents did teach their children skepticism about the outside world; they did so partly to protect them from disappointment. Back in the old country, where families were beset by premature death, lingering illness, and financial uncertainty, it was an unspoken rule not to take on burdens outside one's family. In America, however, family privacy and harshness toward others softened. The second generation seldom interpreted the competition of neighbors as a threat. Boarders and lodgers (some with dissenting views) also altered family life. In 1903, the United States commissioner of labor reported that 22 percent of native-born households and 25 percent of "foreign-headed" households had some income from boarders. Usually these outsiders were

123

lodged in a small house or flat that offered limited privacy, and they occasionally brought new and strange ideas into the immigrant household, some at variance with the father's wishes.

The loosening of kinship bonds, speeded by industrialization, accompanied new job opportunities that made the family no longer a school, a bank, and a center for personal solace. Strangers intruded upon these functions. Children pursued substitutes for the warmth and empathy not forthcoming from important loved persons. With their emotional sustenance increasingly derived from outsiders, children became less amenable to paternal domination.

In Europe a young man followed his father—in character as well as in vocation. This was so natural that a son did not resent his lack of control. One's fellow villagers defined strength of character as rigidity, not adjustment. In order to hold out against enemies, there must be family unity. Peasants who kept personal convictions to themselves taught their children to repress insecurities in the name of "will power," a well-known obsessive-compulsive defense against anxiety and discontent.

Members of the older generation found it easier than did their children to retain simple tastes. They were content to grow tomatoes and basil in the backyard, to drink their morning *caffe latte*, and to savor an occasional sip of *grappa* (brandy), or a tender moment in bed with an aging spouse. Despite the transgressions of a Nick Molise, patience and restraint ruled the lives of most older immigrants. But the United States was not Italy. As they came of age, second-generation ethnics, born on America's soil, sought to wrest from this land those riches so long promised them. They wished to replace the sweat and grime of their fathers and to experiment with new jobs and machinery, new products and techniques. Tuscan cigar smoke and the odor of garlic did not pervade the kitchens of the young. Slowly, there was less guilt about not maintaining *l'onore di famiglia*. Formerly, not to labor for one's family was to risk a *brutta figura*, or loss of dignity. By the sacrifice of all members of a family, and through perseverance, the immigrant had learned to prevail, even over

124

more experienced American neighbors, who were looked upon as spoiled. The immigrant code tolerated few human parasites. Only through frugality could one achieve one's most important ideal—property ownership—and its corollary—financial independence. To make their children fully competitive. immigrant parents taught a thinly disguised brand of materialism.

Although it was undesirable to show off one's wealth, the impression sent home to Italy was another story. Fathers used their hard-earned wages to pay for photographs in which children were lined up in their Sunday best. It was important to show relatives in the old country how prosperous they had all become. One endured almost any privation in order to mail back as much as 75 percent of one's earnings to relatives left behind.

Such frugality and family loyalty proved impossible to maintain. The resultant generation gap resembled breakdowns that occurred during the 1960s in non-immigrant families. In that later decade American parents behaved as though they were immigrants in the land of the young. For the values of mature adulthood were not truly honored in the most democratic of all world societies. Parents, like their children, did not seem to grow up. They remained pals with their children. Unlike older cultures, American society gave children rights that they had never before experienced. The son emerged as a sort of father to himself. In the 1960s, parents were (like the earlier immigrants) in a world they sought to master but could not understand. Youths led their elders into the unknown. Parents grew unsure even of where their children wanted to go.

Long ago, then, in a "reversal of the generations," immigrant children came to interpret the new society to their parents. In Italy the older generation had remained firmly in command. But, as the homeland formed a steadily less significant part of the immigrant child's experience, one of these recalled his parents' loyalty to Italy, that ancient soil which they

> could neither deny nor yet forget completely—the Italy of their childhood, motherland, home, source of all their deepest memories and deepest desires—and mine too? Mine, who had never smelled the

ground my father had trod, who had never known the fields and the grass, the hum of the crickets and the odor of the vineyards at night; who had never lain and looked at the clouds floating across the blue Italian sky? No, for this land which was to my father's generation the source . . . there remained in my veins no more than a distant echo, as of a story dimly told and dimly remembered; and this too was fitting.[10]

VIII

LA FAMIGLIA:
Reaching Out

NO ONE CAN LIVE permanently between two cultures. The older generation of immigrants, who believed in a melting pot, had really projected a wish that fusion might be possible. Instead, the boiling together in a cauldron of so many nationalities produced a growing demand that ethnics crawl out of the pot, indeed, out of the confines of "foreign" family life.

The second generation provided an emotional bridge over which the dissolution of old ties could proceed. Children of immigrants, contoured by new conditioning, resented the halting English used by their parents. They were also eager to discard the folkways and symbols carried off the boats at Ellis Island—the kerchiefs worn by Polish peasant women, the Jewish onion rolls, the Italian pepperoni and Tuscan cigars. To cling doggedly to these relics would be to slip backward into old ways, to lose status. Instead, the young sought escape from the garish tastes of the villagers who were their parents.

Like barnyard fowl under attack from skyborne hawks, most scattered to the suburbs. On Long Island or in Westchester,

Yonkers, or Queens, they came to accept the life-style of their non-foreign neighbors. The dicta of Mulberry Bend were supplanted by those of suburbia. And often new friends outside the ghetto symbolized the overcoming of prejudice via material well-being.

The third generation reached out even further. They moved into still better neighborhoods and insisted upon a new identity. A psychological study of second-generation Italians in New Haven by Irvin L. Child distinguishes three "reaction types"—*rebels*, who gravitated toward the American way of life; the *in-group*, which adhered to the values of the Italian community; and the *apathetic*, who retired from ethnic conflict. One can see denial in the attempts at ethnic liberation. Young married couples sought to minimize memories of parents who remained socially unsophisticated.

Immigrant elders felt that their offspring, now mingling with persons outside the family environment, deprecated the kin group's pride, reserve, and dignity—that crucial *dignità* within which one was expected to remain. Not to "keep one's place" in a static society was a major impertinence. For immigrant children to "make time" at the expense of their personal integrity was not easily understood by the first generation. In peasant Italy one was taught to await one's *destino*. Life remained timeless and unmeasured. Jo Pagano recalled that his immigrant mother, father, and their *paesani* friends "seemed oblivious of the passing of the time, lost in the past, lost in their youth." Their lives

> reached back to a poverty-stricken childhood . . . that swept forward into . . . an America which was, to their eager eyes and hopeful hearts, a truly Promised Land: I saw the barren wooden shacks, the deep shafts striking into the heart of the ground, the coal-dust blackened men coming home at sunset from the mines. . . . I had not transformed it by my young blood and young desire into the fruitful life which for them it had been.[1]

Immigrant offspring who had seen mothers and fathers travel the hard road from poverty to riches (as well as replacement of the horse and buggy by the airplane) asked some new questions: Why continue to live together as a family? Why should daughters not select husbands without parental sanction? It seemed unspeakably old-fashioned, if not intolerable, to turn one's unopened pay envelope over to parents. Yet the immigrant norm dictated that "a son should take care of his father and mother." Otherwise, parents might have to turn to a *Società di Mutuo Soccorso* or to a *Società di Benevolenza.*

As the years passed, immigrant fathers and mothers, too, could feel prosperity in the air. Pagano described the parents' growing security and self-respect as their Los Angeles saloon provided a prosperous living and as their family became "solid members of the community, sober, industrious and well-established."

> Now there was this house in Lincoln Heights, overlooking the city; now there was the street car line into town, to the market, with its clamoring, busily shopping crowds; now there were Saturday nights, with the money sack dumped onto the kitchen table, and the ledger book where my father kept his accounts (the ham with hot peppers and eggs sizzling on the stove, meanwhile, and the jug of illicit red wine waiting; now there was talk of investing in property with the money they were accumulating, and perhaps, a trip to Italy before they died. Then Rose with her second baby, and Marguerite about to get married, and Vincent promoted to teller in the bank. Ever-surging ever-replenishing future.[2]

More than their parents did, immigrant children sought status, better housing and furnishings, an escape from rococo in the living room and from chrome and plastic in the kitchen. Males who wished to validate upward mobility used as symbols better houses, bigger autos, and the ideal of a beautiful, blond wife. For women, no longer adequate were the inelegant, if well-scrubbed, wooden houses, especially those converted from storefronts. About the process by which the children of Jews sought to move their parents out of old neighborhoods, Harry Golden has written that "the second-generation came along and soon the sons took the old folks away, out of Brooklyn, or up to the Bronx."

Pagano recalled further how much material conditions had changed for the better:

> I thought of Coalville and their struggle there. I thought of them as their wedding picture showed them—the stalwart, red-cheeked youth who

129

had been my father, with his swirling black mustache and great barrel chest, the timid, big-eyed girl who was my mother—and I thought of all . . . the promised glory which America, the promised land, had held forth to their eager and hopeful hearts.[3]

Being born again was not easy, even though these immigrants had believed in the promise of a new Eden. There remained much confusion, fear, and doubt. Only occasionally was there what naive newcomers called glamour. The son of the oldsters just described, Jo Pagano, did become a Hollywood movie writer.

Rudolph Valentino also ended up in filmmaking. He was to inspire pardonable pride in Italian men as the most successful lover on the silver screen.

But what did it really mean to be a "Latin lover"? Valentino's modest origins illustrate the impatience that he and other young immigrants felt as they faced an uncertain future. In 1913 this son of a veterinarian in the south Italian town of Castellaneta had been shipped off to America, as a lot of other unmanageable sons had been. His family was through with him, but Rodolfo Guglielmi had ambitious ideas. He quickly cast aside a job as an assistant gardener in New York's Central Park and began to hang around the cabarets near Times Square. In order to attract attention the slender eighteen year old with the slicked-down hair did odd jobs, sweeping out dance halls, washing cars, always showing off his elegant body. John Dos Passos saw him as lazy, vain, but good tempered. Above all he was a born tango dancer.

A series of dancing engagements in ballrooms, vaudeville, and cabarets eventually brought Valentino to Hollywood. He played bit parts in sixteen movies before being cast as the lead in a film entitled *The Four Horsemen of the Apocalypse*. One of the greatest film successes of all time, this movie gave him national exposure. The swarthy hero became, almost overnight, the answer to the dreams of lovesick and lonely women across the country.

Valentino spent his life in the colorless glare of klieg lights, in stucco villas obstructed with bricabrac, oriental rugs, tigerskins, in silk bathrobes, and private cars. He was always getting into limousines or getting out of limousines, or patting the necks of fine horses. Wherever he went the sirens of the motorcycle cops screeched ahead of him.[4]

But "the Sheik," as he came to be called, had a chaotic personal life. He married his dancing partner, then divorced her, wedding the adopted daughter of a millionaire cosmetic manufacturer. He was pursued relentlessly by women and finally broke down in his suite at New York's Ambassador Hotel. An initial diagnosis of gastric ulcer was followed by an operation that revealed that peritonitis had spread from an inflamed appendix throughout his body. Valentino was only thirty-one when he died.

The tens of thousands who mobbed his funeral cortege wanted to identify with the Italian immigrant once despised by his own family. Women fainted on his coffin, covered with pink roses. Notables sobbed bitterly at the loss of America's "Rudy," a new idol. Many of his fellow immigrants would have cherished such adulation, even if it seemed to lead to an early death, with overtones of dissipation and whispers of an unfulfilled internal life. He was known to have consulted H. L. Mencken about a growing rumor that he was a homosexual. Mencken described him as "a man of relatively civilized feelings thrown into a situation of intolerable vulgarity."

This particular immigrant had been more than upraised, but at what cost? His olive skin, dark sideburns, and oiled hair defied the American ideal of manhood. Too graceful and too beautiful, Valentino was hated by men while women lusted after him. He was ill served by them all. His second wife, who bore the phony name Natasha Rambova, made him wear a slave bracelet, to the great derision of American men. In short, Valentino became an exploited plaything of the media. His press agent turned his funeral into an extravaganza in order to enhance box office sales for his last film, *Son of the Sheik*.

Despite the adulation he had received, Valentino found it necessary (and perhaps materially useful) to list himself grandiosely in the 1926 edition of *Who's Who in America* as "Rodolfo Alfonzo Raffaelo Pierre Filibert Guglielmi Di Valentina d'Antonguolla." By August 23 of that year he, and his narcissism, was dead in a strange, new land.

Although Valentino was a sex symbol, there were hidden, conflicted areas of his sexuality and that of other Italian males. These produced damaging results for such persons and for family life.

Immigrant sexuality remains an uncharted sea. Some studies suggest that Italian males are sexually repressed. Others point out that they, although Catholics, are among the most effective users of birth control devices. In contrast, Latin American males, who most closely approach the macho image, are much less permissive as far as the use of contraceptives is concerned. We shall probably never know fully what the attitudes of immigrants were concerning such secret matters.

What does seem obvious is that sexual behavior in America clashed with the mores taught in the old country. There, both church and state encouraged repression in women approaching puberty. A father zealously guarded the chastity of his daughter. She must be delivered to her future husband a virgin; only marriage legalized and sanctified her sexuality. Whenever a girl became *Americanizata*, the inference was pejorative. It meant that she had freed herself from family control. She was attempting (in an age before "Women's Lib" made it fashionable) to buck male authority. As a phrase loaded with special contempt noted: *Si ha Americanizata per fare la no-gooda.* The *no-good-nick* in Jewish immigrant parlance was like the *no-gooda* among Italians—a woman more than arrogant, perhaps even a deflowered female bum.

In pre–World War II Italy, *gli Americanizati* were persons who had grown perverted, incapable of moderate views. The mix between American and Italian values did indeed make it difficult for immigrants to maintain the sexual views of Apennine peasants, in an age when Sigmund Freud was writing that male puberty brought on "an accession of libido." Unrealistic restraints upon female sexuality only served to heighten the urges of young Italians and to overemotionalize sex—legally attainable through marriage alone. In America, females were more difficult for immigrant parents to watch over. Young men were incomparably freer to find sexual outlets. Repression thus remained tied to a watchful familial authority that rested on traditional mores (now in conflict with open-ended ones).

Mussolini once (quite unconsciously) pointed out the immaturity of Italian men when he remarked: "War is to man as maturity is to woman." More recently, writer Luigi Barzini and filmmaker Federico Fellini have been vilified for pointing out the Italian male's need to certify his virility before friends. "I am the Satan of the Italian petite bourgeoisie," Fellini wrote: "During a reception for me in the country some people came and threw stones at my windows. We are in a country that is basically childish." Barzini's *The Italians* also features the childishness of Italian male sexuality. A popular stereotype promotes the Italian man as a consummate Latin lover. Costanzo Constantini's book *The National Lover* (1973) challenges the view that Italians are even attentive lovers. Spoiled by doting mothers (in turn influenced by the church), the passionate Italian treats women in an infantile way. The more certain wives accept their inferior status, the more that husband pursues other women.

What was the Latin of the double standard to do with his sexuality in America—a land whose values sprang from Puritanism? Some fathers became both faithless and faithful, externally lascivious yet loyal within the home environment. However, the quest for women outside the family was an activity more easily pursued by the rich than by the struggling immigrant. Few members of the first generation had the manners and self-esteem vital to the Casanova image. Their children might aspire to having the time and affluence necessary to womenizing.

In a 1973 survey of a thousand Italian housewives, a large proportion of the women complained that their husbands were not good lovers. If such a survey had been taken among immigrant wives, what would the results have been? The few immigrant novels written by women complain of the coarseness with which they were treated. Whether their men were as unfaithful as their prototypes in the old country, we do not know. But frequently the immigrant male stayed in the United States as a single person, while his wife remained in Italy.

Becoming a good mother (especially if left behind by an immigrant husband) came to be related to a rigid suppression of sexuality. Meanwhile the wife, by lavishing attention on her offspring, was apt to carry on the same process that had infantilized her husband. Tied to the memory of mother, the Italian male continued to virginalize his wife. The Italian family had to trowel over a melancholy set of contradictions. The Italian husband demanded absolute faithfulness from his wife. Both looked upon divorce with horror. With his wife transformed into a mother figure, the husband would symbolically be orphaned by divorce. These frustrating circumstances squelched individuality (oddly enough) for the husband himself, splitting his self-image.

A south Italian saying seemed designed to keep the generations together under a symbolic grape arbor, even though the setting might be an urban one: "Be content to remain what your father was. Then you'll be neither a knave nor an ass." Some oldsters clearly resented the material and educational successes of younger and brighter folk. Members of the first generation nursed grudges that they had not had the chance to receive an American education and might have bested their offspring had they been given similar opportunities. A Sicilian proverb advises: "Don't make your children better than yourself." A son wrote: "My father was of the opinion that too much school makes children lazy and opens the mind for unhealthy dreams." Immigrants suspected that America's monolithic school system would make Yankees of all its students. Ultimately it nearly succeeded in doing so. The schools rewarded conformity. Indeed, acceptability depended upon socialization by new educational institutions.

Immigrant community leaders who saw the schools as a means by which the stigma of ignorance could be overcome backed compulsory classroom attendance. Without such laws probably some parents would never have sent their offspring to school. A major product of this schooling, Americanization, was also paradoxically sponsored by ardent Anglo nativists. Americanization teachers introduced immigrant children to a new world of useful knowledge.

Home from school, the child who was accustomed to hearing standard English spoken, listened with shame to the thick accents of his mother and father, who found it difficult to convert their vowel-ridden language into the new tongue. Illiterate parents were outclassed by teachers who taught that Italian values were of a lesser order than Yankee ones.

The schools both questioned and eroded past habits. Youngsters who had never used a toothbrush were taught dental hygiene and even that they should bathe at least once per week. Boys were instructed to wash under the arms and to clean the foreskin of the penis to prevent infection.

Some immigrant children found it difficult to sit still in class and these came to regard school attendance as burdensome. Michael Katz noted that immigrant children were regularly told by school administrators: "You are vicious, immoral, short-sighted, and thoroughly wrong about most things. We are right. We shall show you the truth."[5]

At home the educational message was a different one. As Jerre Mangione put it: "My mother believed that too much reading would drive a person insane."[6] Eventually, children and parents no longer seemed to speak the same language. There were new cracks in the omnipotent parental *imago*. Children gained the upper hand as the family's front stoop ushered in a whole new world that unfolded on America's streets. This was a strange and public world. In the old one, play was a luxury either of the rich or of the very young. At home, play was not encouraged, but it was sponsored by the schools. Time spent at a playground or local park meant the loss of income for a family. Children spilled out onto the ghetto streets, at first with bat and ball, later with knife or gun. Defying both parents and the police, they took to the alleyways in an escape from family, social workers, and the law.

Children embarrassed by their lack of education and status began to lie about family background. It was hard to admit that one's father was a garbage collector, iron molder, or steam fitter. So, a child would claim that his garage mechanic father was an engineer or at least a shop foreman. A gardener's son might transform his father into a landscape architect. A bricklayer's daughter might pretend her father was a terrazzo designer. There were endless possibilities for upgrading one's parents. This phenomenon is related to "the family romance." Blue-collar Italian fathers, as compared to benign Jewish family leaders, often proved to be no great respecters of education or culture. The Italian *paterfamilias* seemed locked into the role of vengeful tribal leader who downgraded the attempts of his children to better themselves.

The Italian forte remained activism rather than contemplation. Italy was a nation of non-readers. American Jews showed a pronounced respect for learning, part of the talmudic tradition. We must, however, remember that the term "Jewish" refers to religious identity, not to national origin. Furthermore, the Jews are a rather atypical group for comparative purposes. They cannot be identified exclusively with any one country. Some Jews arrived long before the great waves of immigration from eastern Europe and they were well situated in America in advance of the Italian migration. Nevertheless, one cannot help notice how much the Jewish attitude toward education, for example, contrasted with the south Italian notion of one's destiny (*destino*). This sense of fate, beyond human control, discouraged knowledge seeking by Italian children.

Jews, with higher occupational aspirations, generally surpassed Italian immigrants in terms of professional attainments. The Latin family, with its lack of faith in the outer world, as well as in government, too often exerted an anti-intellectual influence upon its offspring. Former peasants saw humans as inevitably imperfect. What could education do to change either *destino* or human nature? In contrast, the Jews resembled the Calvinists in their industriousness outside the home. By not associating guilt with surpassing one's father, the Jewish community sanctioned all manner of achievements. Jews, however, produced their own varieties of *angsts!*

Jewish fathers appeared to be less directly punishing than were the Italians. They evoked a patriarchal respect rather than fear. They exercised authority in a generally softer way, with greater care and warmth than were typical of the families described by the Italo-American novelists.

Jews, furthermore, generally used mental health facilities more than did Italians when the stresses of ghetto life became too burdensome. This approach to the resolution of family battles was not sanctioned in most Italian families. Marvin Opler's *Culture and Social Psychiatry* (1967) tells us that blue-collar workers in general prefer to focus on bodily aches and pains rather than upon emotional disabilities. The Italians, not understanding the need for psychotherapy, ridiculed it in a way not characteristic of most Jews. All immigrants, of course, could little afford being stigmatized as mentally ill.

Fights over schooling surfaced in those families that offered little support of their children's education. As early as 1907, the *Bolletino della Sera*, published in New York City, compared Italian and Jewish attitudes toward education:

> But instead of this what a contrast! The schools where the Italian language is taught are deserted. The Italian families falsify even the ages of their children in order to send them to the factories, instead of the schools, showing thus an avarice more sordid than that of the traditional Shylock. There is not a young Italian girl who knows to typewrite in both languages, and our men of affairs must employ Jewish girls or Americans for lack of Italians.

There was precious little learning in the Little Italys of America. Parents saw a "bad" child as one who left home to get an education. The "good" child stayed home to help. The "ideal" child might develop a personality like that of Perry Como or Joe DiMaggio, who, although they became celebrities, remained big-hearted, non-intellectual children. Immigrants who looked upon the New World as threatening raised children who could disarm their anxieties—children who were lighthearted, simpleminded, and tractable. In the entertainment world, a Como, a Dean Martin, or a Vic Damone were models of outwardly unworried adaptation. Jimmy Durante could assure audiences that he was always friendly and ready to please. Calm, smiling, never angry, these stereotyped neo-Italians reassured American audiences of their complaisance.

Various statistics may be quoted concerning the educational attainments of the Italian Americans. According to Richard Gambino, 93 percent of them have not gone to college. Yet, in the late 1970s 50 percent of Fordham University's student body is Italian. Twenty-five percent of the students at the City University of New York are Italian Americans (but only 4.5 percent of the faculty is of that group). The highest concentrations of Italo-Americans historically have attended Catholic institutions, among them Fordham, Notre Dame, and the various Loyola universities. Chancellor Peter Sammartino of Farleigh Dickinson University (which he founded in 1942) has pointed out that there are now forty Italian American college and university presidents.[7] (His institution, incidentally, was materially aided by Colonel Farleigh Dickinson, whose name and background were notably non-Italian.)

Despite their increasing involvement with the educational process, Italian Americans are still described as not interested in learning. Would it be unfair to say that the majority of them *act* rather than *think*? And, how different is such behavior from that of their fellow Americans? One can feel how much certain members of the older generation remain suspicious of, if not hostile to, investigatory writing about them—almost as if family secrets might be aired publicly. The third generation of Italian descent thus remains mostly largely ignorant of its origins, strengths, and weaknesses. There is a defensiveness about sensational books that concern crime, the Mafia, and alleged inferiority. More important, the Italian American child frequently suffers from an identity confusion based upon past unrealistic parental authority and the family's disrespect for learning.

From outward appearances, the descendents of immigrants seem to have "made it." But, to achieve success in American terms has not meant permanent resolution of the anger, hurt, and envy locked up so tightly inside.

Why did some immigrant children rise to the challenge of American life whereas others did not? The quality of the parent-child attachment was the factor that powerfully determined whether a child had a negative or a positive life experience. Too much rigidity in the parenting process threw the child into conflict with the parents. If a child could not verbalize his feelings, he acted them out or kept them under strict control.

A central theme of this book is that the emotions that churned beneath the surface in the lives of immigrants were not those that have appeared in the record. This is because we reveal mostly the history of our outer life. Family turmoil is not a subject that most Italians discuss openly. Instead, the outer record shows that Italians have a genius for dealing with babies, that they are hyperloyal to the family, and that its harmony exists because children subordinate their wills to those of parents.

We must be careful not to stereotype the family experiences of immigrants. One needs to differentiate between particular and individual variables. Some children enjoyed strong nurturing. Erik Erikson has called basic trust the foundation of good parent-child relationships. If such trust breaks down, family loyalty crumbles. Fiorello La Guardia came out of a family in which mutual regard remained high. Books such as *The Americanization of Edward Bok* and Jacob Riis's *How the Other Half Live* describe deprivation outside, rather than inside, the immigrant structure. Riis lived in just as oppressed conditions as did many other immigrants. But there seemed to be a difference in his family life. Although the stench of the city rises from the pages of his book, Riis did not give up hope.

Not all children went down the road to delinquency or despair. It was surely the exceptionally deprived ones who stole cars and motorcycles in order to work out their unresolved conflicts. Others found models in teachers or in corner policemen. Some did not know it, but they sought reintegration of their egos to make up for inadequate parenting. For many of these, father and mother had given up emotionally. For their children the search for love and warmth had to go elsewhere and without shame.

IX
POLITICS

CRITICS ONCE WONDERED whether immigrants in ethnically mixed cities might not be permanently condemned to social and political inferiority under the tutelage of ward bosses. Could they actually strike out on their own, developing new power relationships that were more healthy and permanent than those the ghetto offered? Or would Italians and Poles squander their political power, continuing to be wooed by Irish politicians at election time?

Whereas the Irish arrived in America's cities when political machines were in their infancy, the Italians came too late to shape these institutions. Instead, some sold their votes and egos for a few dollars, as did the blacks in the American South. The Irish, having moved up on the social ladder, no longer needed to engage in such indignities. Indeed, they came to monopolize positions in city and county governments, most particularly, the police forces.

After the first world war a few first-generation naturalized citizens obtained positions as constables, city commissioners, judges, and county supervisors. Francis B. Spinola (1887–1891) of New York and Anthony J. Caminetti (1891–1895) of California were the first members of Congress of Italian descent. Later came

140

Fiorello La Guardia and Vito Marcantonio in New York. In comparison with other nationalities, however, the Italians produced relatively few national leaders.

This was the result not only of discrimination against them. Unlike the Irish, the Italians did not vote in blocs. In the first part of the twentieth century, moreover, today's urban tenant unions, welfare rights organizations, and ethnic power groups did not exist. Group confrontation as a means of gaining power was virtually unknown. In New York the Italian Americans were split between Republicans and Democrats. Between the two world wars they began to move away from the Democratic party, which catered to immigrants. In national elections foreigners increasingly sided with the Republicans while they voted Democratic in local contests. But even at the local level, Italians were politically unpredictable.

In only a few areas of America was ethnicity sufficiently developed to hold together a foreign vote based upon the Italians. One such place was east Harlem (now a black and Puerto Rican area). Harlem's electorate once sent more congressmen of Italian origin to Washington than did any other district in the United States. Somehow, its Italians were able to submerge their individualism.

For almost fifty years (1917 to 1962) La Guardia, Marcantonio, James Lanzetta, and Alfred E. Santangelo represented the district. La Guardia and Marcantonio were reform minded and hypersensitive to slights against Italians. Marcantonio, unlike La Guardia, had ties, however obscure, to a Mafia underboss named Thomas Lucchese (known as "Three-Finger Brown"). It was La Guardia who gained national prominence by excluding New York's Tammany leaders from city hall (which drove them deeper into the ranks of racketeers).

La Guardia's story gives us an opportunity to see how the children of immigrants could overcome ethnic bitterness. He was the first Italian American who became powerful without denying his mixed background and personal tastes. Of Jewish and Italian ancestry, though he later became a Protestant, this extraordinary leader seemed apolitical and atypical. La Guardia, three-term mayor of New York City, was the son of a southern Italian father and a northern Italian mother. His father was from Foggia and his mother from Trieste. This north-south combination may have helped to produce a brash and young Fiorello, who spent his early years traveling around the United States with his army band-master father, once an accompanist to the opera diva Adelina Patti. Although born on the east side of New York City on December 11, 1882, Fiorello was raised out west. His playground was the great Arizona outdoors, where he hunted, rode, "saw what Indians looked like, spoke to miners and cowboys, went camping in the hills with soldiers, tended the chickens and cow that his father kept, and enjoyed his share of schoolboy pranks and fights."

La Guardia's father, leader of the 11th U.S. Infantry Band, included his children in concerts. Fiorello blew the cornet while his sister played the violin. Their father accompanied them on piano. Although there was a rigid distinction between officers and enlisted men, which extended to their families, this barrier did not bother Fiorello: "I would just as soon fight an officer's kid as I would anyone else." As he recalled: "What I saw and heard and learned in my boyhood days in Arizona made lasting impressions on me. . . . For instance, I loathe the professional politician. . . . This attitude had its origin in the badly dressed, slick and sly Indian agents, political appointees, I saw come into Arizona . . . robbing the Indians of the food the government provided for them."

La Guardia also remembered being ashamed of eating apples and cookies in front of hungry Indian kids. In later life he was to do something about the welfare of needy children. About this he wrote: "Another early impression that made its mark on my mind was gained from watching the railroad being built between Ashfork, Prescott, and Phoenix." Little machinery was employed on this particular construction job: "It was all manpower and draft animals. The laborers were all Mexicans and Italians." Even then he was shocked by the fact that there were no social security laws, employer liability regulations, or workmen's compensation provisions to protect immigrants and non-immigrants. Such memories spurred him on to fight for social equality: "It was nearly half a lifetime later, as a member of Congress, that I had an opportunity of taking part in preparing the Railways Labor Act and in passage of the Norris–La Guardia Anti-Injunction Act." Both were designed to protect laborers.

A particularly poignant memory had its effect when La Guardia assumed office in New York. This concerned an organ grinder who had come to town when La Guardia was a boy in Prescott:

> He, and particularly the monkey, attracted a great deal of attention. I can hear the cries of the kids: "Dago with a monkey! Hey, Fiorello, you're a dago, too. Where's your monkey?" It hurt. And what made it worse, along came Dad, and he started to chatter in Neapolitan with the organ grinder. He hadn't spoken Italian in many years, and he seemed to enjoy it. Perhaps, too, he considered the organ grinder a fellow musician. At any rate, he promptly invited him to our house for a macaroni dinner. The kids taunted me for a long time after that. I couldn't understand it. What difference was there between us? Some of their families hadn't been in the country any longer than mine. [1]

While mayor of New York, La Guardia was told by the Police Department that roaming organ grinders posed both a traffic menace and a hazard to small children, who rushed out onto the city streets in pursuit of them. Despite the criticism he received, the mayor banned all organ grinders from New York's public thoroughfares. He claimed that "the advent of the phonograph and the radio," as well as "free public concerts in parks, libraries, museums and other public places," made organ grinders and their monkeys obsolete. But perhaps his action was based on the humiliation and ridicule that he had experienced on the frontier when he was linked with the illiterate, begging organ grinder.

In 1933, La Guardia, congressman for fourteen years, was elected mayor of New York. One of the best known political leaders of his time, he ran an efficient government and participated in many aspects of the city's life. Fiorello—or "Little Flower," as his name translated from Italian—sped to fires, went on rounds with policemen, and reported to the populace via a

143

weekly radio program. During a newspaper strike he kept restless youngsters and adults alike informed about the latest comic strips; he read his favorite Italian recipes over the air as well.

La Guardia hated social gradations, about which he said: "I have no family tree. The only member of my family who has one is my dog Yank. He is the son of Doughboy, who was the son of Siegfried, who was the son of Tannhauser, who was the son of Wotan. A distinguished family tree, to be sure—but after all, he was only a son of a bitch."[2]

Immigrants found in La Guardia a champion of their interests who openly condemned the United States immigration quota system as bigoted. Even the Irish Americans rallied around the mayor. He won everyone's trust, standing against government by favor and connection, which the poor once thought they needed. In 1949, again a candidate for mayor, he protested against a film, *The House of Strangers*, that he considered damaging to Italians.

Beyond the image of honesty that La Guardia projected, he gave America's largest city its first efficient government. With the help of President Franklin Roosevelt, he set out to demolish the Tammany Hall patronage organization. A new fusion ticket, composed of Jews, blacks, Italians, and WASP liberals, kept the mayor in office for twelve years (1934 to 1946). He tried to show the ethnics that they no longer needed the favors dispensed by machine politicians. Racketeers fled into neighboring New Jersey, chased by La Guardia's prosecuting attorney, Thomas E. Dewey.

Between the two world wars the problems that faced all Americans confronted its foreign population as well. Prohibition, unemployment, and the great depression all confused social patterns. Even more threatening than these to Italian and German Americans was the rise of dictators in their homelands. Although Mussolini was initially a source of patriotic pride for immigrants, he ultimately became an embarrassment. One of Clarence Darrow's last cases, that of Greco-Carrillo (1927), involved a bloody conflict between fascist and anti-fascist Italian immigrants.

A 1928 booklet published in California by an immigrant editor labeled fascism the "shame of the homeland." And though

144

twenty-one years of dictatorship (1922 to 1943) convinced some immigrants that their hopes for a Fascist state were misplaced, others were bolstered by Mussolini's African adventures and they began to look at their new homeland as *una terra maledetta*. Puffing crooked "Di Nobile" Toscano stogies, they read *Il Progresso Italo Americano*, New York City's Italian daily—which regularly portrayed Mussolini as a hero.

La Guardia urged his compatriots not to be taken in by fascism. Another public figure who refused to modernize his *Italianità* to fit the Duce's politics was Maestro Arturo Toscanini. The greatest conductor of modern times, he emigrated to America after having planned to retire in his mother country.

The Italian self-image in America might have been bolstered had there been more top-flight refugees from fascism. A prime example was Enrico Fermi, who constructed the first atomic chain reactor at the University of Chicago. He became disillusioned with conditions in Italy, where his Jewish wife had experienced discrimination. After refusing to give the Fascist salute at the Nobel Prize ceremony, Fermi migrated to America. These role models were, however, far removed from the ghetto streets along which most immigrants lived.

The political chasm between Italy and its overseas progeny grew to be unbridgeable. The fervor that fascism stirred up in some immigrants gave way to disgust as they admitted to having been blinded by Mussolini's flashy Ethiopian imperialistic adventure, his draining of swamps, and the building of roads and hospitals. When the United States went to war against Italy in 1941, its immigrants, almost to a man, repudiated Mussolini's regime.

After Italy's surrender to the American forces under General Eisenhower, that nation's co-belligerency on the allied side once more aligned the country with the United States' objectives. Once the war ended, one of these goals was the rebuilding of Europe. In 1948 the Italian Americans played a crucial part in the anti-Communist campaign: that year, despite the appeal of Marshall Plan aid, Italy's Communist party grew so popular that, for a time, its leaders seemed on the verge of coming to power. Immigrants by the thousands wrote letters to their relatives urging them to back Italy's newly established democracy under Alcide De Gasperi.

Back in America the days of La Guardia and Marcantonio had come to an end. Large-scale immigration was virtually halted by restrictive quota laws. This forced postwar Italian American political leaders to strive for a wider constituency. As the 1950s began, three New York City politicos of Italian descent ran for mayor: Judge Ferdinand Pecora, a Democrat, Vincent Impellitieri, an independent, and Edward Corsi, a Republican. Although Corsi sought to link both of his opponents with criminal activities, Impellitieri won. But the charges raised by Corsi during the campaign threw enough doubt upon the incumbent that he served only one term.

In Chicago the Italians and the Poles were a plurality but never a majority. However, they had some political muscle. For example, the Libonati family, using their law firm as a base, represented a powerful constituency in the city's Italian districts. In 1933, when Italy's Fascist air marshal, Italo Balbo, led a mass flight of twenty-four airplanes to Chicago, members of the Libonati family rode with him through Chicago's streets in an open limousine. During the 1950s and into the 1960s Roland Victor Libonati was a member of Congress from the seventh district of Illinois. This sort of power, based on ethnic needs, was, however, an unusual phenomenon in the Middle West. In the eastern states, too, the political unity of the Italians was hard to maintain.

Gone were the days when ward captains put in handshaking appearances at annual *festas* and dances in return for ethnic votes. Block politics and political machines were weakened when Franklin Roosevelt's New Deal provided ethnics and non-ethnics alike with political alternatives. Meanwhile, tens of thousands of blue-collar immigrants had escaped out of south Brooklyn and Flatbush to the suburbs; others had crossed the Hudson River out of Manhattan's Hell's Kitchen into the Bronx, Long Island, and Westchester.

In Manhattan, deterioration of the Italo-American vote was symbolized by Carmine De Sapio's loss of control over Tammany Hall during 1961. De Sapio, the last of the big-time bosses, was not merely an ethnic politico. In 1947 he had driven the Irish out of Tammany Hall; but he also betrayed the ethnic reformist image introduced by La Guardia. De Sapio provided almost a caricature of the big-city machine politician. Dapper and well groomed, he could be counted upon to deliver votes, money, and raw power when needed. Behind his tinted glasses was more than a slick politician; he was also a skillful organization man, who had oiled up the creaky Tammany Hall political machine.

De Sapio started out as a reformer. He is now in prison, convicted of trying to bribe a public official. The Italians of south Greenwich Village, his precinct, look upon him as their betrayer. Forgetting *their* needs, he got himself defeated politically, then jailed. His political demise created despair. An ethnic hero was besmirched, and, in a sense, so were his constituents.

Whereas La Guardia had escaped the fusion of crime and politics in New York, De Sapio could not. Unlike the Jews, Italians had few wealthy merchants to back their campaigns. The Irish drew funds from inside city government, with police support, but the the only real money available to Italian politicians was from mobsters. Both Frank Costello and Lucky Luciano supported Tammany Hall. From the 1930s into the 1940s Costello exercised leverage, including even the selection of Italian judges. He also gave money to Irish politicians on the upper west side of Manhattan and to Jewish leaders on the east side of the island. An affluent quasi-Fascist apologist, Generoso Pope, in company with Costello, used Pope's newspaper, *Il Progresso Italo Americano*, and radio station to influence ethnic voting in each of the boroughs of New York. Pope has, incidentally, been called the first Italian American millionaire.

Italian American politicians sometimes manipulate their ethnicity in ingenious ways. During the 1960s New Jersey Congressman Joseph Minish was elected by constituents who were aware of his national background even though his name had been changed. But his ethnicity was not generally known outside his congressional district and therefore did not work against him. Much the same situation has occurred among other Italian American congressmen, including John Dent, Robert Leggett, Dante Fascell, George Miller, and Domenick Daniels. By 1968 there were thirteen congressmen of Italian origin; six had either changed their names or came from families whose names had been changed.

The politics of ethnicity has yielded its best results within mainstream political organizations. But the vacillating political allegiances of Italians have been costly to them. The Jewish comic Woody Allen has openly made fun of Italian politicians. About Mario Procaccino, Mayor John Lindsay's opponent in 1969, Allen quipped that he was probably sitting at home "in his undershirt, drinking beer, and watching Lawrence Welk on television." Another Allen joke about Procaccino had him removing the rugs from the mayor's mansion so that linoleum could be installed. Another story went: "Do you know that Mario is so confident he will be elected that he has bought a pink plaster flamingo to put on the front lawn of city hall?"

Before and after World War II small-propertied immigrants of the working class, both Italian and non-Italian, grew fearful of losing their hard-won security. These tended slowly to move toward a conventional, center-of-the-road politics, hardly in the explosive reform tradition of Tresca or of Sacco and Vanzetti. Instead, as they began to prosper, the majority of immigrants were attracted to relatively conservative politicians within the two major political parties.

Only quite recently have Italian American leaders reached national prominence. Among the first to do so were Senator John Pastore from Rhode Island and Senator Peter Dominici from New Mexico. Pastore, elected in 1951, was the only Italian American to reach the Senate until Dominici's election in 1972. Anthony Celebrezze was the first cabinet member of Italian descent, serving under President Kennedy. Later, President Nixon named John Volpe (the son of an immigrant), who had been governor of Massachusetts three times, his secretary of transportation. In 1972

Volpe became United States ambassador to Italy. President Carter's first secretary of health, education, and welfare was Joseph Anthony Califano, grandson of a Neapolitan sailor and the son of an I.B.M. executive.

In San Francisco, Mayor Joseph Alioto (the son of an Italian fisherman), like Volpe, was personally affluent. These leaders drew strength from each of the major political parties. Despite Alioto's political base in San Francisco's North Beach, he was never able to become governor of California, in part because of accusations of financial irregularity made by a national magazine. He successfully refuted these charges, but the political fallout so damaged his image that he retired from politics.

In 1973 Congressman Peter Rodino catapulted to national prominence as chairman of the House Judiciary Committee and as head of the impeachment inquiry into President Nixon's fitness to remain in office. For twenty-four years prior to the Watergate investigations Rodino, the son of an immigrant toolmaker, lived in relative obscurity. Above all else he prided himself as the author of the 1965 Immigration Act, which repealed discrimination against south European immigrants.

Rodino's parents came over from the old country "with a tag on," as he described those immigrants who could not speak English. Rodino was four years old when his mother, dying in a Newark slum, turned to his father and said: "Look after him. He's going to amount to something." The father clearly became the most important force in the boy's life. "He believed very strongly in his religion," Rodino recalled, "and always taught me and my brother and sister to be honorable. He cobbled our shoes and made our leggings. He even made the tombstone for my mother's grave. There wasn't anything he couldn't do." An Italian boy from Newark hardly could have imagined that he would ever sit in judgment upon a president of the United States. Not only was Rodino handed the impeachment chore, but his House Judiciary Committee was in charge of implementing the Twenty-fifth Amendment, which deals with selecting and confirming a new vice-president.

The mid-1970s saw the emergence on the national scene of other sons of immigrants. Along with Rodino, Judge John J. Sirica and Leon Jaworski, appointed special prosecutor for the Watergate investigation, stepped forward as guardians of the American ethos. Previously, maintenance of the national honor had been the prerogative of men with names like Marshall, Hughes, and Holmes. Later, the Jewish community produced Justices Brandeis, Frankfurter, and Goldberg. But, even after World War II, few could have imagined that the Yankee ethic would be adjudicated by the progeny of Polish and Italian peasants. Rodino and Sirica, along with Jaworski, became symbols of constitutional processes that (set in motion by the excesses of President Nixon and the men around him) led to the toppling of a president. In 1979 the highest legal office in the land went to Benjamin Civiletti, appointed by President Carter as Attorney General of the United States.

In 1974, Ella Grasso, the daughter of Piedmontese immigrants, became the first woman governor (Connecticut) in the fifty states whose husband did not precede her in the post. A seasoned politician who has never lost an election, Grasso maintains a serious involvement in Italo-American affairs and has not sought to escape her national background.

In Philadelphia Frank Rizzo, a former policeman wedded to the rule of force, was elected mayor during the 1960s. His use of alleged "law and order" techniques in government made him unpopular with liberals while he became the darling of the hard hats.

Federal appointments continue to feature a sprinkling of Italian names, which suggests tokenism. As I noted earlier, President Carter's first secretary of health, education, and welfare was Joseph Califano.

By 1979 there were only thirty Italian Americans in Congress, compared to four in the 1930s and eight in the 1940s. None has ever seriously been considered for the presidency—this despite the fact that some seven hundred judges throughout the country bear Italian names. Franklin Roosevelt appointed the first of these, Matthew Abruzzo, to the federal bench.

The Italians lost the struggle with the Irish over control of the Democratic party at an early stage. Furthermore, they never became a force in the Republican apparatus. On the one hand they craved equality and the benefits of assimilation; on the other they were discontented when their ethnicity was ignored. Politicians were exasperated with such a divided minority.

This ambivalence eroded political power even in New York, where one in four persons is Italian by birth or parentage. The 1970 census recorded their presence in that city at 1.7 million. New York's Italian community constitutes its second largest minority, only 5 percent smaller than the Jewish population. In the boroughs also the Italians are in first or second place. In Brooklyn there are close to 700,000 Italian American residents. Yet, in 1975 the Italians of New York City still complained that there were no deputy mayors from their group—while the Jews, Puerto Ricans, and blacks boasted one each; there were two Irish deputy mayors. Abraham Beame, the mayor, was Jewish; the superintendent of schools was of Irish descent.

Why have the Italians not translated their economic success and large numbers into political power? A simplistic reason is that politics does not seem important to the Italian family. But a political tradition transported to the United States from the old country also gets in the way of success in politics. Gordon J. Di Renzo, using a "dogmatism scale" devised by Milton Rokeach (author of *The Open and Closed Mind*), has made a study of Italian political behavior with results that challenge the devil-may-care stereotype of Italians. A high level of dogmatism characterizes political choice at both extremes of the voting spectrum. In the old country and here there existed an inability to achieve compromises for the common good. The Italians consistently refused to identify with a single political party. By splitting their allegiance, they canceled out power within the parties that might have catered to them.

Italian American voters also grew more conservative as they disassociated themselves from strikes and socialism. Some became nativists of sorts. Their authoritarian past, derived from a

151

Catholic heritage and from respect for stability, made for preservers of order, rather than for radical innovators. As new voters, they emphasized law-abiding and "proper" public behavior. The melting pot had come to mean respect for institutions that represent authority—governments, banks, churches, and the armed forces. Under the protecting umbrella of citizenship, family, and hard-earned business connections, ardent new citizens paraded their loyalty to the established order. If not actual flag-wavers, these ethnic Archie Bunkers wanted to be more than worthy of the new land in which they lived. Their new loyalties sounded deeper than those they had given Italy itself.

American politics has remained linked to material achievement. Few great fortunes, such as those of the Carnegies, Guggenheims, or Kennedys, were amassed by Italians. As compared to the Irish, those Italians who became prosperous did not generally achieve political power. The new money of the Italian community often came from restaurants and taverns, construction, trucking, the marketing of produce, and the unfashionable businesses of road building, cesspool contracting, roofing, and masonry. The wealth of the Italian Americans never quite matched that of America's earlier immigrant stock.

In a few cases economic assimilation has taken place through marriage into the WASP establishment. But this process is hard to trace, and Latin machismo could hardly acknowledge that a man would even wish to enter America's corporate structure via his wife's connections.

There is certainly a relationship among money, politics, and ethnic withdrawal. The concentrating of foreigners in inner-city enclaves has not benefited them either socially or politically. Although some communities, like Wallingford, Connecticut, remain heavily populated by persons of Italian descent (local students reputedly do well in Roman history) such places have produced only a few state or national leaders. Furthermore, local ethnic leaders can be displaced by representatives of other minorities. This has occurred in Newark, New Jersey; there blacks have moved into political jobs once held by Italians. In

Philadelphia the political machine of Frank Rizzo did little for any minority. Italian voters seem threatened by political activity. Therefore, they retreat toward the primitive dividing of power with other minorities—as with the Jews and Irish in Manhattan or with the Jews and blacks on Long Island.

As the immigrant years in America recede into the past, a measure of defeatism regarding politics has built up among Italians. In 1968 a conference of trade union leaders produced the following dialogue regarding ethnics in politics: "Not only wouldn't I send a black to organize in a white shop, or a German into a Polish plant, I wouldn't even send a Southern Italian in to organize a Northern Italian shop!" How much is low self-esteem still responsible for the lack of goal direction and intragroup bickering?[3]

X

THE AMENITIES

THE ITALIAN ACHIEVEMENT in America was rooted in folkways and mores far beyond politics. As we have seen, few immigrants became politicians. Few also became the career criminals of popular legendry. At the very center of the Italian experience has always stood the Roman Catholic faith. The church's spires towered above every town and city of the old country. In America too, small wooden crucifixes hung over the marital bed. Italians respected the church almost more as a temporal power than as a religious force. Historically, most governments have been both hurtful and powerless. Italian men would not defend with their lives either church or state; they repulsed attacks upon their families only.

"If you see a crowd of women, the church is close at hand," an old proverb has it. It was women who were bound to the mass, the sacraments, and confession. They regularly prepared their children to receive communion. A familiar sight outside the Italian-American Catholic church was a line of parochial school children in their first communion suits, sometimes sewn by their mothers. The white knee pants, long white socks, and orders from mama not to get these special clothes dirty, form part of the memories of many immigrant children.

Ignazio Silone once wrote: "Religion is to women what salt is to pork. It preserves freshness and flavor." Italian men who hated the clergy referred to priests as parasitic "blackbirds." Clerics heard the confessions of their wives and were an intrusion into, and a threat to male control over, the family. Mothers and wives, traditionally subsidiary figures, burdened now by doubts about the future in America, embraced the spiritual intensity of the mass and the sacraments. The ornate parish church became the center of their lives.

Male feelings toward the church were more aptly summarized by the damning phrase *"Siamo tutti sotto le unghie dei preti"* ("We are all under the talons of the priests"). Italy's architect of national unification, Giuseppe Garibaldi, once called the priesthood the "very scourge of God." (He, incidentally, was referred to by patriots as "our second Jesus Christ.") Priests seemed to intimidate even good and honest men, perhaps by inducing guilt in these parishioners. The gentle image of the clergy became the opposite of that set forth in Carlo Levi's book *Christ Stopped at Eboli.* Priests were perceived as standing between husbands and their womenfolk. It was difficult for men to compete with an authority invoked in God's name. In the American environment male ambivalence about religion grew stronger. This attitude was summed up by Vincent Teresa, later a criminal *sotto capo:*

> When I was a kid, I was a Catholic, but I didn't attend church regularly. My parents tried to make me. When I was fourteen, my mother would send me to church, but I'd wind up at a crap game in the park. I went a few times, but I didn't see nothing there for me, so I didn't want to go. The Church didn't reach me. That's sort of funny. I've read the Bible . . . and I enjoy it as a book. Let's just say I believe in God, but I don't believe in the stuff that's preached in my Church.[1]

Historically, Italians have made up one of the largest ethnic groups in the Catholic church within the United States. Yet, like the Poles, they nursed continuing grievances against the control of American Catholicism by Irish clergy. Even parish schools, first organized by Italians and Poles, were strongly influenced by the Irish. Poles, Italians and Irish all had come from strongly Catholic cultures. Yet, both Poles and Italians felt inferior to the Irish in church matters. The inability to speak to a wider audience than that of their ethnic parishioners made it impossible to enter the Anglo mainstream of American parish life. Both the Poles and the Italians had to be content with a subordinate status, sometimes literally, as when they were relegated to saying mass in the basements of Irish churches.

At the heart of this inferior status was language. We can see who a person is by the way he speaks, states Beulah Parker, author of *My Language Is Me.* It was difficult for persons who spoke English properly to confess their sins in the confessional booth to a priest who might answer: "I no speak da Eng." Some Italian Jesuits and Dominicans were highly educated, but language and pronunciation barriers cut down their influence outside the ethnic community.

Furthermore, the Irish variety of Catholicism was quite different from the continental. Their priests and churches seemed cold and austere to Latin communicants. A puritanical strain of faith showed up in the very training of the Irish clergy. In contrast, the Italian way of life played a subtle role in discouraging the priestly vocation. Male celibacy, particularly in southern Italy, was widely deprecated. Sexuality provided proof of one's manhood. Numerous Irishmen never married; celibacy apparently posed less of a problem for them. Does this help to explain the large number of priests the Irish sent to America?

Despite their large number of communicants, the Italian Americans remained scandalously underrepresented in the church's American hierarchy. As late as 1973 there were thirty-four American archbishops. Only one was of Italian background. Not until 1950 was an Italian bishop (Francis J. Mugavero) appointed—at a time when there were more than a hundred American bishops. An unhappy history lies behind this condition.

American nativists saw Italian Catholicism as menacing and subversive, as well as steeped in superstition and ignorance. These extremists drew a link between papists and the Mafia. In 1895 the American Protective Association had described "the scum of the Mafia as willing tools of the priesthood who protect them in their criminal occupations," both forming a "Tammany of the vilest kind." The year before, the editor of the Baptist *Journal and Messenger* wrote: "An Irish Catholic is preferable to an Italian Catholic, an Irish shillalah to an Italian knife."

In Italy the local curate was, traditionally, at least among women, the most respected person in a rural village. His advice, invariably conservative, was avidly sought before any major decision, especially concerning marriage, was made. Non-church-going men would marry in a Roman Catholic ceremony to please their brides and families.

I have described how a virtual cult of the Madonna, with important psychological components, was exported to the New World. The virgin mother of God, *Santa Maria*, was the fountainhead of *grazia*, or grace. She represented woman desexualized. A woman's virginity could be violated only through a monogamous marriage, protected by no legal divorce. Despite denigration of religious restrictions by males, the south Italian religious system prevailed. Womenfolk could be sexualized only by the sacrament of marriage, symbolized and sanctified by the church. Whenever a bride, clad in white gown and veil, stood before the altar, the groom's relatives looked forward to verifying the "honor" of the virgin wife by examining the nuptial bed sheets for bloodstains after the wedding night.

America's Protestant denominations succeeded in converting only a fraction of its Italian population. Evangelization proved to be no match for the baffling religious practices and beliefs of south European peasants, a religion that included superstitions, pagan rites, and medieval rituals. The very entrenchment of primitive tradition helped immigrants to fend off Protestantism. Older immigrants also showed a greater loyalty to priests born in their homeland and disdain toward the Irish clerics who staffed local dioceses.

The Salesian Fathers, who labored among southern Italians,

kept alive the feast days of San Rocco, San Gennaro, and Saint Anthony. Some immigrant communities held more than thirty such religious celebrations per year. Saint Anthony's Day might begin with the firing of salutes early in the morning, followed by a procession to the local church, high mass, a community dinner, and games. At night a parade with bands, floats, and fireworks was held.

At Torrington, Connecticut, from 1920 until 1944 the town band (led by bandmaster Frank Catania) held two big annual concerts—the first on July 4, Independence Day, and the second on July 16, the Feast of La Madonna del Carmine. This Italian religious holiday became the occasion for new clothes for the children, a mass, good things to eat, decorations, a parade, a band concert, and, as the finale, a fireworks display. The Torrington band played in front of the city's Catholic church and led the parade that preceded its evening concert. Weddings, baptisms, and funerals were entwined with south Italian religious traditions and beliefs, presided over by a clergy tolerant of superstition and even of peasant ignorance.

As time passed, immigrants grew less dependent upon their native churches, and the Latin of the old mass, a nostalgic security, was slowly abandoned. Primitive Old World notions were sharply modified in America. Beginning with the establishment in the 1860s of parish churches for immigrants, an ethnic church had slowly developed. By the 1880s an "Italian problem" of apostasy faced the Vatican as well as its Irish Catholic hierarchy in America. Both were concerned with the defection of religiously indifferent immigrants. Traditional anti-clerical biases, imported from the homeland and reinforced by socialist dogma, made spiritual "leakage" constant.

At first religion served as a cohesive force among the Italo-Americans. But beyond the ethnic neighborhoods in which the church operated lay divisive feelings. Anti-clericalism was not a good base upon which ethnic parishes could grow. As ethnic identity among the second generation faded, so did the power of the local parish priest. Finally, although the church's confessional offered emotional sustenance (really psychiatric support), Italians were hardly kept in bondage by their religion—as were the Irish. Among the Italians, spirituality remains both mortal and divine. In general, they (and the French, too) take their Catholicism far less literally than do the Irish. Scripture can be interpreted individually, much as the Romans chose individual pagan gods who pleased them.

Such subtleties have perhaps been best portrayed by the second-generation novelists rather than by we historians of immigration. Disguised by the genre of the novel have been the unpopular themes of violence, disorientation, loneliness, alienation, and the struggle to maintain individuality. However, the Italian Americans have not yet produced a novel of quite the power and incisiveness of Ole Rolvaag's *Giants in the Earth* (1927) or Willa Cather's *O Pioneers* (1913) and *My Antonia* (1918). There has been no Abraham Cahan to write *The Rise of David Levinsky* (1917), no Anjia Yeziersha to fashion *All I Could Never Be* (1932). There is no Leo Rosten, Nelson Algren, or Louis Adamic to give a clear-cut Italian version of big-city life and its clash with old values; no Saul Bellow, Philip Roth, Bernard Malamud, or William Saroyan among the Italo-American novelists. Hamilton Basso, Paul Gallico, and Bernard De Voto rejected their heritage. Among other writers of Italian origin who virtually ignored the immigrant theme are John Ciardi, Valenti Angelo, and Frances Winwar (Francesca Vinciguerra).

The best known Italian American novel is Mario Puzo's *The Godfather.* A best-seller (over fourteen million copies published), it features violent descriptions and portrays a brutal sexuality. Puzo's book does little, however, to explain the most glaring and destructive myths about the Italians outside its Mafia setting. Furthermore, his penetration of intrapsychic matters is not deep. Jerre Mangione's appealing nonfictional *Mount Allegro* (1941) comes closer to an analysis of persons caught between two cultures. So do the novels of Pietro di Donato, Jo Pagano, and John Fante.

Fante perceives the impact of the first generation upon the second in catastrophic terms. His books may not be great literature but they are more realistic than some histories of the Italian immigrant. In *Full of Life* (1952) Fante described what it once meant to be a wop by emotion and an emerging Yankee by conviction. In an earlier book, *Dago Red* (1940), the main character is ashamed of his nationality. He detests being called a dago or a wop and is brutal in order to compensate for his alienation. As Fante thinks of the past, he remembers a drunken lout of a father and a long-suffering mother who lived out her life in the family kitchen. Only after coming of age does Fante's principal character realize how foolish he has been to hide his past. Fante treated the same theme in *Wait until Spring, Bandini* (1938), which reflects the feelings of shame caused by the broken English and Old World mannerisms of immigrant parents. His embarrassment extends even to the way in which his mother prepares school lunches:

> At the lunch hour I huddle over my lunch pail, for my mother doesn't wrap my sandwiches in wax paper, and she makes them too large, and the lettuce leaves protrude. Worse, the bread is homemade; not bakery bread, not "American" bread. I make a great fuss because I can't have mayonnaise and other "American" things.[2]

Another of Fante's admonishing books, *Full of Life* (1952), was written as a comedy, but it is as sad as humor can possibly be. With the book's morbidity excised, it was produced as a Hollywood film starring Judy Holliday, a non-Italian.

In the autobiographical novel *Golden Wedding*, Jo Pagano also portrayed the strains of immigrant life, with all its volatile elements. These writers,[3] themselves the children of immigrants, deal with anxieties that created ambivalent feelings. While they may have loved the mandolin playing and the singing at a wedding party, they were sorely embarrassed when American playmates saw the flushed faces of *parenti*, reddened from excitement and wine.

Ideally, members of the first generation should have written their own story, with all their travails. Except for Giovanni Schiavo, they produced virtually nothing that can be called history. Only with the rupture of family life did the second-generation novelists emerge. Italy's major modern writers, among

160

them Ignazio Silone, Carlo Levi, and Cesare Pavese, occasionally mentioned emigrants in their works but in a detached and intellectual way. In short, the Italian story in America was subject to considerable distortion.

As for the Italo-American press, it chose to feature material achievement over cultural news. Except for *La Follia di New York*, it was hardly a distinguished press. Most Italian-language papers (of which there were once more than one hundred and fifty) became four- to eight-page weeklies; the dailies were confined to a handful of large cities. Editors either cribbed material from Italian periodicals or focused on births, marriages, deaths, and trite neighborhood events not reported by "American newspapers." Immigrant communities became as interested in these activities as in canned dispatches from Genoa or Rome.

Immigrant papers were neither Italian nor American but a blend of the two. Because of its flexibility, Generoso Pope's New York daily, *Il Progresso Italo-Americano*, has continued publication into the 1980s, more than twenty years after Pope's death. A technique used to retain subscribers was the publication of tributes to immigrants who had made good. Press accounts lauded them in "jubilee" or "anniversary" editions published in connection with patriotic events and feast days.

As the parents of American-born children died, second-generation Italians canceled subscriptions to Italian-language newspapers. Occasional columns of English material designed to attract the younger generation could not save these journals. Immigrant newspapers folded when their readers did not feel the need to look back to the old country for reassurance. At that point the immigrant was no longer an immigrant. He had become an American.

Perhaps the illiteracy of large numbers of former peasants helps to explain why so talented a people as the Italians were not more interested in "culture." Although the first generation moved into the middle class, they showed little interest in the arts. This generation, occupied initially with pressing economic problems, could not find the time, nor had they the education, to contribute

161

culturally to their new homeland. A natural result of the depreciation of learning among immigrants was the refusal of their
children to speak the language of their parents.

Nowhere in America was there a dramatic movement by
Italians to compare with New York's Yiddish theater. True, Italian
opera stars and composers, including Adelina Patti and Pietro
Mascagni, all performed in American theaters; they were followed
by Enrico Caruso, Beniamino Gigli, Ezio Pinza, and Amelita
Gallicurci. Just as there has been no great Italo-American novel,
so there has arisen no important Italian American composer except, perhaps, Henry Mancini, a popular songwriter. Giancarlo
Menotti barely qualifies, for he is too directly a product of Italian
training, as was Pietro Castelnuovo-Tedesco.

In painting and sculpture, renowned but hardly great craftsmen appeared. Constantino Brumidi, architect of the Capitol,
came to America virtually upon assignment. At San Francisco
Beniamino Bufano left behind a number of monumental pieces of
statuary. He became enamored with the theme of world peace and
produced a statue of Saint Francis of Assisi that is five feet taller
than the Statue of Liberty—which angered his rightist critics.
Before his death in 1970 Bufano revealed that in 1917 he had cut
off one of his fingers, sending it to President Woodrow Wilson as
his personal sacrifice in the cause of peace.

Bufano's eccentricities remind one of the tower builder at
Watts, Simon Rodia, and also of the abstractions of painter Frank
Stella, who has obscured his Italian origins.[4] Does Stella's highly
original art style suggest an unspoken wish to transcend the immigrant past? Is his an unconscious denial of nationality, perhaps
an excision of his heritage?

Elsewhere in the realm of aesthetics, the Italian American
community has produced practically no professional art critics,
certainly none of the stature of Bernard Berenson, who came out
of Boston's Jewish ghetto. A talented illustrator, Leo Politi has
written charming children's books. In his *Little Leo* (1951) he tells
how he revisited Italy in his Indian suit, beginning a western fad
among the youngsters of his father's village, all of whom wanted
to imitate the boy from America.

The so-called Spaghetti Western film was virtually invented by Sergio Leone. Such films are directed and produced in Italy. Among Italian American film producers and directors are Frank Capra, Vincent Minelli, Martin Scorsese, and Francis Ford Coppola, who directed *The Godfather*. Dino di Laurentis and Carlo Ponti, two eminent Italian producers, have moved their operations from Rome to Hollywood.

Sidney Howard's Pulitzer Prize–winning play, *They Knew What They Wanted* (1928), first drew national interest to the Italianate vineyards of the Napa valley. In 1956 Frank Loesser converted Howard's play into a popular Broadway musical entitled *The Most Happy Fella*, a high-spirited show with Verdi-like motifs, which include "Abbondanza" and "Sposalizio." A similar excursion into drama was the 1958 film *Wild Is the Wind*, which starred Anna Magnani and Anthony Quinn; it portrayed ethnic conflicts on a western sheep ranch.

After more than two decades in which America's diverse ethnic composition was ignored on television, the mid-1970s saw a temporary turnaround in network attitudes. In 1975 half of the television series appearing in the top Nielsen ratings dealt with ethnic minorities, especially blacks. The "ethnicizing" of actors, characters, and story lines reached its peak that year as producers of network series went out of their way to affix an ethnic or minority cast to their programs. This belated and contrived concern with ethnicity moved television beyond bland representations of a mythic Anglo-Saxon America.

Although the public was not yet viewing an ethnic renaissance, American television began to reflect changing attitudes. Shows entitled *The Montefuscos* and *Joe and Sons* depicted Italians battling it out with Irish Catholics. WASP television, which had once dominated the industry with shows like *I Love Lucy* and *Gunsmoke*, for a time went ethnic. Television detectives and lawyers came to be called Petrocelli and Colombo rather than Perry Mason. On television Americans were no longer a colorless majority living in a homogenized suburbia, never referring to its origins. Tony Montefusco could now be made to speak of his Anglo son-in-law as "Mr. Mayonnaise" or "Mr.

163

Whitebread." Executives of the three major television networks referred to 1975 as the year of the ethnic.

The bubbly optimism over television's having discovered the immigrant story was temporary, however. By 1977, ethnic programs (except for Alex Haley's phenomenally successful *Roots*) had faded from the television screen. Television, furthermore, tended to portray ethnics as indistinguishable. One minority's identity crises became pretty much those of another. Italians, Greeks, or Poles were made to seem alike.

Such arbitrariness has also affected actors of Italian background. Sal Mineo could not be cast in a film as Giuliano, the south Italian bandit: Mineo had been stereotyped as a Jew in the film *Exodus*. Joseph Campanella is not able to be cast in Italian parts either—primarily because (paradoxically) he is tall, fair, and blue-eyed.

Dramatic presentations of all minorities has, in fact, become a cliché-ridden mishmash. Maligned groups in our society are juggled about interchangeably. Differences among them have been explained in a commercially opportunistic, anti-historical way. The problems of Italians are not those of Chicanos; those of Greeks are not those of blacks. Colombo, Petrocelli, Kojak, Rhoda, the Montefuscos, and Sanford and Son are characters of polyglot background whose way of life can be exploited for the sake of a story line. In short, they are the fake window dressing that makes a television series appear unique.

No discussion of the Italians would be complete without attention to their eating and drinking habits, which television continues to feature. Does the Italian attitude toward both (and opera, too) make them an oral people? The American attitude toward gastronomy confused these immigrants. Unlike Italy's village markets, grocery stores in the United States sold packaged goods. Those who could not read the labels were unable to tell what was in a carton or a can. Furthermore, in the homeland, peasants grew their own vegetables, milked their own cows, slaughtered their own pigs, and made their own pasta.

Italian cuisine is family based. Pasta dishes that became

American favorites include spaghetti, lasagne, and ravioli. Minestrone also became well known outside ethnic enclaves. Bread, however, was a special symbolic staple for all immigrants. The phrase *"buono come il pane"* ("as good as bread") is a compliment stronger than its English equivalent, "as good as gold." Pizza dough became a kind of gold for its makers, either in Naples or in Atlantic City. Italians hounded neighborhood stores that carried Genoese *baccalà, torrone* from Cremona, hard-crusted breads, tuna packed in olive oil from Lucca, and Eureka lemons raised from Sicilian seeds. In such establishments one could also find Florentine Chianti and Milanese *boccie* balls for Sunday afternoon games.

Rich meat courses on Sundays supplanted the *polenta* (cornmeal), pasta, and chestnut bread of earlier days. Old style or new, there was an integrity about immigrant cooking that was unforgettable, as the son of a native Italian family that lived in Salt Lake City recalled:

> The feast was nearly ready. The side dishes had already been heaped upon the kitchen table—platters of tuna and anchovies and pickled olives and mushrooms surrounded by sliced salami and cheese. There were bowls of dried olives, swimming in olive oil and flavored with garlic and orange peel; there was celery, and sweetly aromatic *finnochio*, and wafer thin Italian ham. . . . The roasts and chickens were finishing at the same time; the pastries, heaped on the side table, were flaky and crumbling; the chicken soup was clear yet full-bodied in flavor, the spaghetti sauce was rich and thick.[5]

It was no accident that Ignazio Silone entitled one of his most popular books *Bread and Wine. Un giorno senza vino e un giorno senza sole* ("A day without wine is a day without sunshine") is an expression that sums up the importance of wine in the immigrant household. During America's incomprehensible Prohibition era of the 1920s a child had to reconcile the drinking he saw at home with legal constraints on the sale of alcoholic beverages. Also, a good many Americans found drinking to be socially unacceptable when it was illegal. Yet, immigrants were allowed to make small quantities of wine (one's Anglo neighbors generally did not take advantage of this legal loophole). The sight of a father's purple-

165

stained hands meant grape-pressing time. Each October, railroad cars filled with succulent Zinfandel grapes would arrive from California. An honorable ritual ensued, in kitchen or cellar, where father became the ancient high priest of Bacchus.

Like other Mediterranean people—Greeks, Spaniards, and Turks—the Italians experimented with the food they found in the new land. Yet their kitchens continued to reek with the odors of garlic, rosemary, olive oil, and cheese. Family cooks who began to prepare food and drink for puritanical Nordic neighbors obtained a start in the restaurant business. After trying unsuccessfully to market packaged Italian foodstuffs, an immigrant named Paolucci founded Chung King, a company that produces ready-made Chinese foods.

In south Greenwich Village one could order *polpo alla Luciana* (boiled, then chilled, octopus in oil and vinegar) or *merluzzo al bianco* (cod poached in wine and herbs) or *pastina in brodo* (noodles and broth). And today in New York City, on Sullivan Street between Spring and Prince, one passes sidewalk stands whose owners cook sizzling Italian sausages over charcoal braziers. Between Houston and Canal streets a jumble of small, predominantly Italian, family-run eating places still exists. In these neighborhoods families once made their own wine. For the poor, butchers featured sheep heads, a south Italian peasant delicacy. The brains and tender meat of the head were prized, much as tripe is a staple among France's urban poor.

Immigrant cooking might have been better if the operators of some of America's Italian restaurants had not remained so tied to the memory of their mothers' efforts. They recalled, through the mists of time, aging parents bent over a hot stove concocting victuals that were a mixture of ingredients such as fennel, tomato sauce, and chicory. These assorted products were introduced into a variety of dishes, sometimes with indigestible results. The soggy spaghetti and meatballs served in many a restaurant were unknown in Italy. And they were likely to be peppered in a manner designed to please the sort of American who liked hot chili. In short, so-called Italian restaurants in the United States were too often a gastronomic disaster. In the larger cities a few chefs (as at the famed Colony Restaurant in New York and at Perino's in Los Angeles) came to enjoy real prestige.

An abundant diet did not necessarily blend well with Americanization. By 1973, at the small community of Roseto, Pennsylvania, for example, the heart attack rate of the town's sixteen hundred "heavy-eating" Italians suddenly soared to three times the national average. Since 1882, when the town's founders had come from the rural southern Italian village of Roseto, near Foggia, not one person under the age of forty-seven had experienced a recorded heart attack. The rate of arteriosclerosis was only one-fourth that found in nearby towns. However, as the children of these immigrants became affluent, more stressful times, less exercise, changes in family life, plus the substitution of animal fats for vegetables and fish in the diet, lifted Roseto's heart attack rate.

Within the larger American society immigrants had tried to maintain folk arts, literature, music, and unique habits of food and drink. As they strove to do so, a materialistic America no longer seemed the land of deliverance. Italian travelers who wrote books about America, such as Ugo Ojetti and Giuseppe Giacosa, in fact, were disgusted with the lack of sentimentality and culture among America's Italians.

Foreign-language newspapers, lodges, and fraternal organizations (supported on Columbus Day and July 4 by politicians with an eye on the ethnic vote) repeated all those clichés about how well the "foreign element" had blended into the "spirit of America." They toted up statistics about how many Italians had become federal and state officials, professors, judges, and bankers. Although evidence could be used to "prove" resounding material success, there was less boasting about cultural attainments.

The Italians, having sacrificed a large part of their heritage, could hardly hope to change American culture in more than a few ways. What did they bring to America that lingers today? One can speak, for example, of their authoritarian family structure, based upon a "village square" background; dedication to good food; and a half-forgotten tradition of Mediterranean values, fused with religious pageantry. In almost every American city where there are parks and green places, Italian terrazzo craftsmen, stonemasons, and landscapers have left evidence of their artistry.

Nineteenth-century Victorians of means once responded to the appeal of Mediterranean gardens and architecture. Some sought to create a "garden of Italy," whether at Newport, Rhode Island, or at Santa Barbara, California. American tourists and readers of the novels of Henry James became well acquainted with the poignant antiquity encountered on the "grand tour." So, immigrant artisans found at least a limited role on the estates of the Vanderbilts and the Wrigleys. But, the majority of Americans thought of the Italian language (if they thought of it at all) as that of their vegetable man rather than of Dante. However snobbish the custodians of pioneer historical societies seemed, the foreign born had, however, come to live among their neighbors forever.

XI
MAKING IT BIG
AND SMALL

IN FORMER DAYS Americans might have thought of their Italian neighbors in terms of blue-collar brawn. Today they may envision a mixture of Perry Como and Dean Martin quite as much as they subscribe still to the peanut vendor stereotype. For we have come to rely upon the relaxed entertainment style of such performers. They, in turn, have been rewarded handsomely for stage, nightclub, and television appearances before national audiences.

Martin, born Dino Crocetti, has been described as "the biggest little con man ever to flimflam Steubenville, Ohio . . . but almost everyone loved crooked little Dino." He was a drummer for the Boy Scouts, a boxer at age fourteen, a steel mill worker at sixteen, and a professional gambler at seventeen. Today he commands $150,000 a week as a Las Vegas entertainer and earns enormous sums from record sales. A self-admitted loner, fond of women and liquor, Martin displays many of the characteristics of an oral personality acting out his hedonism. An early school dropout who admits to having read only one book (*Black Beauty*), Martin nevertheless appeals to millions of persons. His attraction is summed up in his favorite refrain, "Everybody Loves Somebody Sometime," with its obvious tranquilizing effects.

Like Martin, the sometimes explosive Frank Sinatra can show his audiences a certain Latinate gentility. On other occasions he seems mystifyingly brutal yet displays an arrogance that ethnic members of his audiences might themselves unconsciously wish to show. Altercations, mostly fistfights and insults hurled in public, are part of the Sinatra style. These elemental (id) impulses have been attributed by the press to the repressed passionateness of Italians. Yet a Sinatra does overturn the caricatures of organ grinders and hoodlums from which Italian immigrants once suffered.

Success that follows years of deprivation can produce an immense disequilibrium. It is not unusual under such circumstances to discharge feelings of malaise by implying that others are responsible for immoral and abusive competition. A hurt and resentful Sinatra followed, almost unconsciously, the vindictive folkways of his forebears. One of these was to force an apology from an enemy. In 1975 he won substantial libel damages from the British Broadcasting Corporation because of an accusation carried on a BBC program that the singer had used Mafia influence to attain his Oscar-winning role in the 1953 film *From Here to Eternity*.

Sinatra and fellow Italian American entertainers ultimately achieved a rather shaky re-identity. In these entertainers one still sees fragments of immigrant stereotypes. In general, their sentimentality and good-heartedness triumph over repressed violence and brutality. Although accused of consorting with Mafia chieftains, Sinatra has become deeply involved with such causes as construction of a new hospital at Palm Springs, California, named for President Dwight Eisenhower. He has also (ambivalently) associated himself with the liberal Kennedys and later with their opposite number, Vice-President Spiro Agnew. Sinatra, however, has courageously spoken out in public about his private problems—sleepless nights, depressions, and a desperate past need to use drugs, as well as liquor.

While making it big in American show business, Sinatra recoiled in disgust whenever politicians accused him of connections with the underworld—links obviously based on national background. He or Perry Como or Lisa Minelli or Ann Bancroft (Anna Italiano) understandably could not accept ethnic slurs aimed at them because they came from immigrant families. As a second-generation child once asked: "What had I known of Italia, that ancient soil which my parents had never been able to forget but which I had never even seen? Why should I be mocked by others because blood flowed in my veins that seemed to unsuit me for the Anglo vision of life eternal?" Was there, however, a measure of repressed guilt about being so separated from one's origins? It would be difficult not to elicit emotional responses from individuals who are here because someone took a chance that life would be better on this side of the ocean.

One way out of the identity dilemma faced by second-generation Italian Americans was to become more American than the Americans. Whether one operated a pizza parlor or a barber shop, it seemed expedient to adopt the Perry Como, Dean Martin, Tony Bennett, or Vic Damone style of the nice guy who made it easy for those around him.[1] These entertainers radiated a closeness that Americans seemed to idealize. Their warmth silenced ethnic criticisms and made these particular Italians appealing.

The theater was a ready path toward recognition, a legitimizing agency for immigrants with talent. George M. Cohan and Irving Berlin provided early examples of success outside the Italian community. Some of the characteristics of Italian American actors are those of show business itself. Not only did Italians play the buffoon, à la Pagliacci, *con la faccia infarinata*; it was absolutely necessary for Jewish and other immigrant performers to cultivate a disarming quality. The American theater, then at a primitive stage of development, thus welcomed the antics of a Jimmy Durante.

Athletics was yet another area in which prejudice against foreigners could be minimized. Muscleman Charles Atlas, who began a nationally successful body-building business, was born

Angelo Siciliano on a farm near Aeri in Italy. He migrated to America in 1904. Atlas's system for building up the bodies of emaciated males involved isometric exercises rather than weight lifting, which was then used in most gymnasiums.

Other immigrant city kids went into boxing. In that sport, as Primo Carnera and Tony Canzoneri were to find out, social layering takes certain negative forms in America. At any given time if one wants to know what ethnic group is at the bottom of the social heap, one need look only at who is near the top of the boxing world. For the Irish, the Italians, and latterly the blacks, boxing has afforded minority members a springboard to success. One thinks first of John L. Sullivan and Jim Corbett and later of Jim Braddock—who brought the Irish to the attention of sports fans. Still later came Carnera, Canzoneri, and Rocky Marciano. In the same way, Harry Wills, Joe Louis, and Mohammed Ali reached their prime when blacks occupied the bottom rung of the cultural ladder. To be "top dog" in boxing meant that the nationality which a boxer represented remained the underdog.

In the world of baseball Jo, Vince, and Dom Di Maggio were followed by Yogi Berra, Phil Rizzuto, and Carl Furillo. Today Tommy Lasorda runs the Los Angeles Dodgers and the feisty Billy Martin is on-and-off manager of the New York Yankees.

Mario Andretti is only one Italian name in the motor racing world. The Alfa Romeo and Maserati racing teams regularly produce drivers who enter the American track circuit.

In a business civilization, no less important is the role of the industrial executive. Before Lee Iacocca of the Ford Motor Company became the head of the Chrysler Corporation, John J. Riccardo (its chairman) headed that company. If one were to make a list of the most successful businessmen of Italian extraction (as *Identity* magazine does annually) one would surely include David Beretta, the president of Uniroyal, John Billera, the president of U.S. Industries, and Jeno Paolucci, founder of Jeno Inc., an important food processor. His latest venture is the new Italo-American magazine *Attenzione*.

One can fall into the trap of equating public success with inner harmony. As with other nationalities, the Italians have produced many successful personalities. In 1976 John Pastore retired after twenty-six years on Capitol Hill; he was then still the only Italian ever elected to the United States Senate. That year they buried Carlo Gambino in Brooklyn—a Sicilian stowaway fifty-five years earlier who became the Mafia's boss of bosses, the archetypal "godfather."

Sonny Bono, Liza Minelli, Connie Francis, Al Pacino, and Robert De Niro are constantly in the news. Yet, three or four generations beyond the Ellis Island landings of their forebears, Italians continue to grope for an understanding of their heritage. It is hard, in particular, to live down accusations that the Italians are a crime-ridden people. To become a singer or an athlete also forms part of the cliché about Italian achievement in America.

As the Italians overcame the insularity of their family life, they displayed some of those outward traits that produced the entertainers I have mentioned. One of the most appealing aspects of the Italian character is congeniality—the great art of being happy, despite adversity and with *buona volontà* (goodwill). The pleasures that Italians call *la dolce vita* were never quite extinguished among the immigrants. Luigi Barzini identified these as food, wine, a day in the sun, a pretty girl, defeat of a rival, good music, holidays, frivolous (yet entertaining) art, absence of regimentation, and avoidance of the stifling effects of a strict morality. In short, a lightness of the human heart liberates us from boredom and orthodox restraints.

In *An Ethnic at Large* Jerre Mangione recalled that none of his American friends had the talent for celebrating life that his relatives possessed:

> Now I found myself admiring . . . some of the qualities I had once found intolerable. There were still vestiges of my childhood resentments, but on the whole I felt lucky to be one of them. It gave me a root feeling, a connection with a substantial past. . . . It was shocking to realize that more than once I had thought of cutting myself off from such a natural source of strength.[2]

Perhaps it was frustration that led another Italian American writer, Mario Puzo, to portray his fellow Italians in New York's

173

Hell's Kitchen as always angry. Puzo's *The Godfather* can be seen as an example of self-hatred. The book suggests a hidden anger about how criminality became almost too gainful a way of life for young ethnics who felt rejected.

As we have seen, Italian Americans, like other ethnics, respond to Alitalia's advertisements of return trips to the villages of their forefathers. They think they can thereby recapture their heritage now that the major indignities of the immigrant past are safely obscured. As tourists, they grow emotional when they hear "Santa Lucia" and "Arriverderci Roma." But it takes more than nostalgia to recapture a rejected heritage.

The native languages have all but vanished for the descendants of immigrants. French and Latin were taught in occasional American public schools although these were sometimes located in neighborhoods with concentrations of Italians, Slavs, and German Jews. To white ethnics it seemed odd that black history finally came into the school and college curriculum while the history of other minorities remained neglected.

In an age when they were no longer so defensive about their past, how could white ethnics recapture the past they had discarded? One way was to voice updated feelings of injury over past slights. In the 1960s anger burst out in ethnic enclaves from Massachusetts to California. In 1965 blacks at Watts tore apart one section of the city of Los Angeles; that same year Cesar Chavez's farm workers battled grape growers and vintners named Gallo and Giumarra. Competition for status among all ethnics in American life had become stiff. In New York City the massive Colombo demonstration of 1970 also reflected an unspent rage by persons of Italian background. At a time when former "negroes" were shouting "Black is beautiful," the Irish produced their first American president. Urban centers, historically dominated by members of the WASP establishment, were unexpectedly besieged by agitators seeking to dethrone an elite that had once subjugated Indians as well as blacks. It was as if injustices heaped upon all minorities were now projected onto the Anglos—a euphemistic term for America's non-immigrants.

Most Italian Americans, however, continue to shun politicization and they ambivalently withdraw from reform activities, even in the field of education. It is difficult, for example, to involve them in Parent-Teacher Associations. Such immigrant groups as still exist are plagued by disorganization and internal bickering. Italian Americans discernibly underuse their neighborhood civic facilities partly because they mistrust authority and partly because they believe in reliance upon the family rather than upon the group.

Among the "American Italians" are reactionaries as intransigent as any non-ethnic ultra-conservatives. These rallied in the late 1960s to the tinny nationalism of Vice-President Agnew and to the Nixon pronouncements about law and order in the streets. Hard hat Italians were also in the vanguard of the blue-collar revolt against black power, radical youth, and big-city crime. They had forgotten, or wanted to, the names of Al Capone, Johnny Torrio, and Frank Costello. To Agnew (the son of a Greek immigrant) and to another ethnic rejectors of their heritage who formed the pre-Watergate "silent majority," the social revolt of the sixties seemed almost to be an unfair plot. They were, one must remember, resentful lineal descendants of immigrants who had no one to look down upon—sons of uncertain heritage and of collective insecurity. Tears came to their eyes when they heard Julius La Rosa sing "God Bless America." Ethnic Americanism of the 200 percent variety turns around a distinctly non-Italian slogan: "My country right or wrong."

For immigrant parents who could not understand America's counterculture, there was no Joan Baez to sing their praises, no hippie rock groups like the Jefferson Airplane. The electronic sounds of frenzied, affluent Anglo youngsters bore no resemblance to the strumming of Neapolitan mandolins. How could such kids believe they were being treated unjustly?

So, during the confusing 1960s, aging immigrants were shocked by what they saw about them. The rules of the game had suddenly changed. Demonstrators who destroyed public property went unpunished. The conservative values that immigrants had been expected to uphold were no longer followed. The protest movement that arose in the sixties encouraged permissiveness and handouts to disaffected malcontents. Young persons sought welfare payments rather than accept inferior employment. Still others evaded the draft and even burned the flag. When blue-collar ethnics objected, they were called honkies, racist pigs, and hard hats.

Italians became the later minority vis-à-vis blacks and Mexican Americans. Older ethnics particularly resent perquisites that *they* had once sought being handed over to young blacks and Chicanos. Blue-collar immigrants who object to the new status of these minorities also seek to escape the taint of criminality. They see the Mafia increase in power as keeping qualified workers out of unions, flooding their communities with narcotics, and tarnishing the Italian image. Some third-generation members yearn for the clout needed to eliminate neighborhood crime, to renovate slum housing, to establish day-care centers, and to improve inner-city schools.

Has there been a history of bigotry among immigrants? Of course, and historians generally have overlooked it. We have but to recall the pecking order of intolerance among many nationalities, and even within nationalities and religious groups, as was the case with German and Polish Jews in New York City. As early as 1849, San Francisco's Italians participated in anti-Chinese activities during the California gold rush. About a hundred years later, in that same city, a popular North Beach Italian restaurant refused the black singer Paul Robeson and his party service at a time when he was thrilling audiences at the Geary Theater in Shakespeare's *Othello*.

Immigrant bigotry continues. We can see the defense of what Carl Jung might have called the collective group ego in 1965 at Syracuse, New York. An experimental park was planned there for the city's Italian district. The Italians, fearing the replacement of a neighborhood school by a mysterious new facility that might attract blacks, led a protest that discouraged the entire program of additional city parks.

Most European immigrants encountered less severe obstacles than those barriers erected against Indians, Asians, and blacks. In a few generations, non-English Europeans had joined the dominant culture. Although blue eyes, blond hair, and fair skin enhanced acceptability, when a black man looked at a white he did not ask whether the latter were an Italian or a German. He saw only a white man.

Paradoxically, the civil rights movement of the 1960s promoted ethnicity on the part of whites and blacks who did not know much about their own history. In that era, officials in the housing, job training, and education fields were hardly on the lookout for persons of European descent. The "new minorities" (blacks and Chicanos) became the darlings of Ivy League college admissions offices. Whereas New Haven, the home of Yale University, has a population of Italian origin estimated at 40 percent, only a small percentage of Yale's student body then bore Italian names.[3]

Although Italians joined in a national move toward the suburbs, they were more likely than were other nationalities to be found in the neighborhoods where parents lived. There some stayed, locked into a struggle with blacks. By 1976 an estimated 40 percent of New York's Italians had not left certain urban neighborhoods. Aged immigrants, reluctant to give up real estate in decaying ghettoes, remain stranded there, struggling to keep up with taxes on old houses. Pride and a sense of property keep these resentful elders from accepting welfare. Unable to fight their way out of the central city, they should be exerting more pressure to improve these slum areas, where they constitute a substantial part of the population. Instead, defiant of change, old-timers cling to rivalries with other minorities. When crowded out of their neighborhoods, Italo-Americans have voted heavily against militant candidates for public office. The term "black power" has inflamed inner-city competition—once carried on against the Irish. But today, the very survival of decaying urban neighborhoods is at stake. Neither whites nor blacks know how to handle the competition against each other. Each group is isolated.

It was a new experience to leave behind Bay Ridge and Mulberry Bend. In the former, "the Avenue" was not Fifth but Thirteenth. Long Island and Westchester were far away. But the Italians established new suburban outposts there and at Canarsie and Ozone Park. They flocked also into Nassau and Suffolk towns where property values seemed good. There were no Little Italys as on Sixty-fifth Street in Brooklyn. Few *paesans* waited to welcome their transplanted countrymen.

Although the outskirts of Chicago also seemed less familiar than its near west side, the Italians escaped from delinquency and crime by heading out into the countryside. That urban neighborhood, incidentally, had been the home of the gangster Al Capone, of the famed social worker Jane Addams, and of America's first saint, the immigrant Mother Cabrini. Another center of Italian activity that they left behind was Chicago's South Oakley Avenue, from which immigrants moved into Melrose Park in suburban Cook County. Unafraid, at Clinton, Indiana, the Italians would paint the fire hydrants red, white, and green.

The 1930s saw a similar exodus from the North Broadway area of Los Angeles (toward Glendale, Alhambra, and Pasadena) and out of North Beach in San Francisco (toward Burlingame, Oakland, and San Mateo). In the suburbs one could grow a garden without competing with concrete for space, as in the cities left behind. There tomatoes, grapes, and figs flourish, but the air does not smell of fried dough or roasted chestnuts. The foods of the past do linger in modified form. The descendants of immigrants still bake cannoli filled with whipped ricotta cheese, pistachio nuts, and cherries. They continue to relish gelati, sausages with finocchio, lemon ices, and lasagne. There are mozzarella factories in almost all the major suburbs.

Like their foods and their garden patches (usually protected by sturdy fences), the Italian Americans remain tied to a Mediterranean past. Not all of them have made it big, whether in the city or in the country. But they have perdured, even without fully understanding their roots.

XII

A NEW IDENTITY
OR ASSIMILATION?

WITHOUT A GRASP of our inner motives, we all have to rely upon outer images, as when one looks in a mirror. By viewing a reflection of ourselves we cannot see either our nobility of character or our self-hatred. The image remains an exterior one. Buried underneath are pervasive impulses carried along, unperceived, for generations. These inner realities are attached, as fragments, to the very core of human existence: to the language, literature, and history of us all—whatever our origins.

As we have seen, the complexities of immigrant life were far more hidden than apparent. I believe that a part of the human mind, which psychoanalysts have identified as the ego, was placed under maximal pressure as confused former peasants sought to mediate between the extremes of the American environment. To preserve self-esteem, they employed a number of defense maneuvers described in preceding chapters.

Previous historians have never really looked at how such immigrants were searching abroad for an identity within themselves. Of course, they also sought economic opportunities not available

179

in their homeland. Theirs was a worrisome quest for wholeness, a borrowing of strength from elsewhere that became instead a major disruption in the life pattern. In seeking a new identity, they experienced strong demands, which led to emotional stresses almost too powerful to withstand. The stories of Signora Corsi and Signora Barzini revealed the problems that immigrant women encountered.

In their search for selfhood the immigrants assumed no single identity. Each worked out an accommodation in unique ways, realigning the personality to fit new realities. The idea that we historians can homogenize the ethnics into one national experience has become ridiculous.

In Italy itself the problem of assimilation is still alive. Immigrants who have migrated toward its northern cities in large numbers remain psychologically defensive, as did their relatives who went to New York or Boston. Many among them absolutely refuse to learn "standard Italian," continuing to speak only in the dialects of their provincial southern towns. This obstinacy has, in turn, created hostility among the Milanese, Torinese, and other northerners who act as unwilling hosts for the poor and often illiterate invaders from south of Rome.

For the north Italians, Apulia or Campania still remain a *terra incognita*, a disagreeable amalgam of dirt, noise, and bad food. We should remember that it was from Italy's south that most of her immigrants came. As the Renaissance hardly spread south of Rome (Naples did bask briefly in its penumbra), it was ripe for the reactionary rule of Bourbon Spain and France. With reforms virtually unknown in the *Regno* (as the area was called), it remains a discredited region even in the eyes of Italians themselves.

In recent years thousands of immigrants, experiencing economic and social difficulties at home, have emigrated anew. Young and middle-aged persons without jobs have badgered American relatives to sponsor their visa applications. From the mid-1950s immigration of western Europeans has been on the largest scale since the great waves of migration lasting from 1880 to 1924. Political unrest in Italy continues, as does terrorism on the streets, a new phenomenon that alarms that country's citizenry even more than the sluggish bureaucracy, which seems inevitable but less harmful. Inadequate political leadership, not only in Italy, has brought vast numbers of immigrants here recently from Asia, Latin America, the Middle East, and Africa.

Saul Bellow, referring to the blacks and Puerto Ricans who have flooded into New York City, declared that today's immigrants have spoiled the slums. He meant that we have lost the color and verve which once existed in the Jewish and Italian ghettoes.

The migrants who came earlier in this century, as well as in the late 1800s, had a rougher time maintaining their center. The successful defense of selfhood once required tempering character armor and bolstering self-esteem. We have seen how this effort was a psychological one, at times relying on denial and projection, for example, in the defense of the ego. This process, properly understood, should help us to see why some immigrants remained aloof, violent, even eccentric. One thinks of Old Jules, Mari Sandoz's feisty father, or of Simon Rodia singing in his Watts Towers, or of Baldasare Forestiere, digging his tunnels.

Historians who have followed in the footsteps of Oscar Handlin continue to examine the immigrant record almost exclusively in urban settings and along economic lines, characterizing the foreigner's past as primarily "a history of alienation and of its consequences." According to this archaic interpretation, the bulk of America's immigrants were of peasant origin, remaining downtrodden, backward-looking, ghettoed, and changeless— enslaved by a pessimism characteristic of eastern Europe. Yet, millions of immigrants were never inside a steel mill or a really big factory. Not all pounded city pavements in search of jobs. Some were brutalized by industrial jobs and anomie. Others were not.

In New York City, according to Nathan Glazer and Daniel P. Moynihan's *Beyond the Melting Pot* (1963), ethnic groups maintained a distinct, if changing, identity from generation to generation. Each remained different from the other in spiritual and cultural values. In addition to their material growth, so well documented in Thomas Kessner's *The Golden Door* (1977), their emotional adjustment also varied. Newcomers sought a different sense of self. The majority of them had only superficially preferred trading their original selfhood for the Horatio Alger image of success. To be more American than the Americans became a major immigrant goal. One thinks of George Mardikian, founder of San Francisco's Omar Khayyam restaurant. He filled the front windows of his establishment with copies of a book he had written, *The Song of America*, in praise of everything in the New World.

John W. Briggs has suggested that the typical immigrant was a self-conscious agent of his own destiny, not a mere victim of fate or a tabula rasa. We cannot ignore the role of choice, as opposed to determinism, in human actions, immigrant or otherwise. Although his book *An Italian Passage* has been harshly (and unfairly) reviewed, it courageously maintains that south Italians came to America with peculiar values and experiences that allowed at least some of them to move upward quite rapidly. Briggs portrayed immigration as itself a selective process that recruited the more resourceful. These exhibited thrift, mobility, and prudence. He viewed many of them as possessed of a bourgeois (rather than a peasant) outlook. In some cases their ideals actually coincided, perhaps superficially, with those "expectations prevalent in the United States."[1]

My addition to this refreshing approach would be that activity on the surface of immigrant life was not what occurred underneath. For example, conflict with other laborers was not alleviated by the reduction of competition for jobs after America's great depression of the 1930s. The unionization of all workers, including ethnics, did create a better standard of living. During the era of President Franklin Delano Roosevelt, Americans also seemed to be carrying out a revolt against the provincialism of their own villages. As if to accompany the mobility of the automobile, the immigrant became more acceptable to his neighbors. The seamy mentality of small-town America was gradually replaced by a greater cosmopolitanism, especially in our larger cities. It became increasingly difficult for the Anglo-Saxon bigotry of the Ku Klux Klan to masquerade as moral idealism.

The role of young Italo-Americans in World War II further softened prejudice. The G.I. sons of immigrants brought them a status never before experienced. One immigrant, asked during the war whether he felt like an Italian or an American, replied: "I consider myself a new American." Some continued to be stuck with a kind of "rebel reaction," a private sensibility that was easily bruised. These refused to be typed as members of any one culture. Irvin Child also identified Italians who responded apathetically to their new status, who ashamedly turned away from any mention of their background. Finally, a minority experienced limited pride in their heritage. This phenomenon Child called the "in-group reaction."

A few third-generation ethnics, like cinematographer Philip di Franco, seem to be fascinated by the search for a hidden identity:

> All my life I have been intrigued with a feeling or an impulse to know my ancestral *roots*, to know where and what I came from, to understand what makes me *me*. There is within my being an all-powerful longing to look back at my Italian (Sicilian) heritage to figure out what makes me *different* from others.
>
> This overwhelming desire to go back has a nostalgic or romantic quality to it. It is enshrouded in a veil of mystery, a mystery which, if solved, will somehow set me straight and explain what makes me tick. Yes, if I can understand my roots, I will certainly know myself better.
>
> This feeling was at its strongest point when I was going through the "identity crisis" of the late teens and early 'twenties. At this time I really felt "out of whack" with my world.

Three further interviews help us to understand how several generations of immigrants are actually working out their problems today:

> *First Generation:* I don't know to express myself. A sixteen year old kid . . . I didn't have no trade, I didn't have no money, only a little education. . . . I can't express you how I was feeling, scared . . . no money, a few dollars I think I had . . . I don't know where to go . . . go to America, what America, what is America . . . where is America? . . . You know where I was sleeping? I had no bed. There was a pile of rope. . . . I was sleeping inside the rope.
>
> *Second Generation:* I'm a second generation Italian. My name is Jodi Desmond, but I was born Josephina Dessimone and oh how I hated

that. For the first fourteen years of my life I was Josephina Dessimone and rebelling every moment.

I was ashamed of my parents, they spoke with a broken accent and I am ashamed of being ashamed now, but I wasn't then. I just ignored them.

Third Generation: Just being part of an ethnic group is really great because you belong to something, and you can't always belong to something if you're just plain old American.

Being a melting pot doesn't mean all the cultures have to combine and lose our identity. It means that all cultures can come together . . . maintain our identity, but still be proud we're American.[2]

In writing such a book as this, the line of least resistance would be to perpetuate the old-style immigration history. Based upon names, dates, election statistics, and other hard "facts," that type of history brushes over the softer data, the internal feelings of individuals and groups. Furthermore, as William Langer has stated, historians tend to be frozen in the molds of the past. Many of them (especially immigration specialists) do not really welcome tentative new findings. They seek consensus, dealing in stereotypes.

It would, thus, be much more comforting to respond in the usual paunchy and cheery way to the clichés that portray the Italians as either romantic, happy, carefree, lovable, and gluttonous, or greasy, dark-skinned, lazy, and insensitive. But, as Isaiah Berlin reminds us (in his book *Vico and Herder*): "Understanding other men's motives or acts, however imperfect or corrigible, is a state of mind or activity in principle different from learning about . . . the external world."

Generally the Italian Americans have not developed the ability to criticize the record of their own attainments below the surface of life. An exception is Jerry Della Femina's *An Italian Grows in Brooklyn* (1979). Despite its humorous passages, this book is a grim account of a culture characterized by intense family pressures, repressed violence, and stunted ambitions. He examined factors similar to those which I have portrayed, including how the Italian family failed its young people in this country. Della Femina noted that at Gravesend, Brooklyn, where he grew up, Italian American life crushed the emotions of its young people and relegated some of them to lives of drudgery, emptiness, alcoholism, and unlawful activity. He identified America's ethnic villages as isolated from the larger society, which was looked upon as evil and alien. The downgrading of education stemmed, he argued, from insistence upon learning a trade rather than the encouragement of higher attainments.

Della Femina finds it almost tragic that the Italians have not assimilated themselves happily, or even sadly, into the American scene: "We aren't a minority; there are more people of Italian extraction living in this country than there are blacks, and in that regard we are a majority." Yet, he continues: "The Italian isolation is still there and it goes to prove that the potential exists for the Italians to remain the only group that has come to this country and *never* assimilated. . . ."[3] In short, according to Della Femina, integration into the general culture by this minority has only been superficial, at least in terms of the Brooklyn community from whence he came. Instead of being uprooted, "in our neighborhood we never felt we left the old country," he writes. The result? A failure to benefit fully from either culture, "a terrible price paid," according to Della Femina.

Today it takes much less courage for the descendants of immigrants to claim an inheritance that their grandfathers either denied or repressed. Likewise, new patterns of historical interpretation have a chance to supersede old ones. We may at last write histories of minorities that do more than repeat clichés about racial melting pots or leave unexplained desolation and disillusionment. While today's ethnic history breathes less of the spirit of apology or of the nativist bigotry of the past, writings about the immigrants also reflect little of the humor that they themselves used to quiet anxieties. The ethnic joke, once a safety valve that caricatured peculiar differences among Italians, Jews, and Irishmen, is now as taboo as reference to *Amos and Andy*, a radio program that insulted black America. Once the ability to laugh at one's national group fitted nicely with the middle-class cliché that it was not a person's appearance but his quality that determined success.

On the surface the Italians have a reputation for affability, good humor, and contentment. I believe, however, following long stays in Italy, that the Italian people are not in close touch with their unconscious feelings. Indeed, they frequently act out their deepest anxieties and rages. Public frustration, open and defiant, reaches its peak in the cities, where poverty and crowding have combined to create the effect of an iron cage, somehow partially escaped by the Swiss, the Germans, and the English. In Italy even a traffic jam can stir up violent emotions. A slight personal affront may lead to a serious altercation.

In their new land, Italians repressed these tensions. Children were told that it was one's daily work that really counted. In Zangwill's melting pot, American materialism cooled family warmth. The banalities of suburban affluence proved to be no palliative for emotional fragmentation. Economic attainments were deceptive. Behind the facade of outward success there remained immaturity. The achievement of maturity is painful, even for persons reared under seemingly optimal conditions.

I have described how, by the 1960s, a few young ethnics openly voiced resentment over their image. Some of these nursed a hatred similar to that of Frank Costello over his parents' timidity. While more orthodox first- and second-generation members were embarrassed by activism, militants remained dissatisfied. Of them, Andrew Greeley wrote: "The self-critics cannot live with their ethnic background, and they cannot live without it."[4] Theirs was a psychological balancing act between past injury and future hope.

For the new ethnic generations one proverb seems peculiarly apt: "That which the parents wish to forget children seek to remember." The "born-again" descendants of immigrants no longer desire to keep their roots hidden in a closet. They communicate a wish that resembles an ancestral collective memory, according to Jung: to get in touch with a distant homeland they have never seen.

In 1911 Arthur Schnitzler, a contemporary of Freud's, wrote *The Undiscovered Country (Das Weite Land)*, a play that remains applicable to America's immigration story. As double entendre,

the "undiscovered country" is both a new land *and* that unruly
territory between id (drives) and superego (conscience). As immigrants reconnoitered this domain, in an effort to find their particular center, they were, of course, mostly unfamiliar with
Hamlet's "To be or not to be" speech, in which Shakespeare has
him say:

> *The undiscovered country from whose bourn*
> *No traveler returns, puzzles the will*
> *And makes us rather bear those ills we have,*
> *Than fly to others that we know not of.*

Typical of both Shakespeare and Freud, they plumbed the depths
of the human heart, and their words have an odd suitability to the
immigrant experience.

By the third generation, there was a scrambling for old country roots among all of America's immigrant nationalities. In most
cases, however, this quest was superficial. Interest in the
homeland remained sometimes metaphorical and based upon
repressed guilt. The subtle offense to be covered over was
disloyalty to one's origins. Eric Hoffer (himself the son of foreign-
born parents) has written about how "our nation of immigrants
attained its amazing homogeneity" Those who came to make
money, he pointed out,

> were more quickly and thoroughly Americanized than those who came
> to realize some lofty ideal. The former felt an immediate kinship with
> the millions absorbed in the same pursuit. It was as if they were joining
> a brotherhood. They recognized early that in order to succeed they had
> to blend with their fellow men, do as others do, learn the lingo and play
> the game.

It is a paradox that only in the 1970s did America discover the
word "ethnicity." By then most persons of Italian background
were well on the way to being alchemized and blended into the
dominant society. Yet, as blacks and Chicanos reminded us, roots
were suddenly something to be treasured as a primary source of
sustenance and means of survival. America's immigrants of Italian
background, estimated at over twenty million persons,[5] have lost
much of their identification with the past. Rushing toward valida-

tion as Americans, the invisible ethnics, as we may call them, have mostly flocked out of the bleak stone cities and cement jungles where their ancestors settled seventy-five years earlier. True, some of the aged, infirm, and diehards among them have remained behind. But, for the majority, gone now are the vegetable carts of Bleecker Street. The lower east side of Manhattan and Mulberry Bend are pale replicas of their vibrant past. There the women no longer shop in black dresses for *baccalà* and *cioppino*. The strains of Irving Berlin's first song, "Mari from Sunny Italy" (1907), now seem innocently remote, lost in memory.

The *New York Times* (December 26, 1976) has maintained that only a "sense of discrimination by news organizations and public institutions" will bring Italian Americans together. In New York alone they now number 1.7 million persons, one of the city's largest ethnic groups. Their so-called new ethnicity seems to mean voting for politicians who pay attention to their aspirations.

D. H. Lawrence once wrote that "the whistlers go to America," by which he meant the optimists. Whether downtrodden, tempest tossed, or yearning to be free, they responded to unfriendliness by adapting. We have repeatedly seen how they used repression to keep the success system going. Outwardly, immigrants and their progeny did not *seem* to be perennial refugees in the promised land. Though some remained unsuccessful, it was unpopular to speak of these within the ethnic enclaves except as misfits.

Philip Slater's *The Pursuit of Loneliness: American Culture at the Breaking Point* (1970) was one of the few books to suggest that we have overdone the "excellence" of the immigrant. He, too, saw some of them as having been disturbed and damaged persons. But, he argued, they fortunately fitted the American pattern of "escaping, evading, and avoiding." In America, men believed that they were masters of their environment. Whatever their interior disabilities or outer accents, this remained the place of hope that all had heard about across the sea. Here they could (in theory) go as far as their talents would take them. If discrimination occurred, they could eventually wear it down. Although life had its grubby and dull side, hard work could create in this New World the utopia all deserved. There was no need to melt in the melting pot. One could climb out of it, if only to enter the confusing fires of American life.

Biologists tell us that the fusion of two phenomena may result in the creation of a third element or force. This concept was suggested by remarks made at a 1979 conference held at Harvard University that dealt with the Italian Americans. Two professors present, one from the west coast, the other from the east, made statements that summed up tertiary feelings not ordinarily heard. Alexander De Conde told the conference: "We are not waiting to join any establishment. We *are* the establishment." Robert Viscusi voiced yet another perception: "We want to become what we are."

Such Italian Americans no longer quite needed their Italian roots. They seemed to have replaced them with American ones. There has occurred, in some instances, a transfusion of culture, as well as the original fusion. Though one can never fully put into parentheses the country in which one's family originated, Jerre Mangione has expressed what happened to him: "I had learned how to . . . cope with the ever-recurring sensation of being a foreigner in my native land."[6]

No one wishes to accept the term "outlander," a denial that all men are brothers. Most immigrants of all nationalities determined to be insiders, not outsiders. Having sought assimilation, they have, therefore, had little use for recording their history as that of an underdog minority. Indeed, those books about their record in America are mostly bought and read by others. For the Italians, denial of the past has become a pronounced part of their search for a believable fantasy that they have overcome all obstacles, that the road to adaptation had been the right one to take, that the enemies of this assimilative route are clearly wrong.

Has this quest for "success" resulted in a history of immigration that is in part a fairy-tale or even an historically psychological lie? Were immigrants upraised, uprooted, defeated,

189

or assimilated? Rather than Handlin's "uprooting," perhaps a withering of their past lives occurred. As with a plant that needs daily watering, the temporary shock of replanting led to an accomodation that was not total. The Italians have not been entirely assimilated. They have, however, been changed by the American experience. It is natural that they should seek to obscure their failures, sufferings, and the reversals of life itself. Oscar Wilde once said that our lives were not really the life which we secretly live.

We began our story with Israel Zangwill's optimism. He had dedicated his play to Theodore Roosevelt, who was enthusiastic about America as a melting pot. Zangwill's protagonist in that play hailed the new land as "God's crucible, the great Melting Pot where all the races of Europe are melting and re-forming." Zangwill spoke for his generation: "The real American has not yet arrived. He is only in the crucible. . . . He will be the fusion of all races, the coming superman."

Today, few would wish to defend the melting pot. This concept has angered militants and non-militants alike. That blackened kettle has become a chunk of perverted psychological imagery. The notion that we would all become intregrated into one bland nationality was bound to give way to the opposite idea, "ethnic pluralism." Zangwill's metaphor may have appealed to Theodore Roosevelt, but it masked too many unconscious gradations between people. As they continue to climb out of that mythical cauldron, the Italians and other nationalities may come to feel that in their emotional search for selfhood the whole immigration process need not have occurred in the way it did. The troubles of the past, however, are becoming merged with the struggles of the present and the hopes of the future. When a new identity is finally attained, the distress of being neither European nor American should be over.

Notes

I A Vision of the New Land

1. Valentine Rossilli Winsey, "The Southern Immigrant Family in the United States," in *The United States and Italy: The First Two Hundred Years*, ed. Humbert S. Nelli (New York, 1977), 202.
2. Angelo Pellegrini, *Immigrant's Return* (New York, 1951), 63.
3. Quoted in Renzo De Felice, "L'emigrazione degli emigranti nell' ultimo secolo," Terzo programa (ERI, no. 3, 1964), 176.
4. Lino Covi in *"The Urban Experience of Italian-Americans"* (remarks made at Queen's College, Flushing, N.Y. 1975), 137.

II Dispersal

1. Lucas Longo, *The Family on Vendetta Street* (New York, 1968), 55.

III Seeking Shelter

1. Canzoneri, *A Highly Ramified Tree* (New York, 1976), 1.
2. Di Donato, *Three Circles of Light* (New York, 1960), 58.
3. "Human Mole's Maze," *Los Angeles Times*, September 12, 1975.

191

4. *Ibid.*

5. Mario Cuomo in *"The Urban Experience of Italian-Americans"* (remarks made at Queen's College, Flushing, N.Y., 1975), 6.

IV Birds of Passage

1. Edward Corsi, *In the Shadow of Liberty* (New York, 1935), 23, 27.

2. Luigi Barzini, *O America, When You and I Were Young* (New York, 1977), 58; see also 171, 324.

3. Antonia Pola, *Who Can Buy the Stars?* (New York, 1957), 209.

4. Arcangelo D'Amore, M.D., in "The Urban Experience of Italian-Americans" (remarks made at Queen's College, Flushing, N.Y., 1975, 145.

5. Michael A. Musmanno, *The Story of the Italians in America* (New York, 1926), 158.

6. Thornton Wilder, *The Cabala* (New York, 1926), 17.

7. Mangione, *An Ethnic at Large* (New York, 1978), 176, 180.

8. Mangione, 186–187.

9. Joseph Tusiani, *Envoy from Heaven* (New York, 1965), 174–202.

10. Anthony Mancini, "Ethnic Travel: When You Find Your Roots You Eat Them," *New York Times*, August 1, 1971.

V The Roots of Discrimination

1. Suggestive is Marvin Opler and Jerome L. Singer, "Ethnic Differences in Behavior and Psychopathology, Italian and Irish, *International Journal of Social Psychiatry* II (1956), 11–23.

VI A Touch of the Gutter: La Mafia and Crime

1. In this same year the death penalty was abolished in Italy, not to be reestablished until Fascist times in 1930. Since 1948 the death penalty has been practically nonexistent there. Letter from Judge Guglielmo Sciarelli to the author, September 9, 1979.

2. Professor Monte B. McLaws of Wayne State College, Wayne, Nebraska, has discovered that Capone had an older brother

named James, who used the alias Richard Joseph ("Two-Gun") Hart. He became a town marshal in Nevada, commander of an American Legion post, state deputy sheriff, a deputy special federal officer, and a bodyguard to President Calvin Coolidge!

3. See Georg Groddeck, *The Meaning of Illness* (New York, 1977), 42.

4. John Goodwin, *Murder U.S.A.: The Ways We Kill Each Other* (New York, 1979), treats the mythology of violence.

5. Pietro di Donato, *Three Circles of Light* (New York, 1960), 112.

6. Leonard Katz, *Uncle Frank: The Biography of Frank Costello,* (New York, 1973) 68.

7. Katz, 39, 153–154.

8. Rodney Campbell, *The Luciano Project* (New York, 1977), 72.

9. Humbert Nelli, *The Business of Crime: Italians and Syndicate Crime in the United States* (New York, 1976), 106 ff.

10. Campbell, 79.

11. *Vinnie Teresa's Mafia,* 111.

VII   La Famiglia: Defending the Old Ways

1. Letter to the author, July 4, 1978. Rita Poleri is the pseudonym of an Italian American psychiatric social worker. For other views of women see *The Italian Immigrant Woman in North America,* ed. Betty Boyd Caroli, Robert F. Harney, and Lydio F. Tomasi (Toronto, 1978).

2. Di Donato, 24.

3. Di Donato, 32–33.

4. Jerre Mangione, *An Ethnic at Large* (New York, 1978), 13, 132.

5. John Fante, *The Brotherhood of the Grape* (New York, 1977), 5.

6. John Fante, "The Odyssey of a Wop", *American Mercury* 30 (1970), 90.

7. Fante, "The Odyssey of a Wop," 92.

8. Leonard Covello, *The Heart of the Teacher* (Totowa, N.J., 1970), 28.

9. Mangione, *An Ethnic at Large,* 369.

10. Jo Pagano, *Golden Wedding* (New York, 1943), 86.

VIII La Famiglia: Reaching Out

1. Jo Pagano, *The Paesanos* (Boston, 1940), 18–19.
2. Jo Pagano, *Golden Wedding* (New York, 1943), 81.
3. *Ibid.*, 251.
4. See John Dos Passos, "Adagio Dancer," in *USA* (New York, 1937), 189–194.
5. Michael Katz, *The Irony of Early School Reform* (Cambridge, 1968), 215.
6. Jerre Mangione, *An Ethnic at Large* (New York, 1978), 14.
7. Letter to the author, July 11, 1979.

IX Politics

1. Fiorello La Guardia, *The Making of an Insurgent* (Philadelphia, 1948), 27–28.
2. Quoted in Arthur Mann, *La Guardia: A Fighter against His Times, 1882–1933* (Philadelphia, 1959), 187.
3. Quoted in Irving M. Levine and Judith Herman, "The Life of White Ethnics," *Dissent*, 0 (Winter 1972), 3.

X The Amenities

1. Vincent Teresa, *Vinnie Teresa's Mafia* (New York, 1975), 89.
2. John Fante, "The Odyssey of a Wop," *American Mercury*, 30 (September 1933), 89.
3. Italian American fiction is described in Olga Peragallo, ed., *Italian American Authors* (New York, 1949) and in Rose Basile Green, *The Italian American Novel* (New York, 1973).
4. Consult Jerre Mangione, "American Artists of Italian Origins," in *The United States and Italy: The First Two Hundred Years*, ed. Hubert S. Nelli (New York, 1977), 213.
5. Jo Pagano, *Golden Wedding* (New York, 1943), 84.

XI Making It Big and Small

1. Russ Colombo, who originated the quiet, crooning style of singing that Bing Crosby emulated, is said to have been in the same room with Crosby on the night when Colombo died of a gunshot wound that was called accidental.
2. Mangione, 175.

3. Was it, however, a coincidence that in 1978 A. Bartlett Giamatti became Yale's nineteenth president? Born in Boston of an Italian American father, Giamatti is a mixture of New England WASP and idealized Italianism.

XII A New Identity or Assimilation?

1. John W. Briggs, *An Italian Passage: Immigrants to Three American Cities, 1890–1930* (New Haven, 1978), 36.
2. *Lost and Found: The Search for Our Ethnic Heritage*, a film produced by Roberts Film Co., in cooperation with the National Conference of Christians and Jews, New Jersey Region, 1978. The Di Franco commentary appeared in the house magazine of the Patrons of Italian Culture, Los Angeles, 1970.
3. Jerry Della Femina and Charles Sopkin, *An Italian Grows in Brooklyn* (Boston, 1977), 197, 202.
4. Andrew Greeley, *Why Can't They Be Like Us?* (New York, 1969), 35.
5. Some five million are members of the first generation; another five million are in the second; and ten million are third- and fourth-generation citizens. Altogether they form about 12 percent of America's population.
6. Jerre Mangione, *An Ethnic at Large*, 367.

ESSAY ON SOURCES

THOSE WHO HAVE WRITTEN about Italian Americans know how remiss this group has been about acknowledging its history. For decades these particular immigrants hardly seemed to want to fill the gaps in their knowledge of themselves. Lacking a unified outlook, this minority still sponsors no regularly published historical journal. In contrast, the *American Jewish Historical Quarterly* dates from 1892 and the *American Scandinavian Historical Review* from 1912. Any psychohistorian of the Italian Americans must take notice of this lack of self-pride. Not until 1974 was the journal *Italian Americana* founded. We are almost led to wonder whether numerous Italo-Americans are not embarrassed to have their story told.

Yet, the time has passed when one could say that there are no adequate histories of the Italians in America. Building upon the earlier work of Schiavo and Prezzolini, the books of Iorizzo and Mondello, De Conde, Rolle, Gambino, and Amfitheatrof have filled this gap.

Other valuable books on the Italian immigrant are out of print. Eliot Lord and others, *The Italian in America* (New York,

1905), is such an early study; Robert F. Foerster, *The Italian Emigration of Our Times* (Cambridge, 1919), is devoted only partly to United States immigration and to its Italian background; Emilio Goggio, *Italians in American History* (New York, 1930), is a useful pamphlet that is also generally unavailable. Luciano Iorizzo and Salvatore Mondello, *The Italian Americans* (New York, 1971), is a more recent interpretation; Michael A. Musmanno, *The Story of the Italians in America* (New York, 1965), is a glorified account of success in this country; Lawrence Pisani, *The Italian in America: A Social Study and History* (New York, 1957), is a sociological interpretation. Along similar lines is Joseph Lopreato, *Italian Americans* (New York, 1970).

Andrew F. Rolle, *The Immigrant Upraised: Italian Adventurers and Colonists in an Expanding America* (Norman, 1968), interprets assimilation, particularly in the American West. For those who read Italian, another version has been published in Italy entitled *Gli emigrati vittoriosi* (Milan, 1972). See also Rolle's *The American Italians: Their History and Culture* (Belmont, 1972). Recent histories are Alexander De Conde, *Half Bitter, Half Sweet* (New York, 1971), and Eric Amfitheatrof, *The Children of Columbus: An Informal History of the Italians in the New World* (New York, 1973).

Luigi Barzini, *The Italians* (New York, 1964), helps readers to understand the Italian character. Pascal d'Angelo's *Pascal d'Angelo: Son of Italy* (New York, 1924), an autobiography, reveals the feelings of a newcomer to America. A Federal Writers' Project volume entitled, *The Italian of New York* (New York, 1938), written before World War II, is also an excellent source.

Giovanni Schiavo's two volumes, *Four Centuries of Italian American History* (New York, 1952), and *Italians in America before the Civil War* (New York, 1934), enumerate the contributions of specific Italians although they do not discuss social or adjustment problems. Silvano Tomasi and Madeline H. Engel edited *The Italian Experience in the United States* (New York, 1970), an attempt to understand the Italo-Americans in light of modern ethnic studies; its ten articles by various authors discuss the impact of Italian and American society on individuals, institutions, and return migration. Rudolf Glanz, *Italian and Jew* (New York, 1970), is a comparison of Jewish and Italian immigrants in their quest for acculturation. Giuseppe Prezzolini, *I Trapiantati* (Milan, 1965), remains untranslated; this excellent work is virtually unknown in this country.

Two bibliographies are Francesco Cordasco and Salvatore La Gumina, *Italians in the United States: A Bibliography of Reports, Texts, Critical Studies, and Related Materials* (New York, 1972), and Joseph Velikonja, *Italians in the United States* (Carbondale, 1963).

Useful are J. H. Mariano, *The Italian Contribution to American Democracy* (Boston, 1921), and Richard C. Garlick, *Italy and the Italians in Washington's Time* (New York, 1933); consult also Garlick's *Philip Mazzei: Friend of Jefferson* (New York, 1942). Howard Marraro has also written on Mazzei's generation in "Italo-Americans in Pennsylvania in the Eighteenth Century," *Pennsylvania History*, 7 (July 1940), 159–166. On that early period also see Goggio's *Italians in American History* and Bruno Roselli, *Vigo: A Forgotten Builder of the American Republic* (Boston, 1933).

For the period of mass immigration see Edward Corsi, *In the Shadow of Liberty* (New York, 1935); Herbert J. Gans, *The Urban Villagers: Group and Class in the Life of Italian-Americans* (New York, 1962); Nathan Glazer and Daniel P. Moynihan, *Beyond the Melting Pot: The Negroes, Puerto Ricans, Jews, Italians, and Irish of New York City* (Cambridge, 1963); Antonio Stella, *Some Aspects of Italian Immigration to the United States* (New York, 1924; reprinted in San Francisco, 1970); William Foote Whyte, *Street Corner Society: The Social Structure of an Italian Slum*, revised edition (Chicago, 1943); and Phyllis H. Williams, *South Italian Folkways in Europe and America: A Handbook for Social Workers, Visiting Nurses, School Teachers*, revised edition (New York, 1938; reprinted in New York, 1969). Previously mentioned volumes are the Federal Writers' Project, *The Italians of New York*; Iorizzo and Mondello, *The Italian Americans*; Nelli,

Italians in Chicago; Pisani, *The Italian in America;* Schiavo, *Four Centuries;* and Tomasi and Engel, *The Italian Experience.*

Articles dealing with Italians and the urban environment are Charlotte Adams, "Italian Life in New York," *Harper's,* 62 (April 1881), 676–684; John Foster Carr, "The Coming of the Italian," *Outlook,* 82 (February 29, 1906), 419–431; Edward Corsi, "Our Italian Fellow-Americans," *American Mercury,* 55 (August 1942), 197–205; William E. Davenport, "The Italian Immigrant in America," *Outlook,* 73 (January, 1903), 27–37; Norman Di Giovanni, "Tenements and Cadillacs," *Nation,* 1877 (December 13, 1958), 443–445; Blake McKelvey, "The Italians of Rochester: An Historical Review," *Rochester History,* 22 (October 1960), 1–23; "Mulberry Bend from 1897 to 1958, Pictorial Story," *Saturday Evening Post,* 231 (August 2, 1958), 34–35; Humbert S. Nelli, "Italians and Crime in Chicago: The Formative Years, 1890–1920," *American Journal of Sociology,* 124 (January 1969), 373–391; J. H. Senner, "Immigration from Italy," *North American Review,* 162 (May 1896), 649–657; Gino Speranza, "Solving the Immigration Problem." *Outlook,* 76 (April 16, 1904); and Walter E. Weyl, "The Call of America," *Outlook,* 94 (April 23, 1910), 883–890, and "The Italian Who Lived on Twenty-six Cents a Day," *Outlook,* 93 (December 25, 1909), 966–975.

For an understanding of Italian political behavior consult Gordon J. Di Renzo, *Personalilty, Power, and Politics* (Notre Dame, 1967), and Giorgio Galli and Alfonso Prandi, *Patterns of Political Participation in Italy* (New Haven, 1970).

The ethnic political situation in Chicago at the turn of the century is described in Humbert S. Nelli, "John Powers and the Italians: Politics in a Chicago Ward, 1896–1921," *Journal of American History,* 57 (June 1970), 67–84. On New York's Mayor La Guardia see Arthur Mann, *La Guardia: A Fighter against His Times, 1882–1933* (Philadelphia, 1959), and Fiorello H. La Guardia, *The Making of an Insurgent: An Autobiography, 1882–1919* (Philadelphia, 1948). For Marcantonio see Salvatore J. La Gumina, *Vito Marcantonio: The People's Politician* (Dubuque, 1969), and Alan L. Schaffer, *Vito Marcantonio: Radical in Con-*

gress (Syracuse, 1966). An early article on Pastore is Samuel Lubell, "Rhode Island's Little Firecracker," *Saturday Evening Post*, 222 (November 12, 1949). Regarding Carmine De Sapio see Warren Moscow, *The Last of the Big Time Bosses: The Life and Times of Carmine De Sapio* (New York, 1971). Recent scholarship about a key election is Salvatore J. La Gumina's "Ethnic Groups in the New York Elections of 1970," *New York History*, 53 (January 1972), 55–71. Regarding recent politicization see Michael Novak, "White Ethnics," *Harper's*, 243 (September 1971), 44–50, and *Rise of the Unmeltable Ethnics* (New York, 1971), an impressionistic series of essays; see also Mark R. Levy and Michael S. Kramer, *The Ethnic Factor: How America's Minorities Decide Elections* (New York, 1973).

Information about the banker Amadeo Giannini is in the already cited books of Marinacci and Rolle, as well as in Marquis James and Bessie R. James, *Biography of a Bank: The Story of Bank of America* (New York, 1954). See also Dwight L. Clarke, "The Gianninis: Men of the Renaissance," *California Historical Society Quarterly*, 49 (September 1970), 251–269, and (December 1970), 337–351. On the scientist Enrico Fermi see Marinacci, as well as Laura Fermi, *Illustrious Immigrants: The Intellectual Migration from Europe, 1930–1941* (Chicago, 1968).

Adjustment to life in America is treated in Pisani, *The Italian in America*; Iorizzo and Mondello, *The Italian Americans*; Rolle, *The Immigrant Upraised*; Tomasi and Engel, *The Italian Experience*; Irvin L. Child, *Italian or American? The Second Generation in Conflict* (New Haven, 1943); Leonard Covello, *The Social Background of the Italo-American School Child* (Leiden, 1967); and E. P. Hutchinson, *Immigrants and Their Children, 1850–1950* (New York, 1936). Consult also Salvatore J. La Gumina, editor "Ethnicity in American Political Life: The Italian American Experience," in Proceedings of the First Annual Conference of the American Italian Historical Association, October 26, 1968; Antonio Mangano, *Sons of Italy: A Social and Religious Study of the Italians in America* (New York, 1917); and Enrico C. Sartorio, *Social and Religious Life of Italians in America* (Boston, 1918).

A frank autobiography tells of an Italian growing up in a Brooklyn ghetto: Joseph N. Sorrentino's *Up from Never* (New York, 1971). A view of the Italians in Buffalo, New York, is in Virginia Yans McLaughlin, "Patterns of Work and Family Organization," *Journal of Interdisciplinary History*, 2 (Autumn 1971), 299–314. Two valuable essays concerning Pennsylvania's Italians appear in John E. Bodnar, editor, *The Ethnic Experience in Pennsylvania*: Clement L. Valletta, "The Settlement of Roseto: World View and Promise," and Richard N. Juliani, "The Origin and Development of the Italian Community in Pennsylvania."

A volume that comes near to the thesis of this book but treats alienation sociologically is Richard Sennett and Jonathan Cobb, *The Hidden Injuries of Class* (New York, 1972). The travails of the Tondi family are recounted in John Spiegel's *Transactions: The Interplay between Individual, Family, and Society* (New York, 1971). Ethnicity, social class, and mental disabilities are discussed in several essays in *Perspectives in Italian Immigration and Ethnicity*, published by the American Italian Historical Association (New York, 1977).

The literature on Sacco and Vanzetti is extensive. A starting point is Herbert B. Ehrmann, *The Case That Will Not Die: The Commonwealth of Massachusetts vs. Sacco and Vanzetti* (New York, 1970), as well as Francis Russell, *Tragedy in Dedham* (New York, 1962). A series of essays about Sacco and Vanzetti and other anarchists has been published by the American Italian Historical Association as *Italian American Radicalism* (New York, 1972).

Regarding criminality see Salvatore Mondello, *Crime, the Italian Immigrants, and the Periodical Press*, 1880–1920 (Florence, 1969). Francis A. J. Ianni (with Elizabeth Reuss-Ianni), *A Family Business: Kinship and Social Control in Organized Crime* (New York, 1972), looks at Italian American crime families, using the methods of a social anthropologist interested in systems analysis; Ianni has examined the cultural characteristics that make up the code of rules that dominate criminal syndicates based upon secret family control. A biography by a respected criminal lawyer is

George Wolf's *Frank Costello: Prime Minister of the Underworld* (New York, 1974). For an overview of the Mafia see Nicholas Gage, editor, *Mafia U.S.A.* (New York, 1972). The Mafia is also dealt with in Frederick Sondern, Jr., *Brotherhood of Evil: The Mafia* (New York, 1959), and in Dwight C. Smith's *The Mafia Mystique* (New York, 1974), which repeats Barzini's thesis, updated, that a Mafia organization does not really exist, as fantasied by the American public. See also Peter Maas, *The Valachi Papers* (New York, 1971), Donald Cressey, *Theft of the Nation* (New York, 1969), and Thomas Pitkin and Francesco Cordasco, *The Black Hand* (Totowa, 1977).

America's criminal network is the theme of Martin A. Gosch and Richard Hammer, *The Last Testament of Lucky Luciano* (New York, 1975), and Thomas E. Dewey, *Twenty against the Underworld* (New York, 1975); the latter forms part of the memoirs of the prosecutor who sent Luciano and many other racketeers to prison. The genuine bravery of a New York Italian policeman has been recorded in Arrigo Petacco's *Joe Petrosino* (New York, 1974). For more on crime, see Joseph Albini, *The American Mafia: Genesis of a Legend* (New York); Luigi Barzini, Jr., *From Caesar to the Mafia* (London, 1971), and his "The Real Mafia," *Harper's*, 208 (June 1954), 38–46. See also Mario Puzo's *The Godfather* (New York, 1969), and Gay Talese, *Honor Thy Father* (New York, 1971), seemingly based on the life of Joseph Bonanno. Other volumes include Harry J. Anslinger and Will Oursler, *The Murderers* (New York, 1961); Daniel Bell, *The End of Ideology* (New York, 1962); and the popular but poorly documented Ed Reid, *Mafia* (New York, 1964). Apt to be overlooked is Giovanni Schiavo, *The Truth about the Mafia and Organized Crime in America* (New York, 1962).

More recent are Humbert S. Nelli, *The Business of Crime: Italians and Syndicate Crime in the United States* (New York, 1976); Dwight C. Smith, Jr., *The Mafia Mystique* (New York, 1975); Anton Blok, *The Mafia of an Italian Village* (New York, 1974); and Richard Gambino, *Vendetta* (New York, 1977). See also Vincent Teresa with Thomas C. Renner, *Vinnie Teresa's*

Mafia (New York, 1975), and Leonard Katz, *Uncle Frank: The Biography of Frank Costello* (New York, 1973).

Some books on the Mafia are rewrites of an early volume by Fred Pasley entitled *Al Capone: The Biography of a Self-Made Man* (New York, 1931), whose unprotected author is dead and whose publisher is long defunct. A book written from the premise that there is a real and dangerous Mafia is Nicholas Gage, *The Mafia Is Not an Equal Opportunity Employer* (New York, 1971).

These books deal with Italians in various areas of the United States: Edmondo Mayor des Planches, *Attraverso gli Stati Uniti per l'emigrazione Italiana* (Turin, 1913); United States Immigration Commission, "Agricultural Distribution of Immigrants," in *Reports of the Immigration Commission*, 41 volumes (Washington, 1900), which includes the largest collection of source materials ever assembled on all facets of immigration to the United States. Unfortunately, an index was never published. Not only are these volumes invaluable, but our national restrictive quotas were derived from them.

A bit miscellaneous but useful are the following works: Diomede Carito, *Nella terra di Washington; le mie visioni della psiche Nord America*, reprinted in Betty Boyd Caroli, *Italian Repatriation from the United States* (New York, 1973); Emily Fogg Meade, "Italian Immigration into the South," *South Atlantic Quarterly*, 4 (July 1905), 217–223; Giovanni Preziosi, *Gli italiani negli Stati Uniti del Nord* (Milan, 1909), and "Settlers in Tontitown," *Interpreter*, 8 (January 1929), 56–58; and Anita Moore, "Safe Ways to Get on the Soil: The Work of Father Bandini at Tontitown," *World's Work*, 24 (June 1912), 215–219.

An excellent affirmation of the theory that many immigrants were "upraised" as well as "uprooted" is Thomas Kessner's *The Golden Door: Italian and Jewish Immigrant Mobility in New York City* (New York, 1977). This can be supplemented with Humbert S. Nelli's *The Italians in Chicago, 1880–1930* (New York, 1970). See also John M. Allswang's *A House for All Peoples: Ethnic Politics in Chicago, 1890–1936* (Louisville, 1971).

For other cities consult G. La Piana, *The Italians in*

Milwaukee, Wisconsin (reprinted in San Francisco, 1970), and Rolle, *The Immigrant Upraised*, regarding Italians in various western states; see also Giovanni Perelli, *Colorado and the Italians in Colorado* (Denver, 1922), and for California, see P. E. Botta, *Observations on the Inhabitants of California, 1827–1828*, translated and edited by J. F. Bricca (Los Angeles, 1952). Ruth Teiser's *An Account of Domingo Ghirardelli and the Early Years of the Ghirardelli Company* (San Francisco, 1945), is helpful, as is H. F. Raup, "The Italian-Swiss in California," *California Historical Society Quarterly*, 30 (December 1951), 304–314.

The relationship between the Catholic church and the Italians is discussed in Tomasi and Engel, *The Italian Experience*, 163–213, and in Rudolph J. Vecoli, "Prelates and Peasants," *Journal of Social History*, 2 (Spring 1969), 217–268. On continuing frictions consult "Has the Church Lost Its Soul?" *Newsweek*, October 4, 1971, 80–89. See also Pietro di Donato, *Immigrant Saint: The Life of Mother Cabrini* (New York, 1960), and Theodore Maynard, *Too Small a World: The Life of Francesca Cabrini* (Milwaukee, 1945).

An inspiring story by an educator, Leonard Covello, is *The Heart Is the Teacher* (New York, 1958). On the artist Frank Stella see Irma B. Jaffe, *Joseph Stella* (Cambridge, 1970). Jerre Mangione has written an autobiography, *An Ethnic at Large: A Memoir of America in the Thirties and Forties* (New York, 1978).

Representative novels are Valenti Angelo, *The Golden Gate* (New York, 1939); Michael De Capite, *No Bright Banner* (New York, 1944); Pietro di Donato, *Christ in Concrete* (New York, 1939), and *Three Circles of Light* (New York, 1960); John Fante, *Dago Red* (New York, 1940), and *Wait until Spring, Bandini* (New York, 1938); Jerre Mangione, *Mount Allegro* (New York, 1942); Jo Pagano, *The Condemned* (New York, 1947), *Golden Wedding* (New York, 1943), and *The Paesanos* (New York, 1940); Leo Politi, *Little Leo* (New York, 1951); and Antonia Pola, *Who Can Buy the Stars?* (New York, 1957).

Olga Peragallo edited, *Italian-American Authors and Their Contribution to American Literature* (New York, 1949), which lists novels dealing with the Italo-American theme. More recent is Rose Basile Green, *The Italian American Novel* (New York, 1973), an anthology that includes such books as Lucas Longo, *The Family on Vendetta Street* (New York, 1968); Jerre Mangione, *America Is Also Italian* (New York, 1969), and *A Passion for Sicilians: The World around Danilo Dolci* (New York, 1970); Joe Vergara, *Love and Pasta* (New York, 1968); Ralph Corsel, *Up There the Stars* (New York, 1968); Joseph Arleo, *The Grand Street Collector* (New York, 1970); and Puzo's *The Godfather.* Puzo's recollections of early life in Manhattan appear in "Choosing a Dream: Italians in Hell's Kitchen," in *The Immigrant Experience,* edited by Thomas C. Wheeler (New York, 1971). Consult also John Fante, *The Brotherhood of the Grape (New York, 1977).*

There is a growing literature about immigrant family and child instability. An important contribution is Rita F. Stein's *Disturbed Youth and Ethnic Family Patterns* (Albany, 1971). Consult also Paul F. Campisi, "The Italian Family in the United States," in *Social Perspectives on Behavior,* edited by Herman Stein and Richard Cloward (Glencoe, 1958); in this same volume is Caroline F. Ware's "The Breakdown of Ethnic Solidarity: The Case of the Italian in Greenwich Village." See also the following: Arnold Rose, "The Prevalence of Mental Disorders in Italy," *International Journal of Social Psychiatry,* 10 (Spring 1964), 87–100; Paul Barrabee and Otto Van Mering, "Ethnic Variations in Mental Stress in Families with Psychotic Children," *Social Problems,* 1 (October 1953), 48–53; Joseph Giordano, *Ethnicity and Mental Health* (New York, 1973); and E. B. Piedmont, "Ethnic Differences in Behavior and Psychopathology: Italian and Irish," *International Journal of Social Psychiatry,* 2 (Summer 1956), 11–23.

Anne Parsons, "Is the Oedipus Complex Universal? The Jones-Malinowski Debate Revisited and a South Italian Nuclear Complex,'" in the third volume of *The Psychoanalytic Study of the Child* (New York, 1964), discusses Freud's interpretation and the changing nature of the family psychoanalytically. She finds the Oedipal conflict to be universal but not necessarily central in all cultures. Instead, "nuclear complexes" vary with time, place, and

social circumstances. On Jewish and Italian immigration and sub-
sequent status mobility see Fred L. Strodtbeck, "Family Interaction, Values, and Achievement," in David C. McClelland and
others, *Talent and Society* (New York, 1958). For more about
family life see Sydel F. Silverman, "An Ethnographic Approach to
Social Stratification: Prestige in a Central Italian Community,"
American Anthropologist, 68 (August 1966), 899–922; as well as
Constance Cronin, *The Sting of Change* (Chicago, 1970).

Other useful references about social factors are Judith Kramer,
The American Minority Community (New York, 1970); David
Ward, *Cities and Immigrants: A Geography of Change in Nine-
teenth Century America* (New York, 1971); Grazia Dore, "Some
Social and Historical Aspects of Italian Emigration to America,"
Journal of Social History, 2 (Winter 1968), 95–122; and Humbert
S. Nelli, "Italians in Urban America: A Study of Ethnic Adjust-
ment," *International Migration Review*, 1 (Summer 1967), 38–55.
This special issue contains various other excellent articles. See also
"Patterns of Kinship, Comparaggio, and Community in a South
Italian Village," *Anthropological Quarterly*, 33 (January 1960),
24–32.

The sociology of the family has been discussed in Lydio F.
Tomasi, *The Italian American Family* (New York, 1972), and by
Francis X. Femminella and Jill S. Quadagno in *Ethnic Families in
America* (New York, 1976), edited by Charles H. Mindel and
Robert W. Habenstein.

Stressing the theme of discrimination is a collection edited by
Salvatore J. La Gumina, *Wop!* (New York, 1973). A recent assess-
ment of the internal effects of being Italian in America is Richard
Gambino, *Blood of My Blood: The Dilemma of the Italian-
Americans* (New York, 1974); consult also his *Vendetta* (New
York, 1977).

Arthur Marx, *Everybody Loves Somebody Sometime* (New
York, 1964), superficially looks at the show business personalities
of Dean Martin and his original partner, the stage comic Jerry
Lewis.

Finally, see Jerry della Femina and Charles Sopkin, *An Italian*

Grows in Brooklyn (Boston, 1979) as well as the valuable essays in Francesco Cordasco, editor, *Studies in Italian American Social History* (Totowa, 1975). Other essays, some too abbreviated, are in Humbert S. Nelli, editor, *The United States and Italy: The First Two Hundred Years* (New York, 1977). For a view of women see *The Italian Immigrant Woman in North America,* edited by Betty Boyd Caroli, Robert F. Harney, and Lydio F. Tomasi (Toronto, 1978).

INDEX

Abruzzi, 2, 8, 64, 70
Abruzzo, Matthew, 150
Acceptance, xv, 30, 65
Accommodation to America: *see*
    Americanization
Achievement
    in entertainment, 169–71
    at expense of sanity, xv, 88, 89,
        172–173
    and rewards, 29
    in sports, 172
Acting out, frustrations, 14, 29,
    37, 38, 71, 101
Adamic, Louis, 159
Addams, Jane, 178
Adjustments (Italian) to America,
    xvi, 9–10, 15, 30–32, 48–49,
    134–39, 185; *see also* Ameri-
    canization
Adorno, Theodor, 30
Agnew, Spiro, 170, 175
Alcohol: *see* wine

Algren, Nelson, 159
Ali, Mohammed, 172
Alienation, xii, 21, 25, 37, 44, 96,
    160
Alioto, Mayor Joseph, 149
Allen, Frederick Lewis, 59
Allen, Woody, 148
American Federation of Labor, 70
American Protective Association,
    68, 157
Americanization, 72, 182–83
    and adjustment, 30–32
    created contradictions, xvi,
        121, 189
    and economic difficulties, 48–49
    through education, 134–39
    failure to attain, 185
    and flexibility, 9–10
    impeded by ghettoes, 7
    interpretation by historians,
        xiii, 45–46, 176
    and sexuality, 132

Americanization (*cont.*)
in spite of discrimination, 188–89
steps toward, 15
Anarchists, 66, 72, 75
Anastasia, Albert, 88
Anderson, Sherwood, 9
Andretti, Mario, 172
Anglicized names, 40–41, 44
Anglo-Saxon mystique, 58, 75, 77
Anti-American feelings, 50–51
Anti-communism, 145–46
Anti-defamation acts, 103–107
Anti-intellectual attitude of Italian immigrants, 134–39
Antin, Mary, 28
Anxieties
displacement of, 14, 34, 37
and feelings of abandonment, 4
of immigrants, 1–2, 96
and sublimation, 34
Arizona, immigrants in, 21
Assimilation, 21, 28, 30–32, 180, 185, 189, 190; *see also* Americanization
Asthma, 13
Athletics: *see* sports
Atlas, Charles, 171–72
Attisani, D. Anthony, 106

Baez, Joan, 175
Baltimore, 85
Bancroft, Ann (Anna Italiano), 171
Bancroft, Hubert Howe, 68
Barzini, Luigi, Jr., 50–51, 81, 133, 173
Baseball, and Italian players, 172
Basso, Hamilton, 159
Battaglia, Patricia, 109
Beame, Abraham, 151

Bellow, Saul, 159, 181
Berenson, Bernard, 162
Beretta, David, 172
Berlin, Irving, 171, 188
Berne, Eric, 89
Berra, Yogi, 172
Bessemer, Henry, 18
Bigotry: *see* discrimination; prejudice
Billera, John, 172
"Birds of Passage" (re-migration), 47–55
Black Hand (*Mano Nera*), 80, 82
Blacks, xvii, 44, 57, 82, 106, 109, 144, 151, 152–53, 164, 172, 174, 176–77, 181, 187
Blaine, Secretary of State James G., 84
Boarding house life, 49, 123–24
Boasting, 14, 31
Boccie, an Italian game, 23, 45, 165
Bono, Sonny, 173
Borglum, Gutzon, 37
Boston, 26, 28, 60, 61, 85, 86, 115, 162
Boston Immigration Restriction League, 77
Boxing, and Italians, 172
Braccianti, 3, 16, 30
Braddock, Jim, boxer, 172
Bresci, Gaetano, 29, 70–71, 73
Briggs, John, 182
Bromfield, Louis, 9
Bronx (New York), 26, 28, 129
Brooklyn (New York), 26, 129
Brumidi, Constantino, 162
Brutality, among Italians, 14
Bufano, Beniamino, 162
Burns, John Horne, 46
Businessmen, among Italians, 172
Butte, Montana, 19

Cabrini, Mother, Saint, 178
Cahan, Abraham, 159
Calabria, 7, 8, 16, 28, 64, 90
Calabria's *Onorata Società*, 79
Califano, Joseph Anthony, 149, 150
Caminetti, Anthony, 72, 140
Campanella, Joseph, 164
Campania, 2, 8, 64
Canzoneri, Robert, 32
Canzoneri, Tony, boxer, 172
Capone, Al, 85, 86, 98, 99, 175, 178
Capra, Frank, 163
Cardellini, Giuseppe, 34
Carito, Diomede, 11
Carnegie, Andrew, 18
Carnegie, Dale, 88
Carnera, Primo, 172
Carroll Gardens (Brooklyn), 26–27
Carter, President Jimmy, 149, 150
Caruso, Enrico, 34, 162
Casanova, as image of Italian men, 132–33
Castellamarese War, 101
Cather, Willa, 159
Catholic church, 21, 123, 132, 152
  importance of to Italians, 111, 112, 154–59
  and the Irish, 156
  as threat to Americans, 67, 85
Catholic Universities, 138; *see also* education
Celebrations, religious, 158
Celebrezze, Anthony, 148
Chavez, Cesar, 174
Chicago, 20, 62, 70, 85, 86, 108 146, 178
Chicanos, xvii, 164, 176–77, 187
Child, Irvin L., 128, 183

Children (immigrant)
  and the church, 154–55
  cruelty toward, 38
  effect of American ideas on, 122, 125, 135
  and labor, 22, 120
  prevented from independence, 112
  and rebellion toward parents, 32–33, 115, 120–121, 122
  and schooling, 39, 121, 134–39
  and "social climbing," 32
  tied emotionally to mother, 113
Chinese minority, 16, 57, 72, 176
Ciardi, John, 159
Civil rights movement, 176–77
Civiletti, Benjamin, 150
Clichés
  about America, 5, 15
  about the immigrant experience, xiv–xv, 6
  about Italians, 10, 56–57, 170, 184
Coalfield War, 20
Cohan, George M., 171
Collective unconscious, xii, 176, 186
Colombo, Joseph, 103–104, 174
Colorado, 20, 71–72
Colosimo, Luigi ("Big Jim"), 86
Company store, 63–64
Como, Italy, 7
Como, Perry, singer, 137, 169, 171
Compulsion, 101–102
Concealment of feelings, xv–xvi; *see also* denial
Confession, as emotional support, 158–59
Conformity, xvi, 38
Conrad, Joseph, 117

Contadini, 2, 3, 38
Contract labor, 17, 59, 61–63
Coolidge, President Calvin, 85
Coppola, Francis Ford, 163
Corbett, Jim, boxer, 172
Corleone, Vito, 102
Corsi, Edward, 50, 146
Corsi, Signora, 50
Cosa Nostra, 104, 105
Cosche (Mafia), 78–79
Costello, Frank, 90–92, 97, 147, 175, 186
Creativity, in Italians, 9
Crime
  and bad parenting, 89
  causes of, 85, 88–109
  and compulsions, 101–102
  dealt with harshly by Italians, 85–87, 103–104, 138
  as escape from stifling family life, 95
  and hierarchy of criminal leaders, 101
  juvenile, 90, 95, 107–108, 139
  linked to discrimination, 78, 82
Cripple Creek strike, 71
Crittenden, O.B., 61
Crowding, 14, 21–22
Cuomo, Mario, 42
Culture and Italians, 161–63
Curti, Merle, 20, 44
Czolgosz, Leon, 71

Damone, Vic, 137, 171
D'Angelo, Giuseppe, 64
D'Angelo, Pasquale, 6, 11–12, 15
Darrow, Clarence, 144
Darwin, Charles, 67
De Conde, Alexander, 189
Defenses
  and forgetting the past, xv, 29, 116

learned in childhood, 38, 116
  and lying, 135–36
  that manipulate the environment, 10
  often result in splitting, 108, 116–17
  psychological, 18–19, 179, 181
De Gasperi, Alcide, 146
Delinquency, 90, 95, 107–108, 139
Della Femina, Jerry, 184–85
Democratic party, 141, 146, 151
Denial, mechanism of ego defense, xv, xvii, 11, 31, 38, 43, 86, 92, 122, 128, 181
De Niro, Robert, actor, 173
Denver, 21
Depression, emotional, 122
  of criminals, 91–92
  on leaving homeland, 4
  in men, 120
  in women, 49–50
De Sapio, Carmine, 147
De Voto, Bernard, 159
Dewey, Thomas E., 93, 144
Dialects, 39, 40, 180
di Donato Pietro, 33, 76, 90, 114, 159
di Laurentis, Dino, 163
DiMaggio, Joe, 137, 172
Di Renzo, Gordon J., 151
Disappointments, among immigrants, 48–51
Discrimination; *see also* prejudice
  different between "new" and "old" immigrants, 67
  against foreign workers, 61, 76
  historical view of, xiii, 45–46, 67–68, 176
  against Italians from other minorities, 16
  linked to crime, 78, 82, 107

against modern-day Italians,
58–59
and the *padrone* system, 61
against Sicilians, 84
after World War I, 66, 72
Distrust, and Italian character,
11, 33
Divorce, among Italians, 134
Dominici, Senator Peter, 148
Dos Passos, John, 73, 74, 130
Dreiser, Theodore, 73
Dunini, Amerigo, 29
Durante, Jimmy, 137, 171

Eating habits: *see* food
Education
in Catholic universities, 138
not encouraged by first generation, 134–39, 175
of immigrant children, 39
and parochial schools, 154–55
Ego strength
and defenses, 181
of immigrant children, 121
and pressures of Americanization, 179, 188–89
Eisenhower, President Dwight,
145, 170
Ellis Island, xiii, 1, 5, 8, 22, 40,
58, 127, 173
El Paso (Texas), 19
Emerson, Ralph Waldo, 77
Emigration: *see* migration
Emotional ties to Italy, xv, 31,
51–52
Erikson, Erik, 98, 113, 116, 123,
139
Ethiopian War, 52, 145
"Ethnic pluralism," 190
Ethnicity; *see also* migration
and jokes, 121–22

and modern-day Italians, 174,
188
and pride, 60
in special neighborhoods, 24–27
and stereotypes, 57
Ettor, Joseph, 71
Exploitation, 3–4, 61

Fairbairn, William, 107
Family life of Italians
and authority, 28, 32, 111, 114
not discussed openly, 139
disrupted by migration, 8, 32–
33, 110, 121
and father-son struggle, 117–20
and loyalty, 110–11
and the Mafia, 80, 96, 97, 110
and the masculine mystique,
111, 118–20
and the neurotic cycle, 113
and rebellion, 115
and work, 114, 134–39
and reliance on, 3, 32
and women's place in, 111–13
Fante, John, 118, 159–60
Fascism, and Italians, 34, 52,
144–45
Father and son relationships,
117–20
Faulkner, William, 9
Fear of strangers (by Americans),
30, 31
Federal Bureau of Labor, 70
Fellini, Federico, 133
Fermi, Enrico, 145
Films
directors of, 163
portraying ethnic criminals, 87
spaghetti westerns, 163
Five Points Gang, New York, 93
Flight to America, reasons for,
2–5

Food
    and ethnic stereotypes, 57, 167
    family based, 164–65
    in ghettoes, 23
    habits by descendents, 178
    in literature, 165
    and restaurants, 166–67
Forestiere, Baldasare, the "Human
    Mole," 34–35, 37, 38, 181
Francis, Connie, singer, 173
Frankfurter, Felix, Justice, 73
Fresno, California, 34
Freud, Anna, 94, 123
Freud, Sigmund, xi, xvi, 9, 43,
    74, 87, 111, 117, 118, 132,
    186, 187
Frugality, 125
Furillo, Carl, 172

Gabello, Umberto, 35, 37, 38
Galante, Carmine, 70
Gallenga, Antonio, 9
Gallico, Paul, 159
Gallicurci, Amelita, 162
Gambino, Richard, 137–38
Gangs, 101
Gans, Herbert, 38
Garibaldi, Giuseppe, 10, 64, 155
Garretto, Vito, 84
Gaudi, Antonio, 37
Generational tensions, xvi, 32–33,
    115, 120–22, 135
Genoa, 52, 81, 161
Genovese, Vito, 92
German immigrants, 16, 43, 72,
    144, 186
Ghettoes, 44
    and children, 135
    contributing to illness, 14
    described, 24–27, 181
    in literature, 6, 23, 114, 128
    perpetuated, 57, 177

and politics, 140
    reasons for, 25
    unhealthy, 21–22
Giacosa, Giuseppe, 167
Giancana, Sam, 108
Giannini, A. P., 19, 29, 60, 105
Gigli, Beniamino, 34, 162
Giragi, Carmel, 19
Giragi, Columbus, 19
Glazer, Nathan, 181
The Godfather (Puzo), 102, 105,
    159, 174
Golden, Harry, 129
Golondrinas: see "Birds of
    Passage"
Grasso, Governor Ella, 150
Greeks, xv, xvii, 164, 166
Greeley, Andrew, 186
Groddeck, Georg, 87
Guilt
    and the Church, 155
    induced in Italian families, 113,
        116, 118, 120, 123, 136
    by Italians about leaving the
        homeland, xv
    repressed, 187
    and tolerance, 77
Handlin, Oscar, 23, 181, 190
Harlem, and immigrants, 24, 50,
    90, 141
Harrison, President Benjamin, 84
Haymarket Riot, 85
Hennessy, David, New Orleans
    Chief of Police, 83
Historians
    ethnic prejudices of, 68
    on immigration, xi, xiii, 15,
        179, 180, 181–82, 184–85
Hoffer, Eric, 10, 87
Hoffman, Richard, 92
Hofstadter, Richard, 85
Horney, Karen, psychoanalyst, 88

Howard, Sidney, playwright, 163
Howells, William Dean, 65
Hungarians, 68, 72
Hunter, Evan, 22
Hysteria, 13

Iacocca, Lee, 172
Ianni, Francis, 109
"Identification with the aggressor," 31
Identity
   and adolescents, 123, 138, 183
   diffusion, 13–14
   hidden by third generation eth-
      nics, 183
   need for, xiii, 115
   with old world, 10
   and re-identity, 170
   of returnees, 55
   search for, 88, 121, 180, 181,
      187, 190
Illiteracy, xv, 65, 70
Immaturity, of Italian men, 133–
   34
Immigration: *see* migration
Immigration Act of 1965, 149
Immigration history, xiii, 15, 68,
   180, 181–82, 184, 185
Immigration laws, 17–18, 72
Impellitieri, Vincent, 146
Indians, xvii, 142, 174, 177
Industrial Workers of the World
   (I.W.W.), 71, 75
Inferiority
   and Italian heritage, 92, 135
   in youths, 123
Intolerance: *see* prejudice; dis-
   crimination
Irish, 185
   and Catholicism, 67, 112, 155–
      59, 163
   and crime, 107

and Italian rivalry, 16, 64, 72,
   100, 101
and politics, 140–41, 144, 147,
   151, 152–53, 174
and prejudice, 75
and sports, 172
Italian-American Civil Rights
   League, 105
Italian American politics, 141–53
Italian influence on America,
   167–68
Italian Labor Bureau, 70
Italian people
   and accusations of deceit, 60
   and authority, 74–75
   and boasting, 14, 31
   and brutality, 14, 57, 70–71,
      186
   and conformity, xvi, 38
   and congeniality, 173, 185–86
   and despondency, 49, 50
   and frugality, 125
   needed acceptance, xv, 30
   and practicality, xvii, 10, 15
   and secrecy, 31
   and status, 12, 31–32, 114
   suspiciousness of, 11, 115, 123,
      138
   vengeance among, 71
Italian war veterans and patriotic
   lodges, 72
"Italianity," 40, 42, 55
Identification with the aggressor,
   123

James, Henry, 58, 73, 168
Jaworski, Leon, 150
Jews, 57, 107, 109, 127, 129,
   136–67, 144, 147, 150, 151,
   153, 162, 174, 176, 185
Julesburg, Colorado, 35
Jung, Carl, xii, 176, 186

Juvenile crime, 90, 95, 107–108, 139; *see also* crime

Kansas City, 99
Katz, Michael, 135
Kearney, Denis, 72
Kennedy, President John, 148
Kessner, Thomas, 46, 182
Kienholz, Dr. L. E., 94
Kleptomania, 14
Know-Nothing party, 58
Kohut, Heinz, 122
Ku Klux Klan, 183

Labor strife, 19–20, 29, 69–71
Labor unions, 63
La Guardia, Fiorello, 19, 139, 141–45, 147
Langer, William, 184
Language
    and acceptance, 31
    bizarre use of, 38–40
    describing hierarchy of crime
        leaders, 101
    "pure" Italian, 174
Lanzetta, James, 141
La Rosa, Julius, 175
Lasorda, Tommy, 172
Lattimore, Owen, 68
Lawrence, D. H., 8, 11, 188
Lazia, Johnny, 99–101
Levi, Carlo, 4, 6, 155, 161
Lewis, Sinclair, 73
Libonati family, 146
Liguria, 48
Lippman, Walter, 73
Literature (regarding Italians), 159–161
    on acting out, 90
    on alienation, 50–51, 160
    on Americanization 15, 33, 48, 114–15, 120–21, 128, 129–

30, 135, 159–60 173, 189
    on crime, 81, 87, 90, 102, 113, 120, 159
    on discrimination, 58–59, 64, 67, 73, 76
    on family life, 44, 112, 115–16, 117, 118, 128, 135
    on ghettoes, 6, 23, 114, 128
    on identity problems, 115, 121, 122, 159, 160
    on Italian character, 11–12, 173
    on religion, 155
    on returning to Italy, 54, 55
    on sexuality, 133
"Little Italys," 6–7
Loesser, Frank, 163
Longo, Lucas, 23, 41
Loren, Sophia, actress, 55
Los Angeles, 35, 105, 129, 174
Louis, Joe, 172
Louisiana, 82–85
Loyalties, xvi
Lucchese, Thomas, 141
Luciano, Charles ("Lucky"), 92–95, 147
Ludlow Massacre, 20, 71–72
Lynching, 83–84

Madonna cult, 111, 157
Mafia, 38, 82–83, 110, 122, 141, 157, 170
    alleged omnipotence of, 79–80
    as alternative to family life, 14, 96
    chieftain's need to be respected, 96–97
    definition of, 81
    as described in media, 87–88, 102
    hatred of, by most Italians, 85–87, 103–104, 138
    in Italy today, 102–103

old *vs.* new, 80
in Sicily, 78–79, 103
and sociopaths, 95–96
as source of criminal activity,
78
symbols copied, 109
in western US, 105
Mafiosi, 79, 80
Magnani, Anna, 163
Malamud, Bernard, 159
Mancini, Henry, 162
Mangione, Jerre, 54, 115, 121,
122, 135, 159, 173, 189
Marcantonio, Vito, 141, 146
Marciano, Rocky, 172
Mardikian, George, 182
Marshall Plan, 145
Martin, Billy, 172
Martin, Dean, 137, 169–70, 171
Martini, Louis, 29, 60
Mascagni, Pietro, 162
Masculine mystique, 111, 132–33
Materialism, xiii, xvi, 12–13, 15,
30, 125, 186
Matteoti, Giacomo, 29
Mazursky, Paul, 116
Mazzei, Philip, 57
Melting pot concept, xi–xii, 28,
46, 127, 152, 190
Memories of "old country," 2
Mencken, H. L., 39, 131
Menotti, Giancarlo, 162
Mental illness, 13, 137
Migration (Italian) to America
ambivalence toward, 1–2
compared to others, 16–17, 64,
65
northern *vs.* southern, 65
numbers of, 2, 7–8, 16–17, 18,
20, 65, 180–81
reasons, for, 2–4, 8
recent, 180–81

as safety valve, 16
seen as rebellion, 4
Millay, Edna St. Vincent, 73
Miller, Glenn, 77
Minelli, Lisa, 171, 173
Minelli, Vincent, 163
Mineo, Sal, 164
Minish, Joseph, 147–48
Mitchell, Attorney General John
N., 104
Molise, Nick, 124
Mortarotti, Franco, 51–52
Mothering process, 94, 96
Motivations for change, xiv, xvii
Moynihan, Daniel P., 181
Mugavero, Francis J., Bishop, 156
Mulberry Bend (Street), New
York, xiv, 24–26, 60, 128,
178, 188
Musicians, among Italians, 162
Mussolini, Benito, 34, 52, 70,
100, 133, 144, 145
Mutual aid societies, 44, 63
Myths
of Anglo-Saxon superiority, 75
in history, xvii
about Italians, 4, 60
McKinley, President William, 71

Name changing, 41–42, 121, 148
Napa Valley, 163
Naples, 11, 36, 46, 47, 53, 180
Native Sons of the Golden West,
76
Nativism, 57–59, 72–73, 76–77,
82: *see also* prejudices; dis-
crimination
Neapolitan Camorra, 79
Negroes: *see* blacks
Nelli, Humbert, 46, 89
"Neurasthenia," 13
New Orleans, 19, 82–85

New York City, 61, 63, 64, 181
  and areas of Italian population, 24–27
  and crime, 85, 86
  and discrimination, 176
  and Italian pride, 103–104, 174
  and labor, 70
  and La Guardia, 142–145
  population of foreign born, 20
  and recent migrants, 181
Newspapers
  of immigrants, 161
  portrayal of Italians, 81
Nin, Anais, 32
Nixon, President Richard, 148, 149, 150, 175
Norris–La Guardia Anti-Injunction Act, 143
North Beach (San Francisco), 25, 105, 149, 178
Northern vs. southern Italians, 64–66
Nostalgia for Italy, 11, 40
Novelists: see literature
Nurturing, 25, 94–95, 138–39

Obesity, 14
Obsessive personality, 37
Oedipal struggle, xvi
Ojetti, Ugo, 167
"Old World" characteristics, xii
Omertà, 103
Opler, Marvin, 137
Orality, 164, 169
Orientals, 16, 57, 72, 176

Pacino, Al, 173
Padrone system, 11, 61–63
Paesani, 114
Pagano, Jo, 44, 55, 117, 128, 129–30, 159, 160
Palermo, Sicily, 3, 54

Palmer, Attorney General A. Mitchell, 72
Palmer raids of 1920, 73
Paolucci, Jeno, 172
Parenting, in Italians, 14
  and character formation, 94–95, 125
  discouraging education, 134–39
  as influential as cause of crime, 88
  often authoritarian, 28, 32, 33, 38, 111, 114
  and parent-child attachment, 115, 138–39
  strict, 111
Parker, Beulah, 156
Parochial schools, 39
Passivity, 38, 40–41, 75
Pastore, Senator John, 148, 173
Patti, Adelina, 142, 162
Pavel, Ferdinand, 37
Pavese, Cesare, 9, 12, 161
Peasant
  pragmatism, xvii
  society, 2–3
Pecking order, among immigrants, 72, 176–77
Pecora, Judge Ferdinand, 146
Pellegrini, Angelo, 8, 48, 54
Pendergast, Thomas J., 99, 100
Petrosino, Joseph, 87
Philadelphia, 61, 85, 150
Piedmont, 5, 48
Pinza, Ezio, 162
Pola, Antonia, 51
Polish immigrants, xv, xvii, 43, 127, 140, 146, 150, 155, 156
Politi, Leo, artist, 162
Politics and Italians, 141–153, 175
Ponti, Carlo, 163
Ponzi, Charles ("the Great"), 86
Pope, Generoso, 147, 161

Population
  of foreign born in New York,
    20, 151, 177
  of foreign born in western
    states, 6, 20, 21, 65
  of immigrants in recent years,
    180–81
  of Italian immigrants in Amer-
    ica, 17, 18, 20–21
  of Italians in higher education,
    138, 177
  of Italy, 16
  leaving Italy, 2, 7–8, 16–17
  of northern *vs.* southern
    Italians, 65
  and re-migration to Italy, 48
Populists and Italians, 82
Portland, 71
Poverty
  in cities, 14, 22–24
  in Italy, 2, 38, 49
  leading to crime, 60
  not main cause of crime, 88
  and personal deficits, xiii
  shame of, xv, 13, 110, 120
Practicality, as trait of Italians,
    xvii, 10, 15
Prejudice, 128; *see also* discrimin-
    ation
  against America by Italians,
    50–51, 114–15
  against Catholics, 67
  denial of, 43
  against foreign folkways, 76
  historical view of, 67–68, 176
  Italian reaction to, xvii, 74, 85,
    188
  among Italians, 16, 72, 176–77,
    180
  as projection, 57
  against Sicilians, 84
  in southern states, 82

during Spanish-American War,
    68–69
  and violence, 82–85
  in western states, xiv
Procaccino, Mario, 148
Progressive movement, 69
Prohibition, 44
Projection, xviii, 37, 181
Protestantism and Italians, xvi,
    157
Psychic wounds, 89
Psychoanalysts, findings of, xv,
    31, 88, 94, 179
Psychohistory, and ethnic studies,
    xiii, xiv, 25, 43, 73
Psychoneurotic ailments, 14
Psychotherapy, avoidance by
    Italians, 137
Puerto Ricans, 151, 180
Puzo, Mario, 87, 102, 113, 120,
    159, 173–74

Quinn, Anthony, 163
Quota immigration policies, 17–
    18, 144, 146

Race revolution in 1960s, xvi–
    xvii, 175–76, 186
Racist feelings, 57–59, 76–77
Railroads and immigrants, 16
Railways Labor Act, 143
Randazzo, Giuseppe, 59
Red scare, and nativism, 72–73
Re-migration: *see* repatriation;
    "Birds of Passage"
Renunciation of the past, xv,
    10–11
Repatriation, 47–55
  emotions concerning, 54
  as psychological cure, 53
  reasons for, 48
  and re-identity, 54

Repatriation (*cont.*)
of women, 49–50
Repression, xi, xiii
as damaging, xv
in defense of ego, 116
of feelings, 96, 124, 186, 188
to hide stress, 29
imposed on families, 114, 132–33
of pride in heritage, 31
of resentments, 38
Republican party, 141, 146, 151
Resentment
in families, 110
of menial work, 91, 93
Returnees
as commuters, 48
description of, 52–53
restless again for America, 55
women among, 49
Revenge, and the Italian character, 71
Revolt of the 1960's, xvi–xvii, 175–76, 186
Riccardo, John J., 172
Riis, Jacob, 24, 139
Ritualization of daily life, 38
Rizzo, Mayor Frank, 150, 153
Rizzuto, Phil, 172
Roberts, Kenneth, 59
Robeson, Paul, 176
Robinson, Edward, G., 87
Rocco, Alex, 106
Rodia, Simon, and Watts towers, 9, 35–37, 162, 181
Rodino, Congressman Peter, 149, 150
Rolvaag, Ole, 159
Rome, 161, 180
Roosevelt, President Franklin, 50, 144, 146, 150, 182

Roosevelt, President Theodore, 69, 190
Rossoni, Edmondo, 29
Rosten, Leo, 159
Roth, Philip, 159
Rural environment, 20

Sacco-Vanzetti affair, 73–75, 148
Salt Lake City, 21, 165
Salvation Army, 75
Samenow, Stanton, 89
Sammartino, Peter, 138
Sandoz, Mari, 37
San Francisco, 19, 20, 39, 45, 72, 105, 162, 176
Santangelo, Alfred E., 141
Saroyan, William, 159
Scandinavians, 16, 67
Scapegoating of minorities, 59, 85, 106
Schiavo, Giovanni, 160
Schnitzler, Arthur, 186–87
Schuyler, Ernest, 80–81
Scorsese, Martin, 116, 163
Scottish immigrants, 57
Second generation Italians, xii, 54, 161
and complaints about parents, 32, 183
as criminals, 81, 90
emotional problems of, 13, 171
and identity, 171
less skeptical, 123
as novelists, 159–161
returning to Italy, 174
and status, 124, 129, 135, 183
Secrecy and the Italian character, 31
Self esteem (ego), 121, 179–80, 181, 187

Separation from homeland: *see* migration
Sexuality among immigrants, 111, 112, 132–34, 156, 157
Shakespeare, William, 187
Sicily, 2, 8, 16, 17, 32, 34, 54, 64, 78–79, 80, 89, 92, 97, 114
Silone, Ignazio, 155, 161, 165
Simon, William, Secretary of Treasury, 106
Sinatra, Frank, 170–71
Sinclair, Upton, 73
Sing Sing Penitentiary, 74
Sirica, Judge John J., 150
Slater, Philip, 188
Slums: *see* ghettoes
Social climbing, 32
Social psychology, xi
Society for Italian Immigrants, 63
Sociology, xi, 89
Sociopaths, 88, 91, 95–96, 107
Southern *vs.* northern Italians, 64–66
Spaniards, 166
Spiegel, John, 115
Spinola, Francis B., 140
Splitting, as psychological phenomena
   and allegiances in politics, 151
   as a defense,116–17
   and the Mafia, 108
Sports and Italians, 23, 45, 165, 171–72
Status
   and anxiety, 88
   and importance to Italians, 12, 31–32, 114
   and second generation, 129
   for youth to change, 127
Steel industry, 18

Stein, Rita F., 122
Stekel, Wilhelm, 101
Stella, Frank, 162
Stereotyping
   and connection to crime, 87, 105
   of families, 139
   fostered by Angelos, 33
   of Italians, xiv, 6, 10, 19, 42, 56–57, 60, 75, 121, 137, 151, 169, 170, 184
   of northern *vs.* southern Italians, 65–66
Stieglitz, Alfred, 47
Storr, Anthony, 96
Sublimation, 34
Subversives, 73
Suburbs, movement of Italians toward, 127–128, 146, 177–78
Subway construction workers, 22
Success
   in business, 172
   among entertainers, 169–71, 173
   effect of, on immigrants, 88, 170–73
   ethic, 29, 89
   as a goal, xv
   and repudiation of previous identity, xvii
   and sports, 172
Suffrage and immigrants, 68
Suicide and immigrants, 13, 95
Sullivan, John L., boxer, 172
Suspicion, and the Italian character, 11, 115, 123, 138

Tammany Hall, 144, 147
Taranto, 47
Television, and depiction of Italians, 87–88, 163–64

Teresa, Vincent, 155

Third generation Italians, xii, 13, 54, 128, 138, 183, 184, 187

Thwaites, Reuben Gold, 68

Torrio, Johnny, 98, 175

Toscanini, Maestro Arturo, 145

Trempeleau County (Wisconsin), 20

Tresca, Carlo, 70, 74, 148

Trust, as basis of good relationship, 139

Tuberculosis, "the immigrant's disease," 13, 22

Turin, 7

Turner, Frederick Jackson, 68

Twain, Mark, 59

Unconscious mind
converted depression, 13
origins of, xii-xiv, xv
as producer of a fantasy of escape, 4

Unemployment, 182
as factor for return to Italy, 48–49
in Italy, as cause for immigration, 3, 17
kept wages depressed, 60

Unico National, 105

Unione Siciliana, 79, 101

Unionism and foreigners, 69, 182

United States Wickersham Commission on Law Enforcement, 84–85

Valachi, Joseph, 104–105

Valdioce, Carlo, 73

Valenti, Angelo, 159

Valentino, Rudolph, 130–32

Vigilantism, 83–84

Violence, among immigrants, 70–71

Viscusi, Robert, 189

Volpe, John, 148–49

Wages of workers, 3–4, 7, 70

Wallingford, 152

Ward bosses, 140

WASP establishment, 57, 109, 144, 152, 163, 174

Watergate investigation, 149, 150, 175

Watts towers, 9, 35–37, 162, 181

Wendell, Barrett, 77

Western Federation of Miners, 71

Western Italian immigrants
emancipation and adjustment, 19, 21, 61
as opposed to east coast ghettoes, xiv
population of 6, 20, 21, 25

Wharton, Edith, 58, 59, 73

Wilde, Oscar, 190

Wilder, Thornton, 53

Wills, Harry, 172

Wilson, President Woodrow, 72, 162

Wine, 44–45, 165–66

Winwar, Frances, 159

Wittke, Carl, 76

Women (Italian) immigrants, 21
and the Church, 154–55, 157
and emotional stress, 50–51, 180
and the "Madonna" syndrome, 111, 157
and role in family life, 111–13
and sexuality, 132–34, 157
spoiled sons, 112, 118, 133

World War II and Italo-Americans, 183

Xenophobia, 30, 31, 57–59, 72–73, 76–77

Yeziersha, Anjia, 159

Yochelson, Samuel, 89

Zangwill, Israel, and "melting pot" concept, xi-xii, 186, 190